# THE GRAHAMS

*Glencoe from the summit of Meall Mor*

# *The Grahams*

## A GUIDE TO SCOTLAND'S 2,000FT PEAKS

ANDREW DEMPSTER

EDINBURGH AND LONDON

First published in Great Britain in 1997 by
MAINSTREAM PUBLISHING COMPANY (EDINBURGH) LTD
7 Albany Street
Edinburgh EH1 3UG

ISBN 1 85158 847 7



A catalogue record for this book is available from the British Library

Photographs by Andrew Dempster
Designed by Janene Reid
Typeset in Adobe Garamond
Printed and bound in Great Britain by Butler & Tanner Ltd

*To Heather*

# ACKNOWLEDGEMENTS

I would like to say a special thanks to Alan Dawson and the late Fiona Graham who between them proposed the original list of Grahams on which this book is based. I would also like to thank Tacit Press whose publication *The Grahams and the New Donalds* is the forerunner to this guidebook.

I would also like to thank all those people who have in any way, small or otherwise, helped to make this book a reality. In particular to Heather Dempster, Katharine Muirhead and Alexandrina Robertson.

# CONTENTS

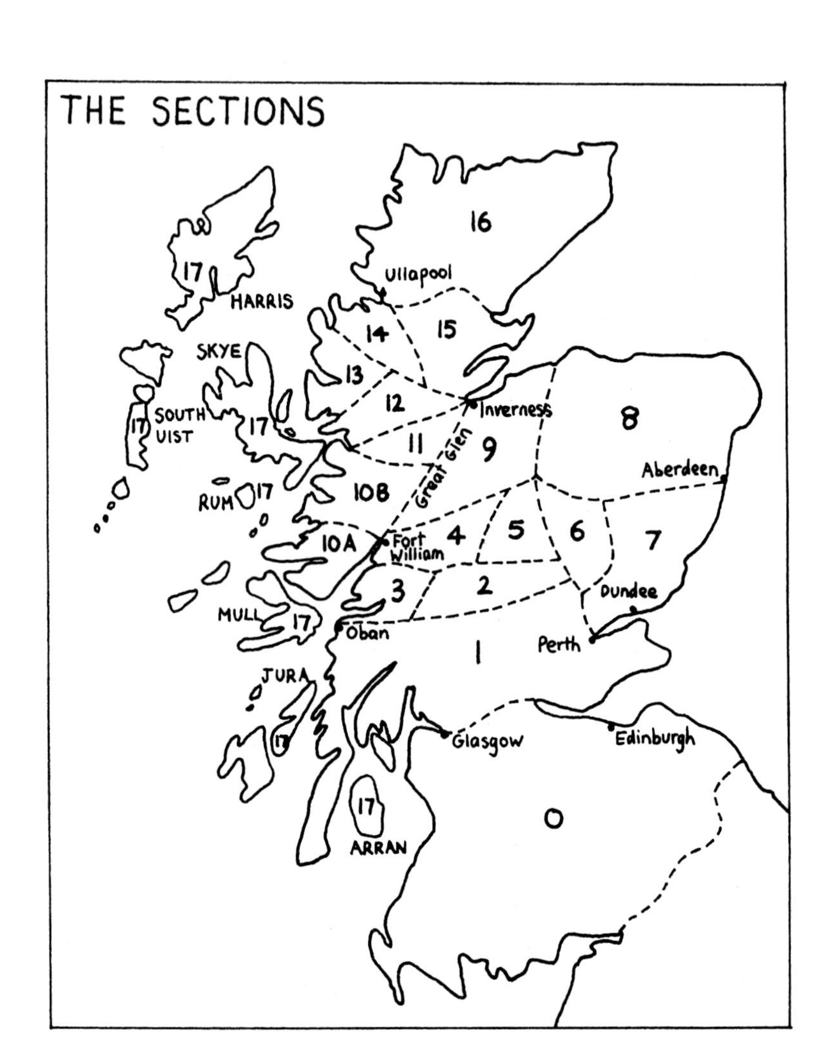
THE SECTIONS
16
Ullapool
15
14
13
12
11
10B
10A
9
8
7
6
5
4
3
2
1
0
17
HARRIS
SKYE
SOUTH
UIST
RUM
MULL
JURA
ARRAN
Inverness
Great Glen
Aberdeen
Fort
William
Dundee
Oban
Perth
Glasgow
Edinburgh

# LIST OF MAPS

# INTRODUCTION

## THE LURE OF LISTS

Once upon a time a man called Hugh Munro compiled a list of Scottish mountains over 3,000ft high and in so doing inadvertently instigated a long-standing tradition of climbing these hills. Today, the growing obsession with 'Munros' has extended to a fascination with lists of hills in general. As more and more people have completed the ascent of all 277 mountains (see end of Introduction) on Sir Hugh's list, they have refused to spend too long basking in the glory of past summit encounters, turning instead to seek out a fresh challenge.

For many, this challenge is another list of hills known as the 'Corbetts', which are between 2,500ft and 3,000ft high. Unlike Munros, Corbetts have the added criterion that there must be at least 500ft in height between each hill and any adjacent higher one. This stipulation, which is implicit in John Rooke Corbett's list though never been openly stated, ensured that the total number of Corbetts has been kept to a manageable figure – there are currently 219. It has also ensured that the reduction in challenge through the reduction in height has been counter-balanced by an increase in challenge due to the distinctive nature of the Corbetts. Baggers hoping for long South Cluanie-type ridges of Corbetts have therefore been disappointed.

As Corbett collectors have neared the end of this secondary quest, many have continued to search for further challenges only to discover that few have been forthcoming. Those who possessed a copy of the SMC guide, *The Corbetts and Other Scottish Hills* (volume 2 following on from the enormously successful volume 1, *The Munros*) would have been aware that the 'Other Scottish Hills' constituted a selection of summits below 2,500ft, over 30 of which are also over 2,000ft. Many may have wondered why there was no definitive list of Scottish mountains between 2,000ft and 2,500ft other than the list of 'Donalds' published along with the Corbetts and Munros in the SMC guide, *Munro's Tables.* Percy Donald's list of hills over 2,000ft in the Scottish Lowlands gave a total of 87 main summits and over 100 subsidiary tops, but used a cumbersome formula for determining what constituted a separate hill. This fact, together with their localised nature, have ensured that

Donalds have never been very popular.

The obvious extension to the Corbetts was therefore to define a list of hills between 2,000ft and 2,500ft with the same criterion of a re-ascent of 500ft. The 224 hills resulting from this classification are known as the 'Grahams'.

## THE BIRTH OF GRAHAMS

In 1992, the popular walking magazine, *The Great Outdoors*, published a list of 244 hills compiled by a woman called Fiona Graham. Her list included every hill between 2,000ft and 2,500ft in height north of the Highland Line 'having a descent all round of about 150m, or being the highest point all round for about two miles'. She had compiled the list while recovering in hospital from a serious skiing accident.

Also in 1992, a book entitled *The Relative Hills of Britain* (Cicerone Press) by Alan Dawson was published. Within its covers is an enormous list of every summit in Britain, regardless of its height above sea-level, which has a re-ascent of at least 150m on all sides. (The rough metric equivalent of Corbett's guideline of 500ft is 150m; that is, 500ft equals 152.4m.) Alan Dawson applied the Corbett re-ascent criterion to all the hills in Britain, and his resolute determination resulted in the current list of 1,551 'Marilyns'. Since 150m is slightly less than 500ft, all the Corbetts have at least this amount of re-ascent and are simply a subdivision of the Marilyns. Similarly, the Grahams are also a subdivision of the Marilyns but are referred to as 'Lesser Corbetts' in Alan Dawson's book.

Having two lists of similar summits with two different names was clearly going to be confusing, so Alan Dawson and Fiona Graham met to agree on drawing up a definitive list of Scottish hills between 2,000ft and 2,500ft. The result of this collaboration was the removal of vagueness as well as some 50 hills from Fiona Graham's list. With the inclusion of 22 hills from the Scottish Lowlands, the pair reached a total of 222. It was agreed that the collective name of 'Graham' would be retained for this class of hill. Since 1992 the number of Grahams has risen to 224 with the promotion of Ladylea Hill (Section 8b) and the demotion of Beiṇn Talaidh on Mull, which had previously been considered a Corbett (Section 17c).

Tragically, Fiona Graham was found murdered while on a hillwalking holiday in the Highlands. She had been listed as missing for almost a year. It is fitting that she will always be remembered in the collective name of these peaks.

This introduction would not be complete without mention being made of a man called William M. Docharty who, in 1948, became the thirteenth person to complete all the Munros. As long ago as this, Docharty had seen the possibilities of climbing hills below 3,000ft, and by 1954 had produced *A Selection of Some 900 British and Irish Mountain Tops* which covered all the main summits above 2,500ft. During the next eight years, he went on to climb and classify all the 2,000ft summits, and in 1962 a second volume was published bringing the grand total of British and Irish mountains to over 2,800. His primary criterion for an independent mountain status was similar to Corbett's but was relaxed in certain circumstances, and it would be true to say that the birth of Grahams had its conception in the volumes of the late William Docharty. (For more information about Docharty see chapter nine of *The Munro Phenomenon* by Andrew Dempster.)

The precursor to this current guide to the Grahams is the booklet, *The Grahams and the New Donalds*, published in 1995 (Tacit Press) by Alan Dawson. This contains a list of all the Grahams together with a revamped list of Donalds which were redefined using a simple drop of 30m rather than Percy Donald's complicated formula. It is stated in the booklet that there is currently no guidebook for the Grahams – which is part of their attraction as many are rarely climbed as part of a series. The book you are now reading is the first (and perhaps the last) guidebook to the Grahams, but its existence will hopefully increase the attraction of these hills rather than making them less popular.

## THE APPEAL OF GRAHAMS

In the introduction to the SMC guide, *The Corbetts and Other Scottish Hills*, it is said that hillwalkers who concentrate their efforts solely on Munros are in danger of missing out on many of the best Scottish mountains. If this sentence was to be changed so that 'Munros' became 'Munros and Corbetts', wouldn't this still leave out many of the best Scottish mountains? Think of hills such as Ben Venue, Marsco, The Storr, the Pap of Glencoe, Stac Pollaidh and Suilven. None of these grand peaks is a Corbett but it would be hard not to include at least a few of them in any list of the hundred best Scottish mountains. Admittedly, all the above-mentioned summits appear as 'Other Scottish Hills' in the SMC guide, and are therefore viewed as worth climbing by that organisation.

Now think of hills such as Stob na Cruaiche, Sgorr a' Choise, Binnein Shuas, Hunt Hill, An Stac, Carnan Cruithneachd, Beinn na h-Eaglaise and Ben Buie. Most hillwalkers could be forgiven for never having heard of any of these, let alone having climbed them. None is listed in the Corbetts guide, but all are Grahams and all have given me some of my most memorable mountain-climbing days in Scotland – and these eight are only a fraction of the scores of others which have hosted equally impressive expeditions.

All of the above hills were ascended in near perfect conditions and not another soul was met on any of them. These two factors play a significant role when assessing the quality of a hill outing and finding the two together is becoming an increasingly rare occurrence on the majority of Munros and many Corbetts. However, the above eight hills, and countless other Grahams, have a lot more to offer than mere solitude at the summit.

In the same way that Corbetts extend the stomping ground of hillwalkers into ever more unfrequented and isolated corners of the Highlands, not to mention Munro-free zones such as the Southern Uplands, Arran and Jura, the Grahams likewise take the hillwalker even further afield into ranges such as the Ochils and islands such as South Uist. The fact that Grahams are found over a very wide area gives them an immediate appeal and presents a challenge which most hill-walkers will find hard to resist. The Grahams range from the rounded grassy tops of the Southern Uplands to the remote rocky summits of Ardgour. They can be isolated heather-clad outposts in Strathspey and Buchan or romantic offshore mountains covering seven different Scottish islands. Those who have visited Mull and only climbed Ben More have missed out on some of the best hillwalking the island has to offer – as well as the Munro of Ben More, Mull contains one Corbett and seven Grahams. The repertoire of hills on Skye has also increased dramatically with ten Grahams to add to the list of 12 Munros and two Corbetts. The Cuillin ridge may well be Mecca for climbers and scramblers, but the relatively unfrequented Trotternish Ridge in the north of the island is a walker's delight and contains two Grahams along its 20-mile crest.

The Grahams too have their share of truly remote summits which will test the determination of the most blinkered hill-bagger. Mountains such as An Stac (Section 10Ba), Creag Mhor (Section 16c) and An Cruachan (Section 12c) are among the remotest hills in the Highlands, with the last staking a claim as possibly the remotest hill in the whole of Scotland. With few paths and fewer people, many Grahams have a distinct feeling of remoteness even though there may be hordes of people on a nearby Munro or Corbett.

It is true that when they are observed in isolation some Grahams are not particularly interesting mountains from a topographical point of view. Many do not possess narrow ridges or fine corries. In fact some are so insignificant that no one has bothered to build a cairn on the summit – that's assuming anyone has actually been to the summit! But lots of Munros and Corbetts are also topographically uninteresting. Many Grahams, on the other hand, do possess fine individual features. But no mountain can be judged solely on appearance.

One of the best characteristics of Grahams is the quality of the views from their summits. Corbetts are often quoted as having finer summit views than Munros. On a Munro you may see more, but it is quality not quantity that is important, and the quality of views from a Graham are often out of all proportion to its modest height. Higher mountains are usually seen to advantage from lower ones, and Grahams often provide the perfect ringside seat to observe the hidden recesses of Munros. A good example is the view of the magnificent triple buttress of Beinn Eighe in Torridon from the summit of Beinn a' Chearcaill (Section 13c). The view across Rannoch Moor to Buachaille Etive Mor from Stob na Cruaiche (Section 2b) is one which will linger in the memory for a long time. The view west from Groban and Beinn Bheag (Section 14a) to the remote mountain fastness of the Fisherfield Forest is a classic.

Summit views, of course, can only be had when low cloud has not descended on the tops. This is another advantage of climbing Grahams as opposed to Munros or Corbetts – the tops of many Grahams are often clear when the higher peaks are submerged in grey. In addition, extremes of weather are not so common, and in winter the snowline may have barely started on the summit of a Graham. This does not imply that less care or less equipment are required on a Graham: every mountain should be treated with respect. Conditions on the summit of *any* mountain (Grahams included) can become severe in the extreme and the usual precautions should be taken. Having said that, it is true *in general* that Grahams provide shorter and easier hill-walking days than Munros or Corbetts, but it must also be noted that the absence of paths on most Grahams can make the going underfoot quite arduous.

The generally less serious nature of these hills make Grahams ideal for a family outing or for your first experience of hillwalking. Many Grahams can be ascended and descended fairly comfortably in less than three hours – it is quite possible to climb a Graham in the morning before descending for lunch then ascending a second one in the afternoon if so desired. Many Grahams can conveniently be climbed during a spare few hours, perhaps while *en route* to part of the Highlands from the south.

There can be little doubt that many hillwalkers enjoy having the framework of a list of hills to work through, whether it be Munros, Corbetts or Grahams. The mere existence of a list gives fresh encouragement to head for the hills perhaps when the spirit or flesh (or both) are weak. But while a list may provide the long-term challenge, it should never become the overriding factor.

Much of what has been written already may indicate that Grahams are only for those staunch hillwalkers who have already completed the Munros and Corbetts. Nothing could be further from the truth. A high proportion of hillwalkers are climbing Munros and Corbetts simultaneously, and Grahams now offer a third option. Whether they are climbed with Corbetts or left until later, or even left for a retirement challenge, they are certainly worth climbing. But don't leave it too late!

## THE USE OF A BICYCLE

A substantial number of the routes described in this book advocate the use of a mountain bike in order to reduce the amount of walking on tracks to reach the more remote hills. The combination of cycling and hillwalking can be extremely satisfying, especially towards the end of the day when the run back out on the bike is almost all downhill. A cool wind blowing on to a perspiring cyclist, happy in the knowledge that another remote Graham is in the bag, can be an addictive pleasure.

I have always held the opinion that wherever motorised vehicles can go then bikes should be allowed too. Unfortunately, some landowners are of the warped belief that simple two-wheeled machines can somehow do more damage than one-ton Land Rovers or all-terrain vehicles. When cyclists go off the beaten track on to walkers' paths then landowners have a valid point – bikes should not be seen on paths designed purely for walking. In the few instances in this book where there could be clashes with a landowner concerning bikes, there is often contradictory advice given by the owners themselves, and it is left to the individual to make his or her own decision as to whether to proceed with a bike. Sometimes a polite phone call before setting out can make all the difference.

## THE SECTIONS *(see map on page 8 and table on page 17)*

The geographical divisions used in this book are identical to those used in the SMC guides to the Munros and Corbetts. The obvious reason for this is to minimise confusion and create some continuity between this guide and the SMC guides. Section 0 was introduced in the Corbetts guide in order to cater for the few Corbetts in the Southern Uplands. Similarly Section 10 was broken down into sections 10A and 10B to allow for the large number of Corbetts in Morven, Sunart, Ardgour and Moidart. One outcome of rigidly adhering to these sections is the large variation in the number of Grahams in each section.

The largest section by far is Section 1 (The Midland Valley to the River Tay) with a total of 43 Grahams, while the smallest is Section 2 (The River Tay to Rannoch Moor) with only two. In fact Sections 5 and 6 (The Southern Grampians) were both so small that they have been combined into one section (Section 5/6) containing just three Grahams. Each main section has been further divided into smaller, more manageable subsections which should prove helpful when planning expeditions.

It is interesting to note from the Distribution Table on page 17 that the Grahams completely dominate the mountain landscape in southern Scotland (Sections 0 and 1) and also the islands (Section 17) with the exception of Skye. In the far north, along with the Corbetts, they also form the major peaks, and similarly Section 10A contains a host of Grahams and Corbetts with no Munros at all. Twelve out of the 18 sections contain more Corbetts or Grahams than Munros, so on the basis of this alone, the smaller hills of Scotland have an assured place.

## Distribution of Scottish Mountains

| Section | Munros | Corbetts | Grahams | Total |
|---|---|---|---|---|
| 0 | 0 | 7 | 21 | 28 |
| 1 | 20 | 21 | 43 | 84 |
| 2 | 25 | 15 | 2 | 42 |
| 3 | 23 | 13 | 12 | 48 |
| 4 | 35 | 7 | 8 | 50 |
| 5 | 7 | 5 | 1 | 13 |
| 6 | 15 | 11 | 2 | 28 |
| 7 | 14 | 5 | 7 | 26 |
| 8 | 17 | 13 | 10 | 40 |
| 9 | 9 | 10 | 9 | 28 |
| 10A | 0 | 16 | 12 | 28 |
| 10B | 26 | 26 | 16 | 68 |
| 11 | 21 | 5 | 7 | 33 |
| 12 | 15 | 12 | 8 | 35 |
| 13 | 7 | 12 | 7 | 26 |
| 14 | 19 | 8 | 8 | 35 |
| 15 | 7 | 5 | 10 | 22 |
| 16 | 4 | 17 | 16 | 37 |
| 17 | 13 | 11 | 25 | 49 |
| **Total** | 277 | 219 | 224 | **720** |

**Note**: The number of Corbetts in the above table is the corrected version of that indicated in the current SMC guide giving 221. Beinn Talaidh on Mull (Section 17) at 761m is now a Graham. Corrieyairack Hill (Section 9) still regarded as a Corbett by the SMC, is now known to be 892m leaving its neighbour Gairbeinn as the Corbett.

### THE MAPS

One major difference between this book and the SMC guides can be found in the maps. Rather than each route being accompanied by its own separate map, it has been deemed more useful to show groups of Grahams on one map. In this way a better idea is gained of their general location and relationship to each other. No attempt has been made to indicate ridge lines or specific routes, and each route description should be read in conjunction with the relevant Ordnance Survey map. In any case, many route descriptions offer alternatives which would not be practicable to show on a location map.

A total of 46 maps cover all 224 Grahams with most maps covering one or two subsections. In all the maps,

Grahams are indicated by black triangles while white triangles indicate Munros or Corbetts; (not all Munros and Corbetts have been marked). Other summits are indicated by white circles. Roads are indicated by dark lines, tracks by dashed lines and footpaths by dotted lines. To avoid clutter and confusion, rivers and forested areas are omitted. Freshwater lochs are marked with random dots while sea lochs are marked with horizontal lines.

## THE ROUTE DESCRIPTIONS

Each route description is preceded by a block of essential information relating to the Graham or group of Grahams to be described. The name of the hill is taken from the relevant 1:50,000 OS map and is followed in brackets by a translation from the Gaelic where appropriate. Where a hill is unnamed on this map then a larger-scale map is used. General names are given rather than summit names where appropriate. The height of the hill above sea-level is given in metres. All spot heights have been taken from Alan Dawson's booklet, which relies heavily on larger-scale maps being generally more accurate than 1:50,000 maps.

The OS sheet number gives the number or numbers of the Ordnance Survey Landranger 1:50,000 map where the summit of the hill is found. If another map is also required, this is mentioned in the route description. Following the map number is the six-figure grid reference of the summit, again using Alan Dawson's information based on larger-scale maps. Where more than one Graham is described, the grid reference of each is given in the order in which the hills are listed.

Information is also given on the length of the proposed route in kilometres (including the return), the total height gain in metres, and a suggestion of how long you can expect to spend completing the route. For instance, a time indication of 3–5 hours would imply that a fairly fast walker could complete the route in three hours while a family or a group of slower walkers might take up to five hours. The number of the sketch map on which the hill appears is also given.

Each route description essentially describes one particular route on which the distance, ascent and time information is based. However, other suggested variations and alternatives are often outlined and these may entail the ascent of additional peaks including Munros and Corbetts. The basic route description in almost all instances gives the ascent of the Graham only and is usually the shortest and most convenient route. Circular routes are generally more satisfying than simply going there and back by the same route, and where possible this has been kept in mind where the situation warrants it. None of the expeditions described requires an overnight stop though a few would certainly benefit from such. This alternative is mentioned where applicable.

Perhaps the most satisfying and fulfilling way of climbing Grahams, and indeed Munros and Corbetts, is during multi-day backpacking trips when body and soul can become totally immersed in the mountain landscape – and also in rain and mist if the weather decides to be unco-operative! Such trips, however, are not the main aim of this book and the majority of routes described can be completed in less than five hours, and a great deal in less than three hours.

## BEYOND THE GRAHAMS

What is left to the Scottish hillwalker who has completed all the 720 Munros, Corbetts and Grahams? Plenty! Any hillwalker worth his or her salt will have climbed many, if not all, of what are known as the 'Munro Tops'; that is, subsidiary summits over 3,000ft which are not ranked as separate Munro mountains. These currently number 240, and, when added to the above figure, produce a mammoth 960 Scottish listed summits over 2,000ft.

Alternatively, you could dispense with the subjectivity of Munros and aim instead to climb all the 'Murdos' – that is, the 444 peaks in Scotland which are over 3,000ft high and have a drop of at least 30m (approximately 100ft) all round. Murdos were the brainchild of Alan Dawson, who found the subjective nature of the Munros and Tops designation irrational and unappealing. A list can be found in the small booklet, *The Murdos*, by Alan Dawson, published by Tacit Press.

Below 3,000ft, the Corbetts and Grahams certainly constitute the main mountain summits, and subsidiary tops are currently not officially listed in any publication other than William Docharty's out-of-print work from the 1960s. An analysis and listing by me a few years ago produced a total of about 240 non-Corbett hills between 2,500ft and 3,000ft with a drop of at least 50m all round. A similar analysis produced about 470 non-Graham hills in the range 2,000ft to 2,500ft. The names 'Corbett Tops' and 'Graham Tops' are not really applicable to these hills as in many cases they are subsidiary not only to Corbetts or Grahams but also to Munros. A better description would be 'Lesser Corbetts' and 'Lesser Grahams', the 'lesser' implying that they do not have the required 150m of ascent all round. The ultimate listing would be to apply the 'Murdo Criterion' (30m of drop) to all hills above 2,000ft. Even with the 50m drop specification used above, the total number of Murdos, Corbetts, Lesser Corbetts, Grahams and Lesser Grahams is around the 1,600 mark. It would be fair to say that the number of Scottish hills above 2,000ft with at least 30m of re-ascent is approaching 2,000 – which is enough climbing for a lifetime.

But why stop at 2,000ft? Classic little hills such as Ben A'n, Sgurr na Stri, Hecla, Ben Shieldaig and Maiden Pap are all under this height but are every bit as worth climbing as a host of higher mountains. All of the above except Ben A'n are Marilyns (i.e. hills with a drop of at least 150m all round). Of the 1,213 of these in Scotland, 565 are below

2,000ft and constitute yet another major challenge – especially since they include the remote and almost inaccessible sea-stacks of Stac Lee and Stac an Armin in the St Kilda group of islands.

Yet it is in the nature of mountains that there will always remain a stubborn few which refuse to drop neatly into any category. Ben A'n, the little jewel of the Trossachs, is possibly the epitome of such a mountain and probably sees more walkers and climbers than many a popular Munro. It is the ascent of hills such as Ben A'n which brings into focus the real reason why we climb hills, or the real reason we *ought* to climb hills – not because they appear on a list, but because they are worth climbing in their own right.

The Grahams may not all be like Ben A'n, but only the walker can decide if some are not worth climbing. The last section of this introduction indicates the enormous scope in Scotland for hill-walking and resolutely confirms the words of Fiona Graham: 'When advancing years bring assorted aches and pains, [and] Munros and Corbetts are done, or not done, you can still feel an explorer in Scotland.'

* The latest revision by the SMC has produced eight new Munros and deleted one existing Munro, bringing the total number of Munros to 284. For details see the new edition of *Munros Tables* published by the SMC, October 1997.

# SECTION 0

## *Galloway and the Borders*

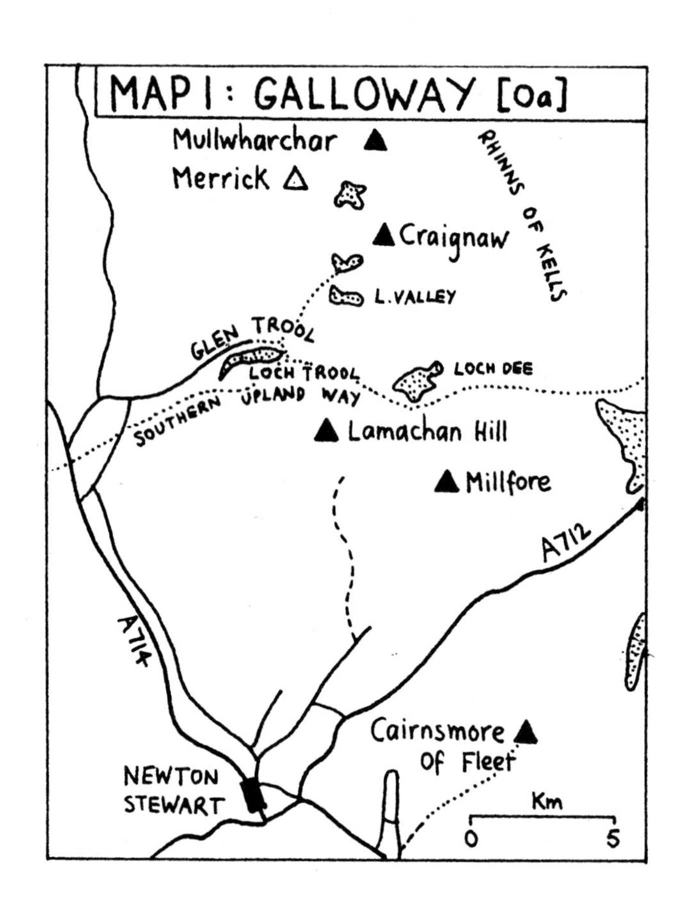
MAP 1: GALLOWAY [Oa]
Mullwharchar
Merrick
RHINNS OF KELLS
Craignaw
L.VALLEY
GLEN TROOL
LOCH TROOL
LOCH DEE
SOUTHERN UPLAND WAY
Lamachan Hill
Millfore
A712
A714
Cairnsmore Of Fleet
NEWTON STEWART
Km
0
5

**Craignaw**; *645m*
**Mullwharchar**; *692m*
*OS Sheet 77; GR 459833, 454866*
*21km/1,100m/6–9hrs*
*Map 1*

The area around Glen Trool is as wild and rugged as many parts of the Highlands, and indeed the vast mountainous area between Loch Trool, Clatteringshaws Loch and Loch Doon to the north exhibits a Highland charm seemingly out of place considering its far southern location. The region is sometimes known as the 'Lake District' of southern Scotland; comparisons are only approximations, however, and the Galloway hills have a unique character of their own. Craignaw and Mullwharchar lie in the heart of the area, and a long circuit from Glen Trool taking in these and the Corbett of Merrick is probably the finest high-level walk in the Southern Uplands.

Begin at the end of the public road in Glen Trool where a track descends steeply to Buchan. Follow this down and cross the bridge over the Buchan burn. Just beyond the bridge go left through a gate and follow the path which makes a gradual rising traverse along the southern slopes of Buchan Hill. Grand views of tree-lined Loch Trool can be enjoyed as the path gains height. Continue on the path which enters a wide glen following the Gairland burn up to a series of secluded high hill lochs. On the map the path appears to end at Loch Valley, but a boggy path follows the west bank to a stone shelter, crossing the burn before Loch Neldricken and then following the southern shore of this loch. At this point the conical mass of Mullwharchar is very evident and the granite outcrops of Craignaw can be seen directly ahead. Wild goats are often found in this area.

At the head of the loch climb tussocky slopes following the line of the burn which flows down to the south of the main crags. The summit of Craignaw lies almost 1km to the north and the abundant granite slabs make the walking easier higher up. It should be noted that Craignaw possesses several false summits and this may be confusing in misty conditions. The actual summit is perched on a granite tor and there is a substantial cairn.

The line of crags known as the Black Gairy continues round to the north of the hill and care should be taken on the descent north to reach the north-west ridge. Good walking on granite slabs leads down to a cairn at the col before Dungeon Hill. A slanting line to the right leads over the lowest part of this hill and down to the final col below Mullwharchar, which is an easy ascent of less than 200m to the cairn at its summit, a grand viewpoint.

Descend south-west and cross the Eglin Lane burn north of Loch Enoch before gaining the eastern slopes of Merrick. Note that any route back to Loch Trool from this point which does not include the Merrick climb is long and fairly arduous. Remember also that an excellent path exists all the way from the summit of the Merrick to the

*Curlywee and Millfore from Lamachan Hill*

starting point, and the Merrick climb is the easiest option even if the thought of another 350m ascent is not pleasant.

Towards the top the angle eases off and a final flat walk leads to the summit cairn and triangulation pillar. The descent path goes south-west over the subsidiary top of Benyellary following a drystane dyke. Beyond this top the path gradually swings south, dropping down through the forestry plantation to follow the Buchan burn back to the starting point.

**Lamachan Hill**; *717m*
**Millfore**; *657m*
*OS Sheet 77; GR 435769, 478754*
*22km/1,050m/6½–9hrs*
*Map 1*

---

These two Grahams lie south of Loch Trool and Loch Dee, the meandering line of the Southern Upland Way separating them from the north Galloway ranges. Lamachan Hill and its shapelier eastern neighbour of Curleywee make a pleasant round from Glen Trool, but the inclusion of Millfore to the south-east adds significantly to the length of time necessary to complete this outing. Despite this, the following is a description of the traverse of both hills which makes a challenging hill walk for the fit.

Begin at the end of the public road in Glen Trool and descend the steep track to Buchan. Follow the track east until a point is reached about 300m short of the farm at Glenhead. A Southern Upland Way sign indicates the point at which you should leave the track and follow a vague grassy path down to the Glenhead burn which is crossed by a wooden foot-bridge. (Note that there is also a disused foot-bridge about 50m downstream of the new one.) Follow the

Southern Upland Way for about 1km through the trees until you emerge on to a forestry track higher up. Go left here and after 200m leave the track to follow the line of Shiel burn steeply upwards through the trees where it emerges suddenly to open hillside.

On the eastern side of the burn a fine little ridge soon becomes apparent and this should be gained to eventually reach a flat area just north of Lamachan Hill and Bennanbrack. The flat summit of Lamachan Hill is easily reached from here either directly or via the col below Bennanbrack. The summit cairn is to the south and forms part of a drystane wall. On a clear day there is a very fine view north to Merrick, Mullwharchar and Craignaw.

The distinctive conical shape of the delightfully named Curleywee is the next objective and is reached by following the well-defined ridge over Bennanbrack. A steep rocky step has to be negotiated on the descent but should pose no real problems. You can either climb the next small top directly or use a path which contours steeply round its north side, to reach a fence below the craggy slopes of Curleywee. This hill can be avoided if so wished but it would be a pity to omit what is probably the finest of the group.

Curleywee has a good summit cairn and is a grand place to linger on a warm day. It is also a good spot to appreciate the extra distance and height drop needed in order to reach Millfore. Those who have had enough for one day can easily descend north over White Hill and regain the Southern Upland Way.

Millfore is best reached by heading south initially then east down steeper slopes to reach the col below Bennan Hill. Climb tussocky, undulating ground to the vicinity of Black Loch before another obvious rise leads to the White Lochan of Drigmorn. This was a favourite spot for curlers in the past and on a warm day is a fine secluded area in which to take a long rest. The summit of Millfore is soon reached from here by keeping to the higher ground on the right before traversing onto the ridge. The actual summit has a triangulation pillar with two cairns on either side.

The most direct way back is to leave the summit in a north-westerly direction, crossing the Black Laggan burn lower down and making a slight rise over a subsidiary ridge before descending to the path coming up from White Laggan. This leads back to the Southern Upland Way which can be followed west to the route used in the walk in.

Millfore can be ascended as a separate expedition from Craigencallie House to the north-east or from the parking area near Black Loch to the south. Both hills can also be ascended from the Penkiln forestry track to the south but this approach involves problems with forestry and is not so aesthetically pleasing.

**Cairnsmore of Fleet;** *711m*
*OS Sheet 83; GR 501670*
*13km/680m/3–5hrs*
*Map 1*

This popular hill lies east of Newton Stewart and is the most southerly of all the Grahams. The easiest route of ascent is a well-trodden path on the western flank, but various other routes are also possible.

Leave the A75 road at GR 457629 and follow a minor road over a bridge before turning right under a stone viaduct into Cairnsmore Estate. Drive up the estate track for over 1km, going round to the rear of some estate buildings before parking at a small signposted area specifically for walkers using the hill track. Walk left to the end of the track and go through a gate into a large field. Head north-east across the field to reach a metal gate higher up behind some gorse bushes. This marks the beginning of the hill path which initially passes through natural woodland then sitka spruce forest.

Cross a forestry track higher up and continue on the path until it emerges from the forest at a height of about 400m. Shortly beyond this point cross a fence at a stile and continue on the path as it zigzags up the steepest part of the hill. Towards the summit the path levels off and passes a granite memorial dedicated to the numerous airmen killed on this hill since 1940. Shortly beyond the memorial a triangulation pillar and large shelter cairn mark the summit of the hill.

The quickest descent is by the route of ascent but the following offers a more interesting variation and the time and distance information given above is based on this option. Cairnsmore of Fleet is actually a long ridge running

*Windmill generators on Windy Standard*

north-west to the south-east and by following the crest of the ridge south-east a fence is joined which leads to a col and a wall crossing the ridge. From the col an easy ascent leads to a cairn (656m) on the Knee of Cairnsmore. From this cairn descend roughly south to south-west on fairly steep slopes for 350m to reach the end of a track which can be followed down by the Graddoch burn on the south side of Crammery Hill. This leads back to Cairnsmore Estate and the starting point in 4.5km.

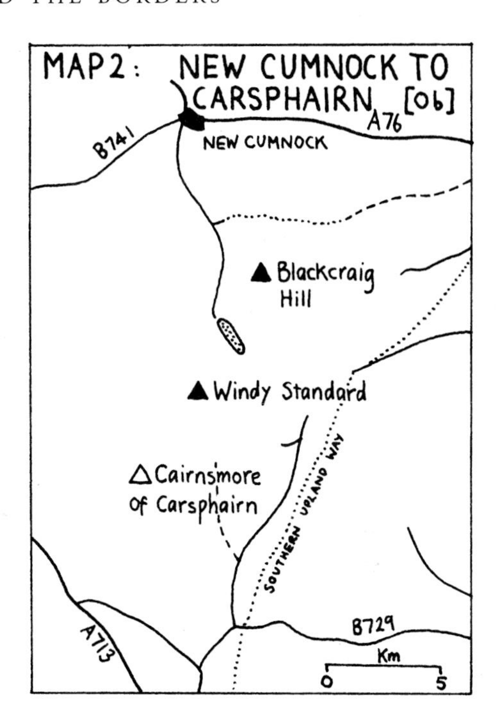


**Windy Standard**; *698m*
*OS Sheet 77; GR 620014*
*12km/580m/3–5hrs*
*Map 2*

The appearance of this hill has altered significantly within the last few years with the placing of scores of 'windmill' electricity-generating pylons on and around the summit. Leaving aside the merits of such man-made intrusions in wild upland moor, the result is that the summit of Windy Standard no longer feels like the remote outpost it once was. On top of this, the serried ranks of sitka spruce are slowly but steadily encroaching from all directions to further confirm man's presence. The approach described here avoids forestry plantations but includes the odd electric fence!

From the B729 road to the south take the minor road at GR 633919 which follows the Water of Ken to the track leading to Nether Holm of Dalquhairn. Park at or near the end of this track and walk the 500m to the vicinity of the farmhouse. After crossing the bridge over the Spout burn, head round to the right of the wooded copse behind the farmhouse. Go through a gate and head directly up the grassy hillside, negotiating an electric fence some distance up. Gradually traverse right to reach the col south-east of Mid Hill of Glenhead. Ascend this hill following a fence and from the summit enjoy a fine view of Windy Standard to the north-west with its wind-powered generators plainly visible. Note that the path shown (on some earlier maps) running along the northern slopes of Mid Hill has all but disappeared and is not usable.

The summit of this hill is a good place to view the unusual drumlin formation in the Upper Holm burn valley to the north. Scores of alluvial mounds formed by the retreating glacier huddle together like a basket of eggs. Continue to follow the fence down to the wide col below Windy Standard and ascend tussocky slopes to a broad shoulder where a large boulder known as the Deil's Putting Stone can be found just off to the left of the ridge. By this stage numerous other wind generators will have come into view and by the time you reach the summit you might feel rather like a modern-day Don Quixote. The triangulation pillar and tiny wind-charger are dwarfed by the alien windmill structures – at least fifty in all – stretching out to Trostan Hill and the north-westerly ridge of Jedburgh Knees.

The time and distance information given above is based on a return by the route of ascent; but if time, weather and inclination permit, it makes a good circuit to descend east to the col below Alhang and ascend this hill. The descent of this hill by its south-east ridge via Mid Rig leads directly back to the starting point.

Other possible approaches to Windy Standard include the forestry track past Moorbrock to the south of the hill. This makes a large loop at the head of the glen which is not indicated in the current (1995) OS map. Access to the col between Mid Hill and Windy Standard is straightforward from this loop.

*The cluttered summit of Green Lowther*

**Blackcraig Hill**; *700m*
*OS Sheet 71, 77; GR 647064*
*9km/450m/2–3½hrs*
*Map 2*

---

This fairly commanding hill sits on the east side of picturesque Glen Afton lying south of New Cumnock. It is surprisingly craggy compared to the surrounding hills and has a girth of crags known as the Black Clints on the steep western flank. The most convenient approach begins at the bridge over the Afton Water at Blackcraig to the north-west of the hill.

Follow the track to the house before turning to the left and climbing the hillside on a muddy path to the left of the small copse behind Blackcraig. Go through a metal gate and gain the marked path which gradually ascends open hillside following the line of a shallow gully and stream course. A cairn on the horizon at Quinton Knowe marks the col to the north of the hill and is plainly visible from the path (and, indeed, the road).

Continue along the sometimes boggy path to the cairn and go past the cairn for a few hundred metres before turning south to gain the broad north ridge of the hill. A fence goes up this ridge to the left of the line of ascent. The ridge soon begins to level off and at least four cairns are passed before reaching the true summit with a triangulation pillar and cairn 50m beyond. In misty conditions these cairns may be more of a hindrance than a help as they have the appearance of summit cairns. The penultimate one is a useful shelter cairn in inclement weather. Descend by the route of ascent.

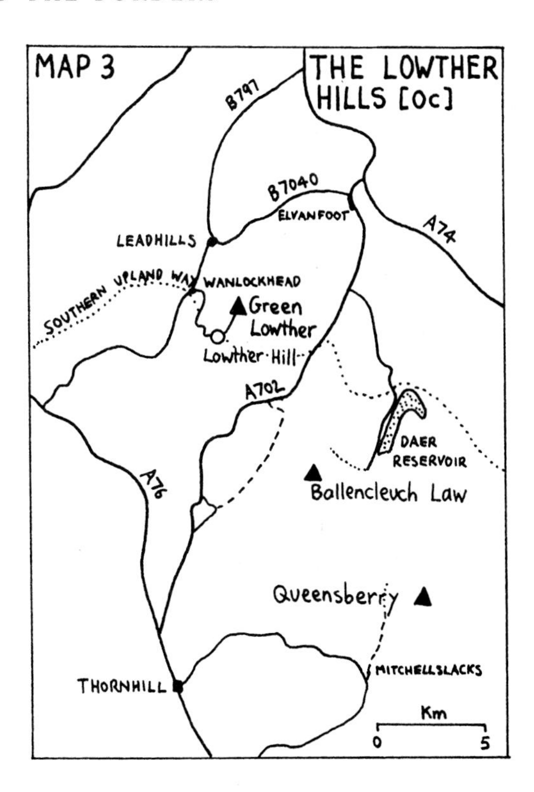


**Green Lowther**; 732m
*OS Sheet 78; GR 900120*
*11km/280m/2–3hrs*
*Map 3*

---

Green Lowther is the highest summit of the district range of rounded hills known as the Lowther Hills which lie between the A74 and the A76 south of Leadhills and Wanlockhead. Both these villages developed as a result of gold, silver and lead mining, and Wanlockhead at a height of nearly 470m stakes a claim as the highest village in Scotland. Both Green Lowther and its smaller neighbour, Lowther Hill, to the south-west possess cluttered and extremely prominent radar installations on their summits which detract somewhat from an enjoyable ascent. Despite this, the advantage of a high starting point and a tarmac service road all the way to the top make for a very quick ascent. Green Lowther is the only Graham, Corbett or Munro with such a road to the summit. Cars are *not* allowed!

Begin at Wanlockhead at the start of the radar installation service road which is followed east and then south over rolling moor before reaching the summit of Lowther Hill in a series of large zigzags. The large white geodesic dome structures are an unmistakeable landmark for miles around. Continue along the road which now heads north-east along the broad ridge to a minor top with further installations. Finally, drop slightly and follow the road to its termination on Green Lowther with its assorted clutter of pylons, dish aerials and buildings. The triangulation pillar is dwarfed by the surrounding structures. (In the depths of winter the summits of these hills give the climber the impression of being at some remote Antarctic station.) Descend by the same road.

An alternative start begins above the village centre and follows the Southern Upland Way for 1km before joining the service road.

**Ballencleuch Law**; 689m
*OS Sheet 78; GR 935049*
*7km/340m/2–3½hrs*
*Map 3*

Ballencleuch Law is the highest point of the clutch of Lowther Hills lying immediately south of the A702 Elvanfoot to Thornhill road. It is best approached from the Daer Reservoir to the north-east, where a minor road ends at Kirkhope Farm to the south of the reservoir.

From Kirkhope a path/vehicle track leads up the spur of Catlow Dod and passes close to the triangulation pillar on Rodger Law. Follow this easily to the summit of Rodger Law where there is also a radio mast. From here continue south-west to a col and follow a fence to the rather featureless summit of Ballencleuch Law where there is a tiny cairn. Green Lowther and Lowther Hill are very prominent partly because of the intrusive radar installations on their summits. Return by the same route.

This hill can also be reached from Durisdeer to the south-west where a track leads up Durisdeer Rig. With two cars or a kind driver it would be a pleasant outing to combine these routes, beginning at Kirkhope and ending at Durisdeer.

**Queensberry**; 697m
*OS Sheet 78; GR 989997*
*11km/490m/2½–4hrs*
*Map 3*

This hill forms the south-eastern termination of the Lowther range and its height and conical shape make it a fairly prominent landmark from all directions. It is situated a great distance from major roads and is perhaps not as popular as some other Border hills, such as Tinto Hill, which are more accessible.

From Thornhill on the A76 road a minor road makes a massive loop on the eastern side of the A76 skirting the southern edge of the Lowther range. The easternmost extremity of this minor road at Mitchellslacks is the most convenient starting point for the ascent of Queensberry.

Follow the track which crosses the Capel Water and goes through the farmyard before ascending to open hillside. The track contours along the west side of the Law above the deep trough formed by the Capel burn. The prominent hill directly ahead is Earncraig Hill and Queensberry itself cannot be seen. About 500m before New House take the minor grassy track which forks off to the right, climbing directly to the wider shoulder of Glengowan hill. The distinctive little cone of Wee Queensberry can be clearly seen from this point. From here the track heads north-east towards the fairly featureless whale-back of Queensberry with the track itself becoming less distinct. A prominent marker cairn on the horizon is a suitable point to aim for but is not the actual summit. This lies a few hundred metres further on and is marked by a large sprawling cairn.

The time and distance information is based on a return by the same route, but the descent could be varied by heading roughly south to the col below Wee Queensberry and ascending this before dropping south-west to pick up the track below the Law.

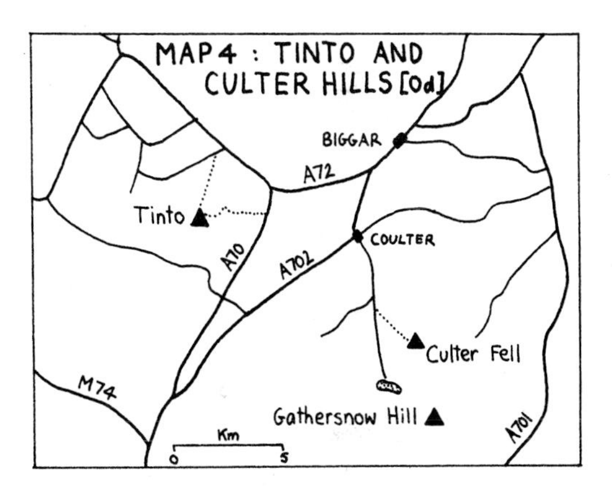


**Tinto**; *711m*
*OS Sheet 72; GR 953343*
*7km/480m/2–3hrs*
*Map 4*

Tinto and the Culter Hills form the north-western extremities of the Southern Uplands, with the River Clyde flowing between them. Tinto is actually situated in the Midland Valley of Scotland as it stands north of the Clyde but is normally regarded as one of the Border hills. Being almost completely surrounded by low-lying countryside it is a conspicuous landmark from all directions and is a popular and frequently climbed hill.

On the A73 Lanark road just opposite Thankerton road end is the Tinto Hill Tearoom (an ideal après-climb spot). The usual starting point for the ascent of Tinto is near Fallburn to the north of the hill. A minor road is followed to a large carpark where a distinct but often boggy path climbs to the shoulder of Totherin Hill, before the final haul to the summit of Tinto. In the latter reaches past the hollow of Maurice's Cleuch, the path follows a fence. The top is crowned by what is probably the largest cairn on any Scottish hill, the width at the base being at least 10m, and is almost certainly of prehistoric origin. The viewpoint symbol marked on the OS map is certainly well deserved, as on a clear day the panorama is unequalled in southern Scotland. Mountains as far away as Skiddaw in the English Lake District and Lochnagar in the Cairngorms have been spotted, while Arran and Ailsa Craig can sometimes be visible on the western horizon.

The distance and time given above are based on a return by the same route, but as Tinto has no less than three distinct paths to its summit it is an ideal hill for a complete traverse. The only drawback of descending by a different route is, of course, a long road walk at the end – unless two cars are available. Descent by the easterly path over Scaut Hill includes about 4km of road walking, whilst descent by the shorter and steeper southerly path to Millrig would involve 11km on the road and it is not a sensible option without a second car. A further option is to make a pathless descent of the broad north-west ridge to Cleuch Reservoir and then follow the quiet minor road for 4km back to the carpark.

*Culter Fell from Gathersnow Hill*

**Culter Fell**; *748m*
**Gathersnow Hill**; *688m*
*OS Sheet 72; GR 052290, 058257*
*17km/730m/4–5hrs*
*Map 4*

Two obvious starting points compete with each other for a convenient round of these two highest summits of the Culter Hills. One is Holms Waterhead to the east and the other is Culter Waterhead on the west. The western approach has the advantage of numerous new bulldozed tracks in the lower reaches (though some would see this in the opposite light!) and this is the approach described.

Having mentioned Culter Waterhead as a starting point it has now to be stated that cars are only allowed as far as the Birthwood junction about 4km short of Culter Waterhead. Various signs at this point make their intention quite clear: 'Walkers Welcome – Their Vehicles Are Not' and 'Unauthorised Vehicles May Be Removed'. However, just half a kilometre beyond here the distinct north-west ridge of Culter Fell is easily gained, initially by the track following Kings Beck, and, a few hundred metres after, by a well-defined stalkers' path passing numerous stone shooting butts. The path is unrelenting for about 250m of height gain before levelling off near a large cairn. The summit of Culter Fell is still about 1km from here and another 200m in vertical height. The summit trig-point stands next to the boundary fence separating Strathclyde region from the Borders, which in misty conditions is a good guide as it leads directly to the summit of Gathersnow Hill.

Follow the fence, more or less due south, and drop over 150m to the boggy col below Moss Law. Continue over this and then descend to Holm Nick where a new Land Rover track ascends from the reservoir. This track can be followed for a short distance (to the left) before it peters out and a faint ATV track takes over, again following the boundary fence. A final sharp turn to the west leads directly to the spacious summit of Gathersnow Hill, where a small cairn sits by the fence.

Gathersnow Hill stands proudly at the head of three stream systems: the Culter Water, Holms Water and Kingledoors Burn, the first flowing to the Clyde and the other two to the Tweed. The name, 'Gathersnow', no doubt refers to its ability to hold snow, which feeds these three streams. Tinto Hill is seen to advantage from here, directly beyond the Culter Waterhead reservoir, and in the opposite direction Fruid and Tala Reservoirs dominate the view.

From the summit descend in a north-westerly direction to pick up another bulldozed track which zigzags down to Culter Water, and the reservoir. Follow the track round the north shore to the dam at Culter Waterhead before a pleasant 3½km walk on the single-track road to the starting point.

A longer day could be made by doing a complete high-level circuit of the reservoir via the tops of Hudderstone, Woodycleuch Dod and Ward Law. From Hudderstone it is also possible to descend north-west to a track leading to Cow Gill and Birthwood.

**Blackhope Scar**; *651m*
*OS Sheet 73; GR 315483*
*11km/370m/3–4hrs*
*Map 5*

Blackhope Scar is the second highest summit in the Moorfoot range of hills which, together with the Lammermuirs, form the northern extremity of the Southern Uplands. In reality the Moorfoots are more a dissected plateau than a distinct range of hills and as a result the going higher up can often be quite arduous with much boggy, poorly drained ground. On the positive side, the view across the Lothian plain to the Pentlands and Edinburgh more than compensates for the awkward terrain.

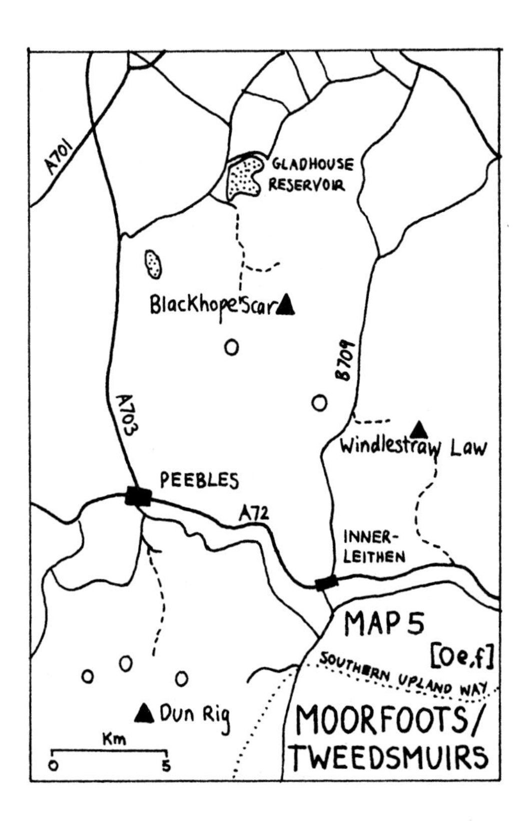


The hill is best climbed from the north at Gladhouse reservoir where cars can be parked at GR 292527 next to the sign relating to the reservoir. It should be noted that cars are not encouraged beyond this point and at least one sign requests drivers not to park on verges or beside gates. Walk along the road to Moorfoot farm and follow the initially muddy track to Gladhouse Cottage. Just short of the cottage take the fork to the left and cross the River South Esk where the ruin of Hirendean Castle is visible above a group of trees on the opposite side. This makes an interesting side excursion.

Continue along the track by the river and at a small hut branch off to the left on a secondary track just south of The Kipps. This track ascends quickly onto the broad heathery ridge north of Blackhope Scar. From here it is 'simply' a matter of following the boundary fence for about 1km directly to the summit. The insertion of inverted commas refers to the tussocky, boggy nature of the ground, which does not make it easy walking. The view from the summit trig-point on a clear day is extensive, with the Pentland Hills, Arthur's Seat and the urban sprawl of Edinburgh distinctly visible to the north. Return by the same route, or vary by dropping west into the Long Cleave to reach the track by the South Esk.

Another possible means of ascent is from the north-east on the B7007 road where a track can be followed past Blackhope to Wooly Law, 2km from the summit of Blackhope Scar. Scenically this is less interesting, however.

**Windlestraw Law**; *659m*
*OS Sheet 73; GR 371431*
*7km/370m/1½–2½hrs*
*Map 5*

This is the highest hill in the Moorfoots and lies north-east of the Borders town of Innerleithen. As with other hills in the area the going underfoot can be quite arduous, especially near the summit plateau. The shortest route to the top begins on the B709 road running north from Innerleithen at a point just south of Blackhopebyre. From here a grass track ascends Glentress Rig, petering out into boggy, heathery ground on Wallet Knowe after about 2km. This point is only just over a kilometre to the summit but the going is hard in deep heather, although a few grassy tongues make things easier. A fence can be followed to the triangulation point which is near the junction of three fences. Descend by the same route.

A more interesting though much longer route begins at Holylee on the A72 road where a track leads up by the Gatehopeknowe burn through a deep glen to end at a height of 420m just east of Seathope Rig. From here the summit can be reached in less than a kilometre by an initially short steep climb. The ideal way to tackle this hill would be to combine the above routes in a complete traverse, though this alternative would obviously create some transport problems.

**Dun Rig**; 744m
*OS Sheet 73; GR 253316*
*20km/650m/5–7hrs*
*Map 5*

Dun Rig is the highest point of the eastern Tweedsmuir hills lying directly south of the pleasant Border town of Peebles. The Western Tweedsmuirs to the west of Manor Water rise to 840m on Broad Law, the second-highest hill in the Southern Uplands. Although Dun Rig occupies a fairly commanding position at the head of Glensax, its gentle summit contours and general remoteness from civilisation give it a shy and retiring character. The usual approach to the hill is via Glensax and this can be combined with a high-level ridge walk to make a varied day's hillwalking.

From Peebles, cross the road bridge over the Tweed before turning immediately left then forking right into Springhill Road. Drive along Springhill Road into a recent housing estate and reach the end of the public road where cars can be parked near an electricity generating station. Directly ahead there is a Scottish 'Rights of Way' sign indicating a footpath to Yarrow by the Gypsy Glen. This is the path marked on the OS map which follows the ridge line east of Glensax, and forms the return route of the following description. The route can, of course, be equally tackled in reverse.

Take the track on the right which leads delightfully for 6km to the deserted wooden dwelling-house named Glensax through the glen of the same name. By this stage the lofty dome of Dun Rig will dominate the view to the head of the glen. Cross the Glensax burn by a wooden bridge and ascend the long curving north ridge of Dun Rig which levels out in the central section. The summit trig point stands at the corner of a boundary fence next to a gate and is a fine vantage point with a remote and spacious feeling.

Leave the summit in a roughly north-easterly direction and pick up a line of old fence posts which leads over Stake Law and down to the boggy col below Birkscairn Hill. By this stage the right of way path will be apparent and this can be followed along the undulating ridge crest. Birkscairn Hill itself is bypassed on the west but can be easily climbed if so wished. The route continues over Kirkhope Law and Kailzie Hill before finally descending through wooded country to the starting point. This completes an extremely satisfying circular route.

The shortest approach to Dun Rig is from the east at Glenshiel Banks but does not do justice to the hill. Another longer route to the hills begins at the northern end of St Mary's Loch to the south and follows the Southern Upland Way to Blackhouse before continuing on forestry tracks to the east of Bught Rig. This southern approach can also be started at Craig Douglas on the A708 Selkirk to Moffat road.

**Andrewhinney Hill**; *677m*
*OS Sheet 79; GR 197138*
*3km/350m/1–2hrs*
*Map 6*

This Graham is the highest point of the long, undulating grassy ridge which connects Herman Law in the north to Bodesbeck Law in the south, running parallel to the A708 Selkirk to Moffat road and also the Southern Upland Way. The hill lies directly opposite the Grey Mare's Tail waterfall, and both this feature and the Corbett of White Coomb are seen to advantage from the vicinity of the summit. The ascent of the hill could be included in an 8km ridge walk connecting the tops mentioned above but is quickly climbed from the road to the north of the summit.

A good starting point is the bridge over Raking Gill, where a faint path ascends the steep hillside gradually fading out higher up. The angle lessens towards the broad heathery ridge and a fence can be followed directly to the summit which boasts a reasonable cairn. This fence stretches the full length of the ridge and is a useful navigational aid in misty conditions. Return by the same route or descend the northern spur to gain better views of the Grey Mare's Tail.

**Capel Fell;** *678m*
**Croft Head;** *637m*
**Ettrick Pen;** *692m*
*OS Sheet 79; GR 163069, 153056, 199076*
*18km/900m/5–7hrs*
*Map 6*

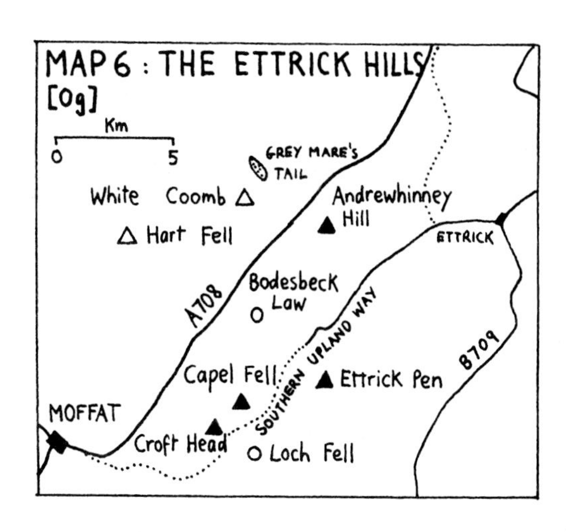


These three hills are part of a little-frequented cluster of high fells known as the Ettrick Hills, situated north-east of the quaint Borders town of Moffat. The Southern Upland Way passes through the area and all three hills could be conveniently climbed as part of this long-distance route. The most convenient starting point is at the end of the public road which follows the Ettrick Water where there is a small parking area.

Follow the Southern Upland Way past Potburn Farm and on to Over Phawhope, where there is an excellent bothy maintained by the MBA. The track continues over a small wooden footbridge and climbs upwards through a forestry plantation to emerge at Ettrick Head at the edge of the forest. Continue for a short distance to the boundary fence and gate dividing the Borders region from Dumfries and Galloway. Follow the fence upwards in a north-westerly direction to reach the cairnless summit of Capel Fell, the actual top being slightly north of the junction of three fences.

Return to the route of the Southern Upland Way by more or less the same way as the route of ascent. This avoids very steep slopes to the south of the hill. The path traverses along the lower slopes of Loch Fell with the waters of the Selcoth burn rushing through a steep gorge below. Above this gorge is the natural feature of Craigmichan Scar where an extensive area of hillside has eroded away to leave bare rock, rubble and scree. At the point where the Southern Upland Way continues south-west and another path follows the Selcoth burn north-west, the obvious grassy east ridge of Croft Head separates the two and an old stone shelter marks the foot of this ridge. An easy ascent of about 250m leads to the featureless summit at the junction of various fences.

To reach the final top of Ettrick Pen, retrace the route to Ettrick Head (avoiding Capel Fell of course) and follow the edge of the forest around the north slopes of Wind Fell. Aim for the prominent cairn near the summit of Hopetoun Craig before traversing this hill and following the rough path to the large cairn at the summit of Ettrick Pen.

The vast area of sitka forest to the south and east is all too noticeable from the airy summit of this hill.

The quickest return route is by the grassy western spur which drops down to a track entering a wide fire-break leading to Over Phawhope and the Southern Upland Way.

**Cauldcleuch Head;** *619m*
*OS Sheet 79; GR 456006*
*10km/430m/2½–4hrs*
*Map 7*

---

Cauldcleuch Head is a lone Graham forming the highest point of a rolling range of hills south-west of the main Cheviot group. As the crow flies it is only 15km from the Scotland–England border and boasts the dubious honour of being the nearest Graham to England! A variety of approaches are possible and if transport can be arranged it is a good idea to make a complete north–south traverse of the hill, incorporating several other summits *en route.* The route to be described, however, begins and ends at Priesthaugh to the north of the hill.

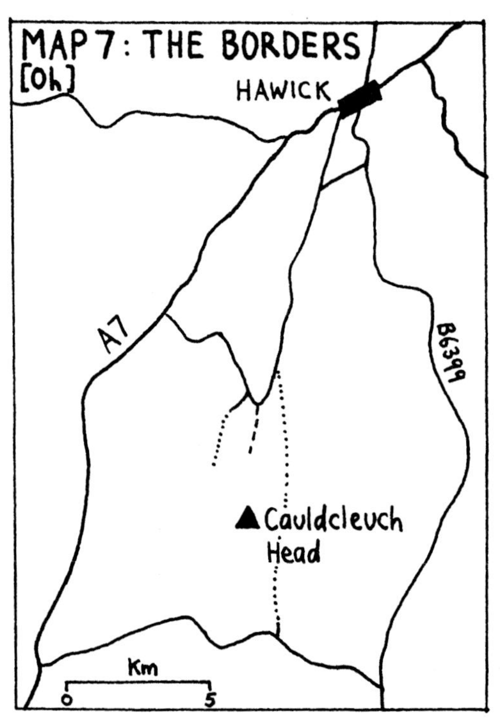


From Priesthaugh follow a farm track south by Priesthaugh burn for about 2km through a pleasant grassy glen, which is often teeming with sheep. The track ends at Priesthaugh Hill and at this point make a direct ascent of Skelfhill Fell following the edge of the forestry plantation. Continue to follow the edge of the forest south over this hill, dropping slightly to the col below Cauldcleuch Head which is easily reached in less than a kilometre. Three fences meeting at the summit are useful aids to navigation in misty conditions.

The return route can be varied by retracing steps over Skelfhill Fell then continuing along the grassy ridge of Holywell Rig before dropping directly to Priesthaugh. Alternatively, descend to Skelfhillhope and follow the path by the Skelfhill burn leading to the farm at Skelfhill.

Other routes from the south are also possible and there is a good path leading north from Braidlie, which crosses the col to the east of Cauldcleuch Head. A pleasant circuit of the Gorrenberry burn could also be made over the subsidiary tops of Dod Hill, Crossbow Hill, Pennygant Hill and Stob Fell.

## SECTION 1

# *The Midland Valley to the River Tay*

**Stob an Eas** (Peak of the Waterfall); *732m*
*OS Sheet 56; GR 185073*
*6km/510m/2–3hrs*
*Map 8*

This fine little peak lies south of Glen Kinglas about 3km west of the note worthy Corbett of Beinn an Lochain. Despite being quickly dismissed in the SMC guide to the Southern Highlands as not being of much interest, when combined with its neighbour, Beinn an t-Seilich, it offers a satisfying horseshoe route from Hell's Glen to the south. The 'Waterfall' in the name is only a seasonal feature of the hill, no doubt referring to the burn which descends steeply from near the summit, and only resembles a waterfall in spate conditions.

The quickest approach route starts at the beginning of a forest track in Gleann Beag (Hell's Glen) at GR 168074. Follow the track through the forest, rounding two sharp bends, and take its continuation beyond the point shown on the map where it appears to end. Reach the above-mentioned stream where there is a wide break in the forest, and the sharp profile of Stob an Eas becomes very prominent.

An obvious spur with crags in its upper reaches lies immediately to the right of the stream and this provides a convenient ascent route. Climb the spur easily until a large crag is reached just short of the summit. This gives a short but entertaining scramble on sound rock with numerous incut holds. In poor conditions the crag can easily be avoided on the left. After another short rise the summit trig-point suddenly comes into view, surrounded by a ring of stones. Summit views were non-existent when the author completed the

*Stob an Eas from Cruach nam Mult*

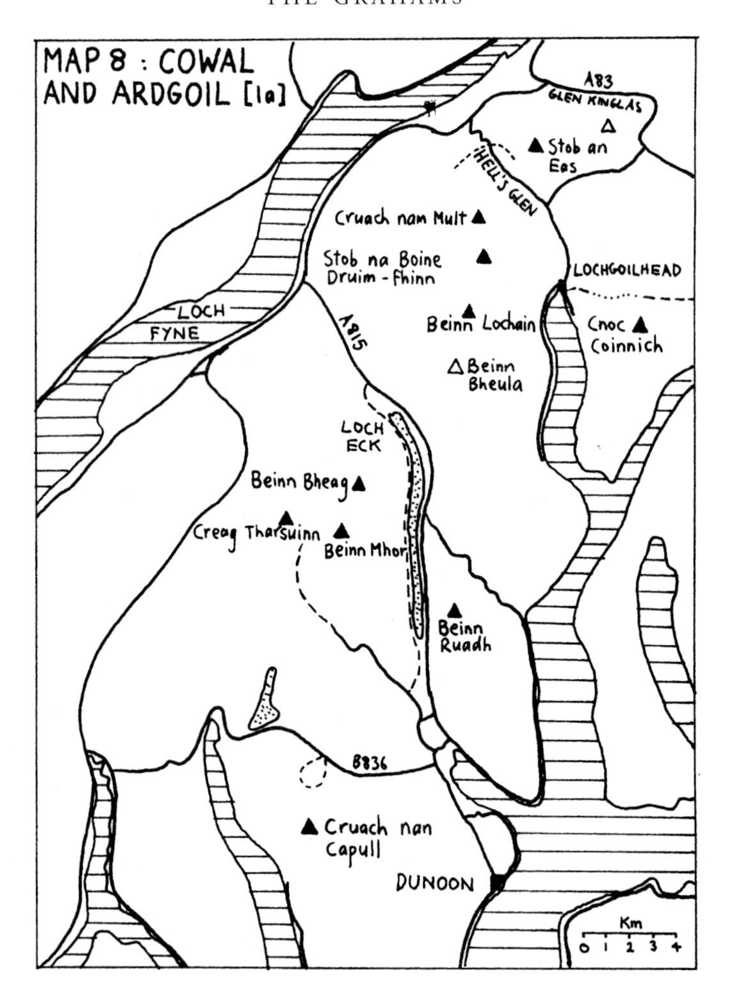


climb but on a clear day the vista east to the Arrochar Alps and beyond is doubtlessly fine.

The distance and time information given above is based on a return by the same route but on a good day it would make sense to continue north-east along the knobbly ridge and descend to a bealach before climbing the subsidiary top of Beinn an t-Seilich. This can be descended by its south-west ridge over another subsidiary top.

Stob an Eas can also be climbed from Glen Kinglas to the north but involves greater distance and ascent.

**Cruach nam Mult** (Rocky Stack of the Young Sheep); *611m*
*OS Sheet 56; GR 168055*
*3km/480m/2–3hrs*
*Map 8*

---

On the opposite side of Hell's Glen to Stob an Eas, Cruach nam Mult is one of a handful of Grahams whose height is a shade above the 2,000ft contour. It could fairly easily be combined with Stob an Eas despite the large drop between them.

Begin in Hell's Glen at GR 178062 where a stream can be followed up the hillside by its right bank, and initially through trees with quite a steep ascent. On emerging from the trees, the angle lessens to some extent, and a final steep section avoiding any crags must be negotiated before arriving suddenly on the undulating summit area. There are two main tops, the westerly one being the higher with a tiny cairn. To the east the Arrochar Alps make a fine picture, while to the west Inveraray and the castle are distinctly visible across Loch Fyne. Descend by the same route.

This hill could also be ascended using the same starting point as for Stob an Eas where a forest track heads south-west into Coire No to the north-west of the hill. This has the advantage of a higher start but some forestry has to be negotiated before open hillside.

**Beinn Lochain** (Hill of the Little Loch); *703m*
**Stob na Boine Druim-fhinn** (Dropped Peak of the White Ridge); *658m*
*OS Sheet 56; GR 160006, 168025*
*11km/910m/4–6hrs*
*Map 8*

---

To the west of Lochgoilhead a contorted ridge of five distinct summits stretches from Hell's Glen in the north to Curra Lochain in the south. Three of these are Grahams, the ascent of the most northerly being described elsewhere and the ascent of the remaining two here. On a long day it would be perfectly feasible to traverse the whole ridge in a single expedition but transport could be a problem and an area of dense forestry occupies the eastern slopes of the whole ridge, making escape routes impractical. The route to be described ascends the above two hills with the option of including the intervening peak of Beinn Tharsuinn. It is interesting to note that the peculiar cleft summit of Mullach Coire a' Chuir (Summit of the Snow Hollow), lying north of the above two Grahams, just fails to make Graham status by only 8m of relative height, i.e. it is 8m short of the required 150m drop between summits; however, it is still worth climbing!

Begin at Lettermay, just south of Lochgoilhead, where a forestry track can be followed west through the forest. Just after a kilometre take a right-hand fork which descends quickly to Lettermay burn. Cross the burn by a concrete weir and make a short climb through forest to reach a horizontal fire-break. An indistinct and very boggy path follows this fire-break and this should be taken for a few hundred metres before breaking off to the right through the trees to open hillside above. Climb the steep slopes and skirt round to the right of a false summit to reach a flat grassy col below the main summit of Beinn Lochain. A short climb from here leads to the top where there are fine views of

*Beinn Lochain and Stob na Boine Druim-fhinn from Cnoc Coinnich*

the surrounding peaks, particularly the Corbett of Beinn Bheula, only 2km to the south across Curra Lochain.

Descend easily to the col north of Beinn Lochain and either climb Beinn Tharsuinn or contour round its eastern flank on an obvious grassy promontory to reach a second col below Stob na Boine Druim-fhinn. From here it is a straightforward grassy ascent to the triangulation pillar situated at the north-western end of a knobbly ridge. The quickest return to Lettermay involves a traverse of this ridge followed by a descent of the south-east ridge avoiding the numerous rocky bluffs. This leads directly to a wide break in the forest which can be followed to Corrow and the road at Lettermay.

**Cnoc Coinnich** (Mossy Knoll);
*761m*
*OS Sheet 56; GR 233007*
*9km/760m/3–5hrs*
*Map 8*

---

Cnoc Coinnich occupies a commanding position south of the twin Corbetts of The Brack and Ben Donich and stands on the Ardgoil peninusla separating Loch Goil and Loch Long. Until the demotion of Beinn Talaidh on Mull from a Corbett to a Graham, it had (and possibly still has) the honour of the highest Graham – both Cnoc Coinnich and Beinn Talaidh are currently credited with 761m of height.

It is possible to combine the ascent of Cnoc Coinnich with The Brack (and even Ben Donich) starting in Glen Croe to the north, but the shortest and most natural ascent is from Lochgoilhead to the west. There is a large parking area opposite the shop/post office and the start of the route goes to the right of the public toilet block up a small lane leading over a stile to a forestry track. Cross the forestry track and continue through a gate where the excellent path traverses up the hillside with the forest on the left.

As height is gained, the view west to the hills on the opposite side of Lochgoilhead begins to open up. The Corbett of Beinn Bheula is on the extreme left while the Grahams of Beinn Lochain and Stob na Boine Druim-fhinn form the main skyline. The sharp summit with the obvious cleft on the right of the skyline is Mullach Coire a' Chuir which, though over 2,000ft high, fails to reach the ranks of the Grahams as it does not quite possess the 150m drop between itself and its Graham neighbour to the south.

Some distance later, the path descends to a bridge and immediately forks beyond the bridge. Take the right-hand fork marked Coilessan until the path reaches the base of a wide fire-break. Here the path deteriorates somewhat and follows a line of white posts directly up the break. Follow this route, ignoring any paths diverging to the left, until the tree-line is reached at a fence and stile. From here the path is less distinct but still follows a line of white posts to reach the wide pass between The Brack and Cnoc Coinnich. At the pass, leave the path and follow the rough line of the north-west ridge, keeping to the right of any crags.

The cairn at the summit is poised precariously on the edge of a large crag and is, not surprisingly, a superb viewpoint. The northern skyline is dominated by The Brack and Ben Donich, while beyond lie the rugged complexities of The Cobbler and the other Arrochar Alps. Further round to the north-east, the shapely cone of Ben Lomond rises in splendid isolation, while to the east and south-east the more gentle lines of the Luss Hills arrest the eye. Directly south, the long arm of Loch Long points its finger to Gourock, Greenock and the industrial south.

A descent can be made by the same route, but a pleasant variation is to drop south-west along the main spine of the hill, gradually curving in a clockwise direction over various knolls to reach the vicinity of The Steeple (GR 210009). Just after leaving the summit there is a fairly steep descent and care should be taken in wet or wintry conditions. From The Steeple, the main path can be reached by following the edge of the forest in a roughly northerly direction.

For those whose appetites have only been whetted on Cnoc Coinnich, a much longer alternative is to continue south on the knobbly ridge to Beinn Reithe (653m) and then on to The Saddle (519m). This is a pleasant undulating ridge walk. A return to Lochgoilhead can be made via the marked path north of Corran Lochan and a forestry track.

**Beinn Mhor** (Big Hill); *741m*
**Beinn Bheag** (Little Hill); *618m*
*OS Sheet 56; GR 107908, 125932*
*18km/1,300m/7–9hrs*
*Map 8*

---

These two rugged hills rise sharply from the western side of the narrow ribbon of Loch Eck. It is in fact Clach Bheinn or Stone Hill, a rocky outlier of Beinn Mhor which, though lower, dominates the view down the loch. A traverse of all three hills is a superb but demanding expedition. The route described includes ascents of both of the Grahams but omits an ascent of Clach Bheinn, although this can easily be included if so wished.

A glance at the map would indicate Bernice House, halfway down the western side of Loch Eck, to be an ideal starting point for the ascent of Beinn Mhor and Beinn Bheag. Unfortunately, the forest road down this side of the loch is private and not accessible to cars. However, the track is an established cycling route and for those with two wheels it would make sense to cycle to the head of Bernice Glen and make the ascent from there.

The following route description begins in Glen Massan to the south of both hills and does not require the use of a bike, but is longer with some re-ascent. Drive up Glen Massan to the end of the public road just beyond Stonefield and continue on foot to the farm at Glenmassan. A short distance beyond this point, after crossing a bridge, a track forks off to the right and zigzags its way up through the forest on the west side of the Allt Coire Mheasan. Take this path and follow its continuation beyond the point shown on the map.

In actuality, the track goes well beyond this point, emerging from the forest and making a rising traverse to pass very close to the summit of Beinn Mhor. A welcome bonus! The summit trig-point is perched on a small crag and is an unrivalled viewpoint on a fine day. To the south, the island of Arran and its distinctive ridges are well seen beyond the jostling smaller hills of South Cowal, while the Paps of Jura are visible to the west. Beinn Bheula and the Arrochar Alps are prominent to the north, while Ben Cruachan and other Highland giants pepper the horizon.

Almost lost in all this magnificence is the 'little hill', Beinn Bheag, which is the next objective. A heart-stopping drop of some 400m in vertical height has to be negotiated before the ascent of Beinn Bheag – and more to the point, most of this has to be re-ascended on the return journey. The north-east ridge of Beinn Mhor, which leads directly to the col, contains some extremely dramatic cliffs and crags in its middle reaches and offers superb vistas down to Bernice and Loch Eck. On reaching the boggy col, cross a couple of fences and begin the 300m ascent of Beinn Bheag, which may be enlivened by the odd pocket of scrambling on some opportune crags. A frustrating series of false tops are passed before the actual summit is reached; the want of a cairn there is an indication of how little visited this summit is. The views up and down Loch Eck are particularly fine, with Clach Bheinn and Beinn Ruadh (another Graham) forming a suitable frame for Loch Eck to the south.

Return to the col by the route of ascent and begin the final climb of the day to the area east of the summit of Beinn Mhor. Note that it is possible to descend to Bernice from the col and walk back along the track by the loch, but then it is still quite a distance to get round into Glen Massan and up to Stonefield. In an emergency or in deteriorating weather this would be a sensible option, however. From the area east of the summit of Beinn Mhor, descend the broad south ridge to the vicinity of Capull Cloiche where the option of visiting Clach Bheinn presents itself. For those who have had enough for one day, head south-east over Creachan Mor and descend to the col between it and Creachan Beag. From here it is possible to descend the steep grassy hillside and go through a gap in the forestry to reach Glen Massan near Stonefield.

**Creag Tharsuinn** (Rocky Transverse); *643m*
*OS Sheet 56; GR 088913*
*14km/560m/4–5hrs*
*Map 8*

---

Creag Tharsuinn is a rarely climbed and retiring Cowal hill lying to the west of Beinn Mhor on the other side of Garrachra Glen. It is the highest point of a long, undulating ridge stretching 7km from Carn Ban in the south to Sron Criche in the north. The shortest approach is from Glen Massan to the south-east, of which Garrachra Glen is a continuation. Cars can be parked at the end of the public road just beyond Stonefield.

From Stonefield, continue on foot to the small white cottage called Garrachra. At this point the day's objective is very prominent at the head of the glen. Follow the track beyond the cottage but branch off left before the bridge, aiming for the large gap between two forest plantations. (At the time of writing some new trees were already planted in this gap.) Climb steeply up through the gap on mainly tussocky grass for about 250m until the top edge of the forest is reached. Contour across the hillside and make a gradual rising traverse to reach Bealach nan Sac after crossing a deep stream channel.

Less than 150m of vertical ascent separates this bealach from the summit of the hill, which is easily reached in less than a kilometre. The summit is the second obvious rise in the ridge and lies a few metres beyond a lone fence post. Like Beinn Bheag to the north-east, Creag Tharsuinn has no cairn and the summit area is also similar in character, with the top poised on the edge of steep craggy slopes to the east. The best views are to the south where Arran's distinctive profile is plainly visible beyond the South Cowal hills.

The best route of descent is to return

*Creag Tharsuinn from Garrachra Glen*

along the ridge for some distance before descending to the forest plantation corner at GR 086905 and following the edge of the forestry from here down to the glen. Cross the river and gain the track at its closest approach to the forest edge a short distance along the glen. This leads back to the bridge north of Garrachra cottage.

**Beinn Ruadh** (Red Hill); *664m*
*OS Sheet 56; GR 155883*
*7km/630m/2½–3½hrs*
*Map 8*

---

Beinn Ruadh rises on the east side of Loch Eck at its southern end and is almost directly opposite the craggy summit of Clach Bheinn. It is a rarely climbed hill but rewards the determined walker with some fine situations. A glance at the map shows it to be surrounded by forestry plantations on all sides, but on closer inspection a small break is evident at the southern end of Loch Eck. In fact, just south of this break a forestry track follows the north side of the Inverchapel burn and this gives the start of the route.

Begin on this track but almost immediately break off to the left and follow the Inverchapel burn on a vague path, crossing over to the north side higher up. The walk here is characterised by pleasant waterfalls and pools with a good cover of larch, birch and other broadleaf trees. Once beyond the tree-line, climb directly up the open hillside to reach the broad south ridge of the mountain. A subsidiary top of height 620m is soon reached and in clear weather the main summit should be clearly visible less than a kilometre to the north, with only a small dip between the two. Loch Eck is not visible from the top but fine views can be had of Beinn Bheula and the Arrochar Alps, while to the south the Firth of Clyde and its associated urban clutter form a marked contrast.

The quickest descent is to drop south-west on initially steep slopes, bypassing Point 620 on its northern side. This option provides fine views down the length of Loch Eck but becomes quite hard going in the latter stages in the vicinity of Creag Liath, where steep bracken-covered slopes have to be negotiated with care. The road which is a short distance away, is not far from the starting point. In wet or wintry conditions it is probably advisable to descend by the route of ascent.

**Cruach nan Capull** (Heap of the Mare); *611m*
*OS Sheet 63; GR 095795*
*7km/510m/2½–3½hrs*
*Map 8*

This hill has the distinction of being the most southerly 2,000ft-elevation in the Scottish Highlands, and anyone planning a major south to north jaunt taking in the best of the Highland hills would do well to begin here. The hill commands fine views of the Firth of Clyde and of the higher mountains to the north.

The quickest and easiest ascent begins on the B836 road to the north, at the entrance to Corrachaive, where limited parking is available. The latest 1989 Landranger map is already out of date as it will be apparent that Corrachaive Glen is now planted out with sitka spruce and this is not evident from the map. Oddly enough, this has made access to the mountain easier, as a good forestry track makes a circuit of the lower part of the glen and can be used initially.

Follow the track along the east side of the glen under Meall Criche until it begins to bend round to the right before heading back along the west side of the glen. Just after crossing the stream which flows down the glen, a rough path forks off to the left and zigzags up the hillside, eventually to emerge from the trees below the north ridge, and south of Mid Hill. Follow this path to reach the ridge below a steep grassy rise. Climb this and one more steep section to arrive at the broad summit which is festooned with various fences and a small cairn. As already mentioned, the view south to the Firth of Clyde and Arran is quite stunning on a clear day, as are the views north to the other Cowal Hills and the Arrochar Alps. The long, undulating ridge topped with fence posts going south from the summit provides another ascent route and is briefly mentioned later.

From the summit descend fairly steeply to the east and follow the fence round the head of Corrachaive Glen, staying on the crest of the ridge leading to Meall Criche. From here it is possible to descend to the track through numerous breaks in the trees, thus completing a satisfying high-level circuit of the glen.

Another possible route of ascent (though longer) begins at Stronyaraig on Loch Striven to the south of the mountain and ascends the long south ridge via Stron Dearg. A circuit can be made by including the subsidiary top of Leacann nan Gall and dropping down to Bealach na Sreine to reach a path which follows Inverchaolain Glen to the starting point. This also gives an extremely satisfying horseshoe route, and for those with more time, it may well be preferable to the route already described. It should also be noted that Dunoon, which lies on the coast south-east of the hill, is accessible by ferry from Gourock across the Firth of Clyde.

**Beinn Eich** (Horse Hill); *703m*
**Cruach an t-Sidhein** (Stack of the Fairy Hill); *684m*
**Doune Hill** (Fort Hill); *734m*
**Beinn Dubh** (Black Hill); *657m* (previously known as Mid Hill)
*OS Sheet 56; GR 302946, 275965, 290971, 321962*
*15km/1,300m/7–8hrs*
*Map 9*

---

The Luss Hills are a compact range of smooth and grassy hills lying between Loch Lomond and Loch Long. Comprising eight Grahams in all, they are separated by well-defined ridges and low cols and offer delightful hillwalking only a short distance from the industrial central belt of Scotland. Indeed, Helensburgh lies only 9km south of the group. Their rounded, smooth nature makes them particularly suited to ski-touring and an absence of rock ensures only a thin layer of snow is necessary. Glen Luss and Glen Douglas neatly separate the group into three manageable subgroups, and the route about to be described is the ascent of the central four Grahams lying between the two glens.

It is a consequence of the compactness of the Luss Hills that enables four Grahams to be climbed in a day and this is the only route in this book in which four are ascended in a single excursion. Of course it is quite easy to shorten the route to include only two or three Grahams, and it is the nature of these hills that many combinations are possible.

From the A82 Loch Lomond road near Luss, drive up the narrow Glen Luss road to the vicinity of Edentaggart, where limited parking space is available. Go through the cluttered farmyard to the track beyond and strike off almost immediately to the right to gain the broad grassy east ridge of Beinn Eich. During the ascent the views down Glen Luss to Loch Lomond and its wooded islands become quite magnetic. The small cairn is a magnificent little perch to while away some time.

Continue north-west along the easy ridge descending to a col before traversing off to the left and contouring round the south side of Beinn Lochain to reach the col to the east of Cruach an t-Sidhein. This manoeuvre saves some

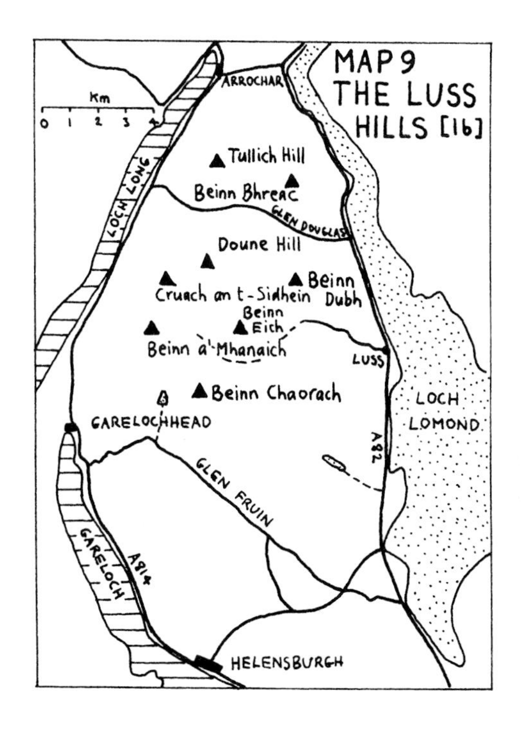

*The Luss Hills: Tullich Hill from Doune Hill*

ascent and re-ascent. A steep little push of about 150m leads to the small grassy summit table and a small cairn. Retrace your steps to the col then ascend nearly 200m to the spacious summit of Beinn Lochain. From here the top of Doune Hill is just a short ridge walk of about half a kilometre. Doune Hill sports a trig-point and is the highest of the Luss Hills with good views across Glen Douglas to Tullich Hill, while beyond Loch Long the giants of the Arrochar Alps jostle for attention.

Beyond Doune Hill lies another top of exactly 700m which can be included in the round if so wished, but the thought of the relentless 400m slog to the top of Beinn Dubh is probably enough to contend with. Descend fairly steeply but safely to the col at the head of Glen Mollochan before beginning the final ascent of the day. Less ambitious and saner mortals will no doubt opt for the gentle stroll down Glen Mollochan and leave Beinn Dubh for another day. It should be noted that this glen is boggy and trackless until about halfway along when a track begins north of the river (unmarked on the map).

Those opting for Beinn Dubh will find the broad west ridge the obvious means of ascent. After a flattening out at around 600m, a final push leads to the highest point, but the actual cairn lies about 150m north-east of this. Descend by the grassy ridge between Glen Mollochan and Glen Striddle to the starting point.

If Beinn Dubh has been left as a single excursion it can be included as part of a circuit of Glen Striddle including Beinn Dubh's outlying top. It is also worth mentioning that Cruach an t-Sidhein can be climbed from Glen Douglas via the long north ridge. This could be combined with Doune Hill to complete a pleasant high-level horseshoe round Cona Ghleann.

**Beinn Chaorach** (Hill of the Sheep); *713m*
**Beinn a' Mhanaich** (Hill of the Monk); *709m*
*OS Sheet 56; GR 287923, 269946*
*12km/940m/4–5hrs*
*Map 9*

---

These two Grahams are the southernmost of the Luss group and Beinn Chaorach is the second highest of the range. The southern approach, from Glen Fruin, is described here, being slightly shorter than the Glen Luss approach although, as is the nature of the Luss Hills, numerous possibilities present themselves.

A new road runs through Glen Fruin to the north of the old one (unmarked on the 1989 OS map) but the old road provides the best starting point just past Auchengaich at the start of a track. Follow this track, crossing the new road higher up, to the reservoir at its head. Head right from here past a wooded area and ascend the grassy western slopes of Beinn Chaorach for about 450m to the summit trig-point. The view from here on a clear day must be quite magnificent but the author was accompanied only by low cloud and sheep so any glorious vistas must remain in the imagination.

To reach Beinn a' Mhanaich, the ridge can be followed to the north-west before descending 300m to the broad and boggy col at GR 275935. A direct ascent of about 350m from this col leads to the summit of Beinn a' Mhanaich. A fence crosses the ridge very close to the top and is a useful guide in thick weather. The cairn at the summit is quite substantial and again the views are undoubtedly fine!

The return route follows the long and obvious south ridge of Beinn a' Mhanaich which presents pleasant high-level walking. Unfortunately, the western slopes of this hill are used for military training and live firing. Subsequently, a long series of Ministry of Defence danger notices are strung out along the crest of the ridge about 50m apart. These are a fine guide in misty conditions but an eyesore to say the least. Reach the new road at a gate and cross over to another gate before traversing a field back to Auchengaich. This completes a satisfying horseshoe route.

For those hillwalkers wishing a longer day with more ridge-walking, Beinn Chaorach can provide the termination of a splendid ridge traverse starting at Beinn Ruisg about 4km to the east. Ben Ruisg can most easily be reached via the Finlas Glen and reservoir between Glen Fruin and Glen Luss. A complete high-level circuit of this glen would be a pleasant day's hillwalking. It is awkward to accommodate Beinn a' Mhanaich in this alternative without much re-ascent but it can easily be climbed on a separate excursion.

## **Tullich Hill** (Hillock Hill); *632m*
## **Beinn Bhreac** (Speckled Hill); *681m*

*OS Sheet 56; GR 293006, 321000*
*9km/860m/4–5hrs (omitting Ben Reoch)*
*Map 9*

---

These two hills lie north of Glen Douglas and together make a pleasant horseshoe from Invergroin. Another 'top' called Ben Reoch lies to the north of both and can be included in the round if so wished. They are more rugged than their counterparts south of Glen Douglas and possess a little of the character of the Arrochar Alps just a few kilometres to the north-west.

Drive up Glen Douglas and park near the deserted cottage at Invergroin. Just beyond the bridge a gate on the right leads to open hillside, and the grassy south-east ridge of Tullich Hill is easily gained. The summit area can be slightly confusing in misty conditions with various knolls and dips. From the summit descend in a roughly north-easterly direction, taking care to avoid any crags which are a feature of this side of the hill. Reach the col of Ant-Sreang where the decision must be made to climb Ben Reoch or to head directly for the second Graham. In some ways the direct ascent of Ben Reoch may be the easier option, as the rising traverse to reach the col north of Beinn Bhreac is quite hard going across initially steep bracken-covered hillside and awkward gullies. Ben Reoch itself, though not a Graham, is a fine little viewpoint, especially to the Arrochar Alps and across neighbouring Loch Lomond to Ben Lomond, only 6km away.

Beinn Bhreac, the highest of the trio, is easily gained by its north ridge. The summit trig-point is perched on a craggy platform and is again a wonderful viewpoint with almost the whole length of Loch Lomond stretching out from south to north. Directly below Beinn Bhreac to the east is Rubha Mor, where a Mount Rushmore-style rock cutting of ancient Celtic mythical figures will possibly be sculpted in the future (according to a well-known Scottish Sunday newspaper) but time will tell if this will become a reality. The return to Invergroin involves a fairly easy descent of steep grass slopes to the south-west, in the latter stages following a rather boggy all-terrain vehicle track.

**Beinn Damhain** (Hill of the Stag Rut); *684m*
*OS Sheet 50, 56; GR 282173*
*12km/660m/3–5hrs*
*Map 10*

This hill lies north-west of the northern extremity of Loch Lomond and south of the Corbett of Meall an Fhudair. Like its Corbett neighbour it has few outstanding features other than a fine craggy profile above the lochan of the same name.

Begin in Glen Falloch opposite the farm with the same name where a track ascends steeply in a series of zigzags up the eastern slopes of Troisgeach. At the junction turn left and continue for almost 2km to the end of the track where there are numerous hydro catchment concrete constructions. Leave the track and head directly for the fairly well-defined east ridge where a few knolls and rocky outcrops make the ascent more interesting. There is an obvious false summit higher up the ridge, and the true summit crowned with a small cairn is a short steep climb beyond this. On a clear day the views are extensive, especially of Ben Vorlich to the south and the Crianlarich Munros to the east. Descend by the same route.

It would be quite possible to combine the ascent of this Graham with the Corbett of Meall an Fhudair although the drop between the two is quite substantial.

**Meall nan Gabhar** (Hill of the Goat); *744m*
*OS Sheet 50; GR 237240*
*25km/720m/4–6hrs (bike)*
*Map 10*

The above time estimate is based on the use of a bike as far as GR 261224 on the track which follows Gleann nan Caorann from Glen Falloch. This is not the shortest route to the hill but avoids dense forestry and is a more pleasant approach than from the A85 Tyndrum to Dalmally road to the north. Meall nan Gabhar is not easy to reach from any direction but its extensive summit views make the challenge worth while.

Take the track which begins on the A82 road opposite Glen Falloch farm and follow it steeply initially until the junction at GR 309197. Turn right and continue at an easier angle along the northern slopes of Meall an Fhudair where numerous concrete access ducts are passed, leading to an underground pipe which is visible at a later point. After a right turn the track follows the pipe and eventually ends at a ruined iron hut where a bike can be left. After a 1½km plod north-west on reasonably well-drained grassy terrain, you will reach the steeper eastern slopes of Meall nan Tighearn, which is the southern top of a wide ridge containing three summits. The middle of these is the actual summit of Meall nan Gabhar which is basically a flat grassy knoll with no cairn. The summit gives unusual views of Ben Lui and also of the Arrochar Alps and Beinn Bhuidh to the south. On a clear day Mull, Arran, Ben Nevis and Ben Cruachan should all be visible. Return by the same route.

Note that this hill and its Graham neighbour, Beinn Bhalgairean, could both be attempted from Corryghoil on the A85 road to the north, but forestry is a potential problem.

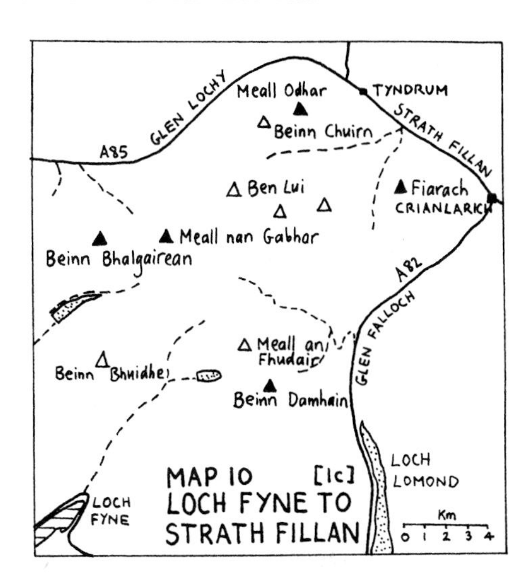


**Beinn Bhalgairean** (Hill of the Foxes); *636m*
*OS Sheet 50; GR 202241*
*10km/590m/3–4hrs*
*Map 10*

---

The close proximity of this hill to Meall nan Gabhar would suggest that both could be climbed together, but on closer inspection this is possibly not the best method of attack. Both Grahams lie south of the A85 Tyndrum to Dalmally road and could be regarded as foothills of the extensive Ben Lui group to the east. Forestry plantations separate them from the road, and a wide finger of forest separates one Graham from the other. A round of the two *could* be attempted from Corryghoil on the A85 using forestry tracks and fire-breaks, but is not described here.

The shortest route to Beinn Bhalgairean begins on the A85 at the Brackley Farm road end, where there is very limited parking space. Follow the rough track to the farm and go through the farmyard before crossing a railway bridge. Almost immediately, leave the track and cut off to the left making for the edge of the forest on a rather boggy all-terrain vehicle track. At the forest corner continue on the ATV track until it begins to peter out. Beyond this, a series of knolls and dips eventually lead to the final steepness.

The cairn at the summit sits slightly off the true highest point and is a fine viewpoint, particularly north-west to the Dalmally horseshoe and the Ben Cruachan range. In the other direction is the enormous bulk of Ben Lui, which at 1,130m is nearly twice the height of humble Beinn Bhalgairean!

The terrain around this Graham is quite complex with many knolls and false summits, so in misty weather good compass work is essential. Return by the same route.

Another much longer route to this hill, and only suitable for avid mountain bikers, would be via Glen Shira to the south-west. This alternative involves at least 40km of cycling for the round trip but only about 5km of walking. Note that Meall nan Gabhar could also be included in this scenario.

**Fiarach** (Grassy Pasture); *652m*
*OS Sheet 50; GR 344261*
*9km/480m/2–3hrs*
*Map 10*

---

Fiarach could be viewed as an after-thought of the chain of Ben Lui Munros, lying east of them but con-

*The Crianlarich hills from the summit of Fiarach*

nected by a 480m high bealach at Cruchan Cruinn. It is a hill of little note, rarely climbed, but on a clear day has tremendous views, the hallmark of many otherwise undistinguished Grahams. It could conveniently be combined with an ascent of Meall Odhar to the north of Glen Cononish as the starting point is the same.

Begin at the Dalrigh junction on the A82 road at the concealed carpark (the usual Ben Lui start point). Follow the old road south-east across the bridge where there is a gate, then turn off at the right along a track which crosses the railway and soon enters a picturesque remnant of the old Caledonian forest (Coille Coire Chuilc). Leave the track just before the gate into the sitka plantation and follow the boundary fence directly up the western slopes of Fiarach. The summit area is rather a clutter of fences, lochans and knolls and would be confusing in misty conditions. The actual summit lies about half a kilometre to the south of Lochan Fiarach and a fence leads almost directly to the top. The small cairn is perched on the edge of a craggy spur facing south and offers fine views of the Crianlarich hills and the Ben Lui range. To the north, Beinn Odhar and Beinn Dorain are also prominent. Return by a similar route.

**Meall Odhar** (Dappled Hill); *656m*
*OS Sheet 50; GR 298298*
*12km/450m/3–4hrs*
*Map 10*

---

The elegant bulk of Ben Lui (Munro) together with its close satellite Beinn Chuirn (Corbett) significantly dwarf this rather overlooked and rarely climbed Graham. Meall Odhar has little in the way of redeeming features save for grandstand views of its more alluring neighbours. Nevertheless, it provides an interesting half day's 'leg stretcher' and could conveniently be combined with nearby Fiarach (see page 56) to make a full day's outing.

A glance at the map shows Meall Odhar to be completely surrounded by forestry plantations but on close inspection these do not prove to be as formidable as they appear. Begin at the Dalrigh junction on the A82 road (GR 343292) where a fairly large but concealed parking area is situated. This is the usual starting point for Ben Lui. Follow the Cononish track for 3km until the first main break in the forestry where a gate can be climbed to enter an upward sloping field. At the top of the field an obvious break in the trees leads up for a few hundred metres before reaching another broad fire-break contouring round the hill. Go right here for about 50m then immediately left up yet another obvious break following a line of all-terrain vehicle tracks. Some way up here the view begins to open out, especially to Ben More and the Crianlarich Munros.

The most direct route to the summit follows another obvious break which is passed on the left, but it is possible to continue on along the same break and emerge on to open hillside some distance further on. From here a short but steep little climb on heather and rock leads on to the summit plateau. A fairly large prominent cairn is quite a surprise considering the rather featureless nature of the hill. Big cairns and fine views are a hallmark of many Grahams, however, and Meall Odhar is no exception. Beinn Chuirn and the Ben Lui group can be seen to advantage, while in the opposite direction the Tyndrum Corbetts and Ben Challum provide a worthy backdrop.

Either return by the route of ascent, or to make a more circular route, a pleasant traverse above the tree-line could be made on the little top of Sron nan Colan (590m), lying just west of Tyndrum. Descent south from here could prove problematic if a good fire-break is not found, but these are visible from near the summit and lead down to a forestry track which in turn leads to the main Cononish track. It is also worth mentioning that from the lower station in Tyndrum, a path follows the railway line before climbing up and finishing a short distance from the summit of Sron nan Colan. For those based in Tyndrum it would be perfectly possible to use this as an ascent route before traversing on to Meall Odhar. A return could be made using the aforementioned forestry track which ends at the lower station. This would provide a satisfying circular route of around four hours.

For hardier souls there is the option of continuing on to the Corbett of Beinn Chuirn, but forestry problems again have to be tackled on the south-west slopes of Meall Odhar. Gold explorations are presently taking place on the slopes of Beinn Chuirn, creating an ugly scar on the hillside.

**Cruinn a' Bheinn** (Round Hill);
*632m*
*OS Sheet 56; GR 365051*
*14km/630m/3–4hrs*
*Map 11*

Cruinn a' Bheinn is a classic example of a Graham totally overshadowed by a Munro neighbour, the Munro in this case being Ben Lomond, lying only a shade over 2km to the south. The high connecting col between the two (over 450m) rightly suggests them both being climbed together, and if the time is available this is indeed a fine option. The following route, however, describes a 'Graham only' excursion and is the shortest route assuming the absence of a suitable vessel to cross Loch Lomond to the west of the hill!

Begin at the Inversnaid Hotel on the east side of Loch Lomond where there is ample parking space. Cross the bridge over the Loch Arklet outflow and follow the route of the West Highland Way south through natural forest on an extremely boggy well-used path. After about 2½km you will reach a second

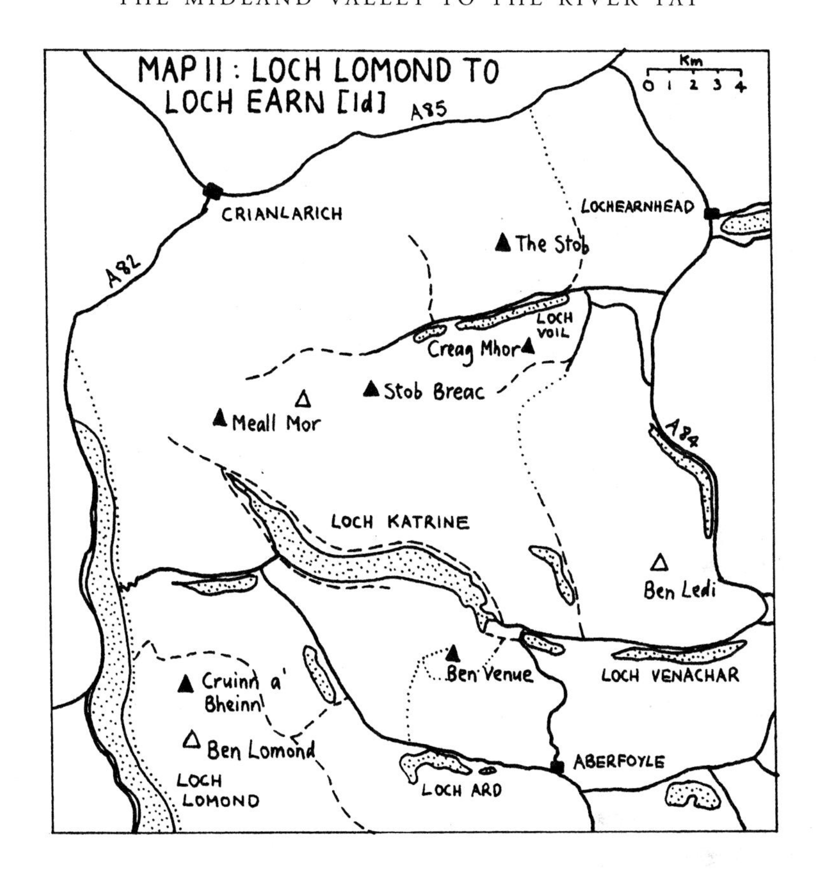


clearing where a track descends from the hillside above to the house at Cailness. Leave the West Highland Way and gain the track, which makes a long rising traverse northwards before zigzagging upwards and southwards to a flat boggy col north-west of Cruinn a' Bheinn. Leave the track and cross the col to gain the grassy north-western slopes of the hill. An easy ascent of 300m leads directly to the undistinguished cairn at the summit. Classic views can be enjoyed of Ben Lomond's little frequented northern ridges and corries, while to the west the Arrochar Alps can be seen well beyond Loch Lomond. Return by the same route.

The best starting point for tackling this hill and Ben Lomond together is at the south end of Loch Chon, where a track can be followed over the hill to Stronmacnair and through Gleann Dubh to the farm at Comer.

**Ben Venue** (Hill of the Caves or Stirks); *729m*
*OS Sheet 57; GR 474063*
*10km/650m/3½–5hrs*
*Map 11*

Ben Venue is the only Graham in section 1d which can truly be said to belong to the Trossachs, an area of

Scotland which has long been regarded as one of the most scenic in the whole of the country. The combination of tranquil lochs, rugged hills and natural wooded glens gave Sir Walter Scott and Wordsworth the inspiration for much written praise both in prose and poetry. Ben Venue epitomises the district, lying directly south of beautiful Loch Katrine, the source of Glasgow's water supply. The finest view of the hill is from across the placid waters of Loch Achray to the east and an approach from this side is recommended.

Begin at the Loch Achray Hotel, south of Achray Water, where a forestry road can be followed westwards. After about half a kilometre go left at a junction and continue on the track until a path forks off to the right up Gleann Riabhach. Follow the path up the glen through fairly dense sitka forest which often involves very wet and muddy conditions, particularly after a wet spell. Once out of the forest the path can be followed upwards for about 1km to reach a large cairn on the south-west ridge. Turn right and continue along a well-used path to the north-western top which is the highest point on the mountain. The south-eastern top at 727m is 2m lower and has a triangulation pillar. Views from the summit are extensive, espeically to the north across Loch Katrine, where the main peaks of the southern Highlands form a magnificent array, especially when speckled with the first snows of winter.

Descend by continuing to the south-east top before dropping down a wide grassy gully where a vague path can be

*Ben Venue from Loch Achray*

followed on its right-hand side. Fine views of Loch Katrine and its tree-girt islands can be enjoyed during the steep descent. Some distance to the left is the little notch in the hillside known as Bealach nam Bo or Pass of Cattle, through which the Highlanders from Glen Gyle (and Rob Roy in particular) drove their stolen cattle. Just below the pass is Coire na Uruisgean which contains the alleged Goblin's Cave from which the name of the hill is possibly derived. On the lower part of the descent gully pick up the path which continues south-east to the sluices at the south-eastern end of the loch. Shortly beyond this point a forest track begins which leads pleasantly back to the Loch Achray Hotel on the south side of the Achray Water.

The other popular route begins at Ledard Farm near the west end of Loch Ard to the south of the mountain. From here a good path follows the Ledard burn, eventually joining the route already described. Note that Ben Venue is not seen well from the south, being partly hidden by the intervening top of Beinn an Fhogharaidh. An ideal way to tackle the hill is by a complete traverse either beginning or ending at Ledard but this would involve either two cars or an obliging driver. Note also that the hill has numerous subsidiary tops, all of which are worth visiting. In particular, Beinn Bhreac to the west is a very fine little summit standing at exactly 700m.

**Meall Mor** (Big Hill); *747m*
*OS Sheet 56; GR 383151*
*16km/720m/4½–6hrs*
*Map 11*

This relatively inaccessible hill lies in the heart of Rob Roy country, north of Glen Gyle and the western end of Loch Katrine. It is essentially the highest point of an undulating 4km ridge of knolls and false summits which is dominated by the more shapely but lower Stob an Duibhe at the eastern end of the ridge.

The shortest route begins at the end of the public road near Inverlochlarig to the north-east where a large parking area exists. Go through the farmyard and follow the track west by the River Larig for about 4km until the steep grassy slopes of Stob an Duibhe come into view on the left. Leave the track and cross the river before tackling the relentless north-eastern slopes where the odd knoll and rocky outcrop relieve the monotony. Finally, reach the prominent pointed summit where glorious views can be enjoyed on a clear day.

The main summit, Meall Mor, still lies 1½km away along the wide bumpy ridge where a line of old fence posts aids navigation in thick weather. At least three false summits are passed before reaching Meall Mor where there is a small cairn. Grand views can be enjoyed of the clutch of Crianlarich Munros to the north and Loch Katrine to the south-east. Descend Meall Mor directly by the northern slopes and cross the river to reach the end of the track which leads back to the start. Note that the northern slopes of Meall Mor contain a small area of steep cliffs, which are not shown on the OS map and these should be avoided on the descent.

Another possible route, though much longer, begins at the eastern end of Loch Katrine where a track can be followed for about 12km along the northern shore of the loch to a point below the southern slopes of An Garadh, a top lying about 1½km south-east of Stob an Duibhe. An Garadh can then be climbed along with Stob an Duibhe and the main summit before descending south to the end of the loch and the track. A bike would obviously be of use here and the ascent of Meall Mor could be included with a complete cycling circuit of Loch Katrine, a popular route, though trackless for the last few kilometres. The Loch Katrine approach, though long, wins hands down in terms of scenic beauty and character and should be given serious consideration if a bike is available.

**Stob Breac** (Speckled Peak); *688m*
*OS Sheet 57; GR 447166*
*7km/540m/2½–4hrs*
*Map 11*

---

Stob Breac is the highest point of a 3km-long ridge running south to north between Loch Katrine and Loch Doine. It is surrounded by higher mountains, having Corbetts to its east and west and Munros to its north, and because of this, it is a grand viewpoint.

Park at the public carpark at the end of the Balquhidder road and follow the forestry track over the River Larig, eventually traversing along the western flank of the hill. There is much new forestry here and this is not shown on the recent OS map. Once established on the track for about 2km, strike off to the left using a suitable fire-break in the trees. Once clear of the forest ascend open grassy hillside to the summit ridge. The actual top is not obvious and there is no cairn at the summit but it is just south of the most northerly high point.

The descent can be varied by dropping down the east flank of the hill to reach another forestry track which traverses the east side of the hill – this again is not shown on the OS map. Follow this track north and west round the side of the hill where it merges with the route of ascent. A much longer expedition would be to begin at Strone on Loch Katrine and follow the Strone burn before ascending Beinn Mheadhonach and making a complete traverse of the ridge. Unless returning to the start point this would require two cars or a kind driver.

**Creag Mhor** (Big Rock); *658m*
*OS Sheet 57; GR 510185*
*5km/460m/1½–3hrs*
*Map 11*

---

This hill is very prominent from Balquhidder at the eastern end of Loch Voil and rises above heavily forested slopes to the south of the loch. Creag Mhor is effectively an outlier of the higher Stob Fear-tomhais, a Corbett lying further to the south-west, and these two peaks could conveniently be climbed together. However, the following is a description of the ascent of Creag Mhor only.

Begin at Ballimore Farm on the small road up Glen Buckie to the south of Balquhidder. Follow the track north of the farm to a junction before making a more or less direct ascent of the south-eastern slopes of the hill. The summit ridge is broad with a series of knolls and false tops, the highest point being well to the west. The finest views are those looking up and down the length of Loch Voil. The descent can be varied by dropping south to the track and following it back to Ballimore. Note that part of this track passes through a private deer farm and caution should be exercised.

## **The Stob** (The Peak); *753m*

*OS Sheet 51; GR 491231*
*11km/620m/3½–5hrs*
*Map 11*

---

The Stob is the highest point of the Braes of Balquhidder lying between the Ben More–Stob Binnein group to the west and the twin Corbetts of Creag MacRanaich and Meall an t-Seallaidh to the east. This area of high ground is a confusing jumble of knolls and lochans and would be tricky to navigate in misty conditions.

Begin on the Balquhidder Road to the south shortly past the entrance to the Monachyle Mhor Hotel where the Monachyle glen forestry track starts. This is on OS Sheet 57. Follow the track north, crossing the river after about 2km, eventually reaching its termination in about another 2km. At this point a marked trail continues up the glen over 'Kerry's Brig', and several small wooden huts can be seen on the left. None of this is indicated on the 1986 OS map.

Ascend the steep western slopes of The Stob before reaching an undulating area of knolls and peat bogs. Even in clear conditions the actual summit shows no great wish to be discovered and is situated on a small knoll near a tiny lochan but is crowned by a reasonable cairn. A line of fence posts passes close to the summit which would aid navigation in thick weather.

The descent can be varied by heading south over Stob Caol and Creag nan Speireag before dropping down the south-west spur of this latter hill to Monachyle Farm.

## **Uamh Bheag** (Little Cave); *664m*

*OS Sheet 57; GR 691118*
*10km/470m/3–4hrs*
*Map 12*

---

This little hill sits on the border between Tayside and Central regions, north-east of Callander and south-east of the Ben Vorlich range of mountains. There has been much recent discussion over its new status as a Donald, that is, a 2,000ft hill lying south of the Highland boundary fault line. Admittedly it does (only just) lie south of this line so it is technically a Donald, but the more liberal and broad outlook would still suggest Uamh Bheag to be a Highland hill with Highland characteristics. At least there is no question of it not being a Graham! The Gaelic translation of 'Little Cave' refers to some unusual fissures and caves on the south-western shoulder at Uamh Mhor (Big Cave) where there is also a miniature rift valley known locally as Rob Roy's Cattle Fank.

The closest approach by road is from Glen Artney to the north from where a right of way leads south-west to Callander. This approach is more interesting and satisfying than alternative routes from the south. A large purpose-built carpark exists about 2km from the end of the Glen Artney road, and although it is possible to park beyond here at the side of the road it is not encouraged. Leave the road just before the bridge over the Water of Ruchill and follow the river along a faint path crossing the Allt Ollach after a kilometre. From here enjoy a fine view of Am Beannan, the sharp-pointed northern spur of Uamh Bheag, which is the next objective. Climb the steep and grassy slopes of Am Beannan to arrive on a broad, poorly drained ridge which leads on to Meall Clachach, a subsidiary top containing a huge boulder at the junction of various fences. Meall Clachach means 'Hill of the Stone' and so is quite apt. A short drop and further rise following a fence lead directly to the flat-topped summit of Uamh Bheag, where there is a good cairn. On a clear day the view to the north-west is dominated by the fine northern aspect of the twin Munros of Ben Vorlich and Stuc a' Chroin.

The descent can be varied by follow-

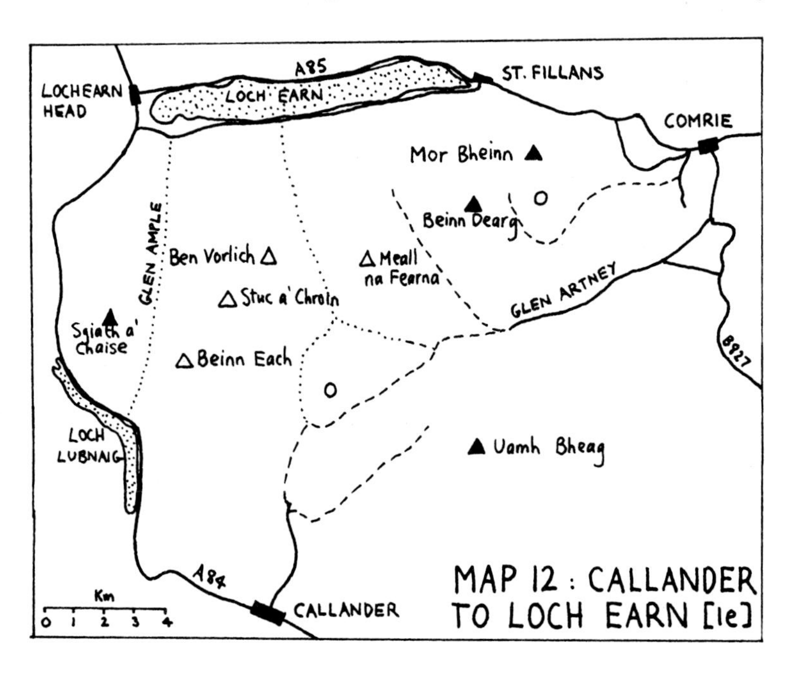

MAP 12 : CALLANDER TO LOCH EARN [1e]

*Mullwharchar from Craignaw* (Section 0a)

*Beinn Ruadh and Loch Eck from Beinn Bheag* (Section 1a)

*Ben Lomond from Cnoc Coinnich* (Section 1a)

*The Ben Lawers range from Shee of Ardtalnaig* (Section 1e)

*The Blackwater Reservoir and the Mamores from Stob na Cruaiche* (Section 2b)

*The Appin hills from Loch Etive* (Section 3b)

*Meall Mor and Aonach Eagach from Sgorr a'Choise* (Section 3c)

*The Pap of Glencoe* (Section 3c)

ing the fence east to a twin summit with a trig-point, before descending north then north-east down the ridge which forms the eastern boundary of Coire na Fionnarachd. Cross the Allt Ollach and skirt round the south-western side of Auchnashellach Hill before dropping to the Water of Ruchill and the route of ascent. This completes a pleasant horseshoe route.

Two other routes from the south are also possible but neither shows the best aspect of the hill or is as satisfying. The first begins by driving up the Bracklinn Falls road from Callander and taking the track by Meall Leathan Dhail. An awkward descent and re-ascent in deep heather then leads to the summit. The other route begins at Severie near Loch Mahaick, which has the advantage of being able to visit the above-mentioned caves and fissures, but only after a tedious grind of 3½km across heathery moorland.

### **Sgiath a' Chaise** (Steep Wing); *645m*

*OS Sheet 57; GR 583169*
*7km/520m/2–3hrs*
*Map 12*

---

Sgiath a' Chaise is the highest point of a long, broad grassy ridge running south to north between Strathyre and Glen Ample. The southernmost top of this ridge is well seen when driving north up the eastern shore of the delightfully scenic Loch Lubnaig. Being dominated somewhat by its more alluring popular eastern neighbours of Ben Vorlich, Stuc a' Chroin and Beinn Each, Sgiath a' Chaise is a sadly neglected hill, but its lack of popularity is part of its charm.

Begin at the southern approach to Glen Ample, where a Scottish right-of-way path continues all the way through the glen. Follow this steep path up through an area of trees until it meets the forestry track a short distance further on. Turn left and continue on the track through a gate at the edge of the forest and out to open hillside on the right. Just over a kilometre from this point leave the track and strike off to the left up open hillside beyond the last vestiges of trees. You will reach the wide summit-ridge of tussocky grass and a few peat hags near the subsidiary top of Creag a' Mhadhaidh, meaning 'Crag of the Fox' – which is well named, as foxes are often spotted around this area. The true summit lies less than a kilometre further north on a broad grassy area with a fence, but no cairn. The best views are across Glen Ample to the Ben Vorlich group.

Rather than descend directly to Glen Ample, it is more interesting to continue south along the ridge to the southern top of Meall Mor, which is a grand viewpoint for Loch Lubnaig and the surrounding hills. Descend the steep southern slopes of this hill to the forestry plantation, which is mainly larch and not dense sitka spruce. Drop down through the forest to reach the road and the start of the route.

**Beinn Dearg** (Red Hill); *706m*
*OS Sheet 57; GR 696197*
*14km/610m/4–6hrs*
*Map 12*

On the north side of Glen Artney, a grassy, horseshoe ridge lies east of Meall na Fearna and the Ben Vorlich range. It contains two high points, both the same height, with the north-easterly one, Beinn Dearg, designated as a Graham. A complete circuit of this ridge is a fine expedition from Glen Artney.

Begin near the unoccupied house at Dalchruin, where a road leads down to the Water of Ruchill and crosses it by a bridge. Head right then left on a track which leads to the ruined cottage of Dalclathick. From here continue west across open heath and moor for about 2½km, climbing steadily to the shoulder of Sron na Maoile. At this point striking views of Ben Vorlich and Stuc a' Chroin open up to the west. Continue north-west, and drop slightly before heading north and upwards to the first high point on the ridge at 706m. The ridge continues in a north-easterly direction on pleasant grassy terrain with several knolls before rising to the summit of Beinn Dearg where there is a small cairn. From here there are good views of the neighbouring Graham of Mor Bheinn to the north-east. An easy and pleasant descent of the south shoulder leads back to Dalclathick and the starting point.

**Mor Bheinn** (Big Hill); *640m*
*OS Sheets 57, 51, 52; GR 716211*
*17km/600m/3½–5hrs*
*Map 12*

Mor Bheinn is a craggy hill situated south of the A85 road about halfway between Comrie and St Fillans. It is seen well on the drive west along Strathearn shortly before reaching Comrie. It is unfortunately surrounded on three sides by forestry plantations which make access rather a problem. This, together with the fact that it appears on three separate OS maps, none of which show the whole mountain, make route planning awkward. Sheet 57, however, shows the whole route about to be described.

Take the road from Comrie which crosses the River Earn, forking left immediately to reach Craggish where a track begins. Follow this track, which passes through a pleasant forested area of oak, chestnut and beech, to GR 748211, where a path goes off to the left up through a field and just before the entrance to Aberuchil Castle. Take this path, which leads to another track, and follow it west, climbing steadily, to the junction at Tomanour. Leave the track at this point and head north-west round the craggy north-eastern flank of Ben Halton, the southern outlier of Mor Bheinn. The going here is not easy and is characterised by deep bracken, trees and outcrops with some vegetation on them.

Reach the burn flowing down the corrie between Ben Halton and Mor

*Beinn Dearg from Glen Artney*

Bheinn and climb the steep, heathery eastern slopes of Mor Bheinn to a false summit. The actual summit has a small cairn and a triangulation pillar and fine views compensate for the tricky ascent. Loch Earn, Ben Vorlich and Ben Lawers are all visible on a clear day.

Descend by the craggy south ridge to the col below Ben Halton. The route now descends the western slopes and contours round to reach the end of the track at GR 714198, but an ascent of Ben Halton could also be made from this point. Once on the track it is still a long loop of 4½km back to Tomanour followed by another 3km to Craggish. During the descent of Mor Beinn, the fine north-eastern ridge of Beinn Dearg is seen to advantage and this Graham could conceivably be included with Mor Bheinn using the Dalchruin start in Glen Artney to the south.

**Creag Each** (Horse Rock); *672m*
**Creag Ruadh** (Red Rock); *712m*
*OS Sheet 51; GR 652263, 674292*
*16km/880m/4½–7hrs*
*Map 13*

---

These two hills lie north-west of St Fillans on the eastern extremity of Loch Earn, and both are unnamed on the 1:50,000 map. A bulldozed track loops round the head of Glen Tarken and both hills can be conveniently combined into one expedition by using this track.

Begin on the A85 road north of Loch Earn where a large parking area is situated just past the beginning of the track which leads to Glen Tarken. Follow

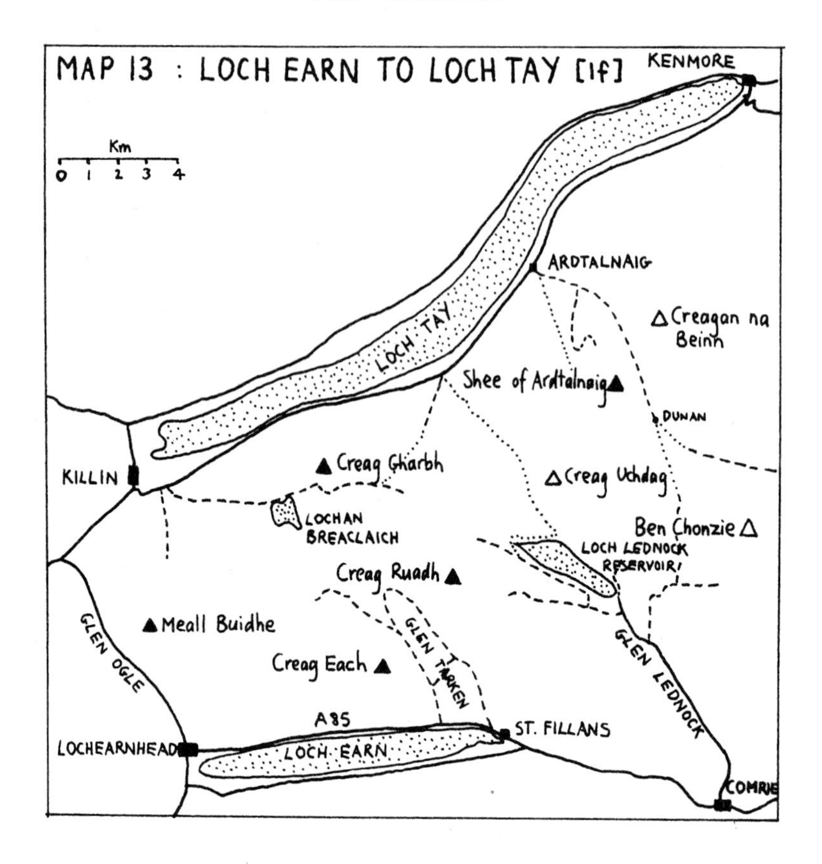


this track, which makes a big dog-leg past some old farm buildings and continue for just over 1km until a stream is reached which flows down from Creag Each. Leave the track at this point and head west, climbing steadily through deep heather to reach eventually the broad southern shoulder of the hill. The summit lies to the north and is girdled by a ring of crags. The top itself is a craggy outcrop with no visible cairn, and is a fine viewpoint, particularly across Loch Earn to the Ben Vorlich group.

Descend to the north for about 250m and rejoin the Glen Tarken track, being careful not to take a left fork which leads to Glen Beich. Follow the track round the head of the glen until it crosses the stream which flows down through a gorge from just west of the summit of Creag Ruadh. Leave the track and ascend the heathery slopes east of the gorge which eventually lead to the small cairn at the summit. Creag Ruadh contains three separate tops, the most westerly being the true summit. In misty conditions care would be needed on this hill.

Descend more or less south from the top to regain the north Glen Tarken track, and follow it to a second track branching off to the right to join the track used on the initial walk in. Both these hills can be ascended on separate outings if so wished, and Creag Ruadh can be approached from Glen Lednock via the track which follows the Allt Mathaig to the east of the hill.

**Meall Buidhe** (Yellow Hill); *719m*
*OS Sheet 51; GR 576275*
*2km/440m/1½–3hrs*
*Map 13*

---

The craggy south-western slopes of Meall Buidhe are very prominent during the drive north up Glen Ogle from Lochearnhead. On a sunny autumn day the yellow, gold and russet tones of grass and bracken provide ample justification for the name 'Yellow Hill'. Meal Buidhe is an ideal objective for a short half day when possibly *en route* north or south.

Park on the A85 Glen Ogle road at a small lay-by near a bridge opposite the railway viaduct. This is more or less directly beneath the summit of the hill and is only a kilometre from the top. Almost any line can be taken though the going is relentlessly steep through mainly heather and bracken. Numerous slab outcrops pepper the hillside but are usually too steep to provide worthwhile scrambling. The actual summit is the more southerly of two tops, the more northerly being Beinn Leabhainn, which translates oddly as 'Hill of the Bed'. The cairn is a grand viewpoint for the Ben Vorlich group to the south and to the twin Corbetts of Creag MacRanaich and Meall an t-Seallaidh to the south-west across Glen Ogle. The area east of Meall Buidhe is a relatively unfrequented

*Ben Vorlich and Stuc a' Chroin from Meall Buidhe*

terrain of knolls and lochans inhabited by little more than deer, grouse and ptarmigan, and is a haven for lovers of solitude. Return by a similar route to that of the ascent.

**Creag Gharbh** (Rough Rock); *637m*
*OS Sheet 51; GR 632327*
*14km/490m/2½–4hrs*
*Map 13*

This little hill is located about 2km south of Loch Tay near its south-western extremity. Like many of the hills in this area it has few distinguishing features, but offers fine views across Loch Tay to the Ben Lawers and Tarmachan ranges.

The most convenient route begins on the south Loch Tay road at the bridge over the Achmore burn. Here a track begins which can be followed upwards through the trees and eventually after 4km to the dam at the western end of Lochan Breaclaich. The 'track' is actually a tarmac road as far as this dam. Continue on the track for another 2km to the big bend just south of Creag Gharbh. Leave the track and head north for about 1km climbing less than 100m to reach the triangulation point perched on a craggy knoll. In clear conditions the view north across Loch Tay to the Munro giants is particularly grand. To vary the descent drop down easy slopes to the north-west and reach the south Loch Tay road from where it is a 4km walk back to the start.

A bike may be found useful in tackling this hill, and a good circuit could be accomplished by returning to the track after climbing Creag Gharbh, then cycling further on to the point where a path and track lead north-east to Ardeonaig. The south Loch Tay road can then be followed back to Achmore.

**Shee of Ardtalnaig** (origin uncertain); *759m*
*OS Sheets 51, 52; GR 729351*
*12km/560m/3–4hrs*
*Map 13*

The name of Shee of Ardtalnaig applies to the whole long whale-back ridge west of the Corbett of Creagan na Beinne and south-east of Ardtalnaig on the southern shore of Loch Tay. Both the Graham and Corbett could be combined in a circuit beginning and ending near Ardtalnaig, but the following is a description of the Graham only.

From Ardtalnaig it is possible to drive up the tarmac road before finding a parking space about halfway to the farm at Claggan. Continue on foot through the farmyard and immediately branch off to the right along a track which climbs steadily up the north-west flank of the hill. After one or two zigzags the track ends about 30m below the broad heathery northern end of the ridge. Climb directly onto the ridge, where grand views can be enjoyed across Loch Tay to the Ben Lawers group of Munros. The summit of the hill is seen from this point as the final steepness of the 2km-long ridge. To reach it requires a very pleasant ridge walk, albeit with the odd peat hag to slow the rhythm. The summit area is flat and a tiny cairn adorns the highest point. There is a grand feeling of spaciousness on top of this hill and it is a fine viewpoint.

To vary the descent drop south-east for 200m to reach a track which descends north to the main Gleann a' Chilleine track leading back to Claggan. Note also that there is a right-of-way from Newton Bridge in the Sma' Glen which follows the River Almond to Dunan before using the track just mentioned to Claggan. Shee of Ardtalnaig would make an interesting start (or finale) to this route.

**Beinn na Gainimh** (Hill of Sand);
*730m*
*OS Sheet 52; GR 837344*
*9km/450m/2–3½hrs*
*Map 14*

This retiring flat-topped heathery hill is fairly typical of the hills to the west of the Sma' Glen. The area is characterised by attractive deep-cut glens and high rolling moorland, and this particular hill lies between Glen Almond and Glen Lochan. The shortest and most scenic approach is from the north-eastern end of Glen Lochan just opposite the entrance to Glenquaich Lodge, where a track continues to a small fishing hut on the north side of tranquil Lochan a' Mhuilinn. Rising up steeply beyond the lochan are the northern outliers of Beinn na Gainimh separated by a col.

Continue on past the hut on a rather boggy path until it begins to hug the northern slopes of the hill just above the aptly named Lochan Uaine (Green Lochan). Climb directly up from here on steep heather slopes interspersed with the odd rocky outcrop. Eventually reach the extensive and featureless flat summit plateau where there is no obvious cairn. To the south-west there are good views of Auchnafree Hill and Ben Chonzie. Return by the route of ascent.

A complete traverse of this hill could be accomplished by continuing to the southern top of Sron Bealaidh, then ascending its south-eastern ridge to pick up a track which descends to Glen Almond. The Glen Almond track can then be followed east for 4km to the A822 road at Newton Bridge in the Sma' Glen. This could equally be used as a means of ascent, with possibly the inclusion of a round of the tops east of

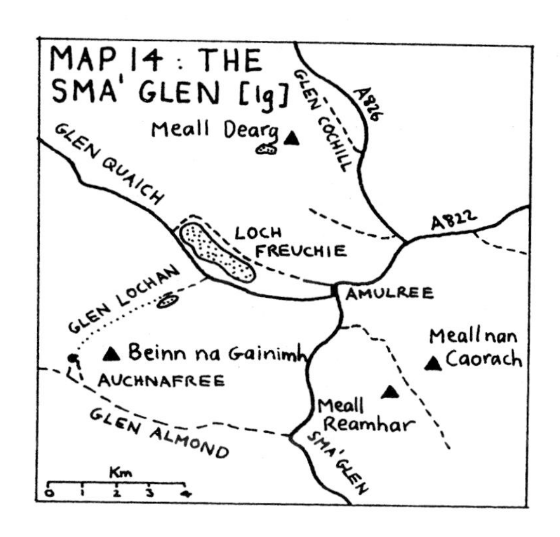

Beinn na Gainimh as far as Meall Reamhar.

**Meall nan Caorach** (Hill of the Sheep); *623m*
**Meall Reamhar** (Fat Hill), *620m*
*OS Sheet 52; GR 928338, 922332*
*10km/500m/2–4hrs*
*Map 14*

---

These two rather reclusive hills lie north-east of the Sma' Glen and are the highest points of the large mass of high ground between the A822 and the A9 to the east. Their summits are only a kilometre apart and they are separated by a high bealach which makes their combined traverse a relatively easy undertaking.

Begin on the A822 road just south of Amulree, where a track can be followed across a bridge to the farm at Girron. Go round a big bend in the track and continue for some 4km to the bealach between the two hills. Ascend Meall nan Caorach by easy heathery slopes to the summit triangulation point, where fine views can be enjoyed of Loch Freuchie and the hills to the west.

Descend to the track and make a similarly easy ascent of Meall Reamhar, which has a substantial cairn at the summit. Descend north to reach the track and follow it back to the start point.

*The view west from Meall nan Caorach*

**Meall Dearg** (Red Hill); *690m*
*OS Sheet 52; GR 886414*
*5km/370m/1–2hrs*
*Map 14*

This fairly nondescript little hill lies to the west of Glen Cochill and north-east of Glen Quaich. Apart from fine summit views of Schiehallion and Faragon Hill to the north, the hill has few redeeming features.

Begin at White Cairn on the A826 road to Aberfeldy, where part of Wade's Road can be used to gain access to the heathery eastern slopes of the hill. Climb these slopes directly to the vicinity of a false summit with a few crags on the southern side. The actual summit lies across a boggy area of peat hags and the final ascent leads to a triangulation pillar. Return by the same route.

A longer excursion could be made by dropping west to Loch Fender, then ascending the subsidiary top of Creag an Loch before descending to the track in Glen Fender. This would require two cars, a kind driver, or a long road walk!

**Ben Cleuch**; *721m*
*OS Sheet 58; GR 902006*
*9km/720m/3½–5hrs*
*Map 15*

The Ochils are well seen from the A9 road driving north to Stirling, and are a continuous range of grassy, rounded tops dropping steeply to the hillfoot towns of Alva, Tillicoultry and Dollar. The highest of the group and the only Graham is Ben Cleuch, which is the only hill in the Ochils to rise above 700m. There are numerous other tops over 600m (and above 2,000ft) but none of them aspire to Graham status as they do not possess the necessary 150m drop on all sides. In fact, the full 10km range from Glen Devon to Sheriff Muir

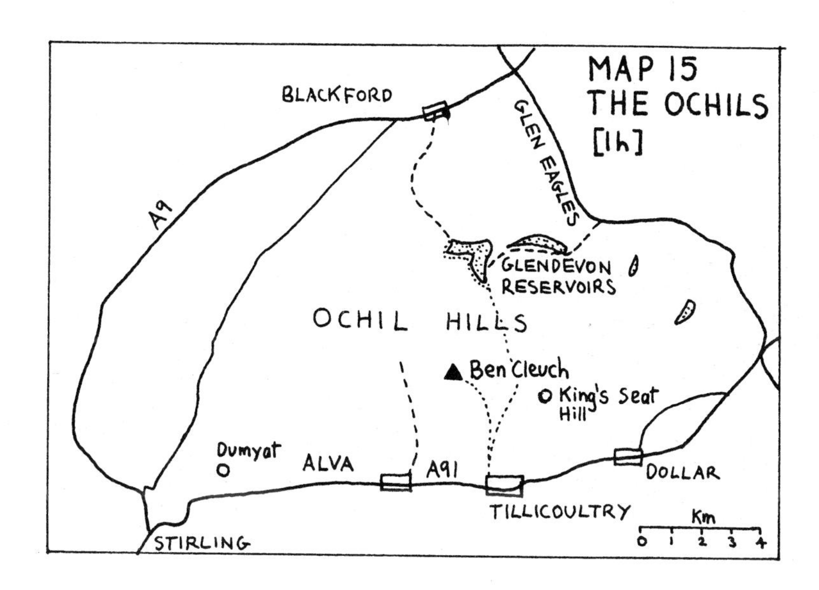

never falls below 540m and the Ochils are ideal hills for long traverses taking in several tops. The route described is a pleasant horseshoe ridge involving three distinct summits.

Begin in Tillicoultry at the entrance to Mill Glen, where limited parking space is available. A signposted route winds its way up the delightful wooded steep-sided glen, and crosses the burn at various places on well-constructed footbridges. Reach an obvious hairpin bend in the path just beyond the last bridge and take the secondary path which drops down to the burn and cross it by a wooden footbridge. This point is near the junction of the Gannel and Daiglen burns, where the steep south ridge of The Law rises up between them. Follow the path which ascends this ridge and levels off higher up.

Continue on up to reach the cairn at the summit of The Law (638m) just beyond a boundary fence. This is a good place to sit and admire the view across the valley of the Forth to the south. The summit of Ben Cleuch lies about 1½km further round to the north-west and is easily reached by following the line of the fence along the broad grassy ridge. The summit contains a cairn and triangulation pillar.

Continue past the broad summit along the wide ridge and drop steeply to the col below the final top of Ben Ever (622m). Traverse this top and head south along the grassy ridge, passing several minor tops before descending steeply down the south-eastern spur to the foot of the south ridge of The Law. The Glen path can then be followed back to the start of the route. Note that a hill path begins at the carpark as well as the Glen path and both these meet at the hairpin bend mentioned earlier.

*Ben Cleuch from near Tillicoultry*

## SECTION 2

# *The River Tay to Rannoch Moor*

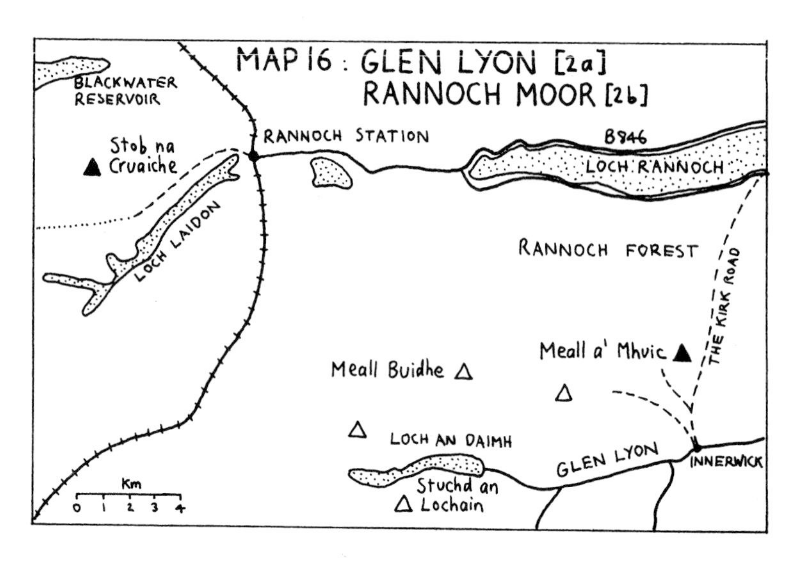


**Meall a' Mhuic** (Hill of the Pig); *745m*
*OS Sheets 51, 42; GR 579508*
*9km/550m/2–3hrs*
*Map 16*

---

This well-defined hill lies north of Innerwick in Glen Lyon and is a lone Graham amongst a host of Munros and Corbetts. It provides a pleasant short outing from Innerwick but could be combined with some of its loftier neighbours. It could also be included in a walk along the right-of-way from Innerwick to Loch Rannoch, which is also known as the Kirk Road. The route described uses part of this right-of-way.

From the church at Innerwick follow the track up the east side of the burn before entering the forest and continue through the steep-sided glen to Lairig Ghallabhaich. At the point where the track crosses the stream (GR 592511) strike off to the west and ascend easy heathery slopes for less than 300m to reach the broad summit of the hill topped by a small cairn. The view is extensive, with Ben Lawers and the Tarmachans looking particularly grand to the south-west across Glen Lyon. Descend by the broad southern flank and pick up another track at a height of 530m which zigzags down to meet a second track leading back to Innerwick. This completes a satisfying half day's outing.

**Stob na Cruaiche** (Peak of the Peat Stack); *739m*
*OS Sheet 41; GR 363571*
*16km/540m/4½–6hrs*
*Map 16*

---

This isolated hill stands on the north-eastern extremity of vast and lonely Rannoch Moor, and between Loch Laidon and the Blackwater Reservoir. As such it requires a fair amount of fitness and determination to reach, but its marvellous summit views far outweigh the effort involved, and Stob na Cruaiche should be kept for a good clear day.

The shortest approach is from Rannoch station to the east, which is unfortunately on OS Sheet 42, thus involving two maps for the route. Cross the railway line and take the track which heads north-west to the forestry plantation. After about half a kilometre take a right fork which climbs through the trees and terminates on open hillside well above the tree-line. Follow a faint ATV track and several cairns to the rounded, heathery top of Liath na Doire. From here it is still nearly a 4km trudge along a broad ridge with a minor top *en route* to the summit of Stob na Cruaiche, which is crowned with a cairn and triangulation pillar. On a clear day the view from the summit is a revelation with a colossal array of magnificent peaks girdling the extremities of Rannoch Moor. The Lyon and Orchy peaks, Blackmount, Glencoe, the Mamores, Ben Nevis, the Grey Corries, Ben Alder, Schiehallion – all are clearly visible in a near 360-degree arc from this unrivalled viewpoint.

The descent can be varied by dropping south-east to the end of the forestry at Loch Laidon. A path from Black Corries Lodge to the west appears to end about half a kilometre from the forest but actually continues to a gate and wooden steps at GR 385556 at the edge of the forest. Climb the steps and follow a vague path along a wide firebreak until it is possible to climb up steeply to the left to reach a good forestry track leading back to the start of the route. This particular track is shown on OS map 42 but not on OS sheet 41.

A right-of-way connects Rannoch Station and the Kingshouse Hotel in Glencoe and it would be quite possible to climb this hill in conjunction with a walk between these two end-points. The Kingshouse Hotel is another possible start point for the ascent but involves a much longer walk. Finally, it should be noted that the footpath shown on OS Sheet 42 along the northern shore of Loch Laidon is more a figment of the mapmakers' imagination than a reality. The aforementioned forestry track provides the best route through this plantation.

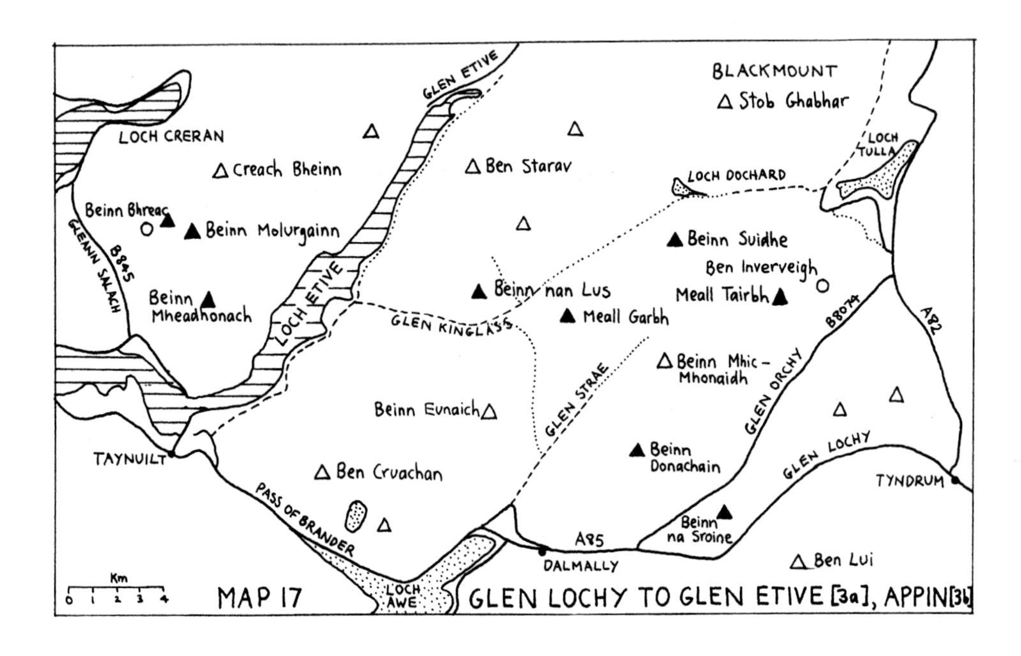
BLACKMOUNT
Stob Ghabhar
LOCH TULLA
GLEN ETIVE
LOCH CRERAN
Creach Bheinn
Ben Starav
LOCH DOCHARD
Beinn Bhreac
Beinn Molurgainn
GLENN SALACH
B845
Beinn Suidhe
Ben Inverveigh
Beinn Mheadhonach
LOCH ETIVE
Beinn nan Lus
Meall Tairbh
Meall Garbh
GLEN KINGLASS
B8074
A82
Beinn Mhic-Mhonaidh
GLEN ORCHY
GLEN STRAE
Beinn Eunaich
Beinn Donachain
GLEN LOCHY
TAYNUILT
Ben Cruachan
TYNDRUM
PASS OF BRANDER
A85
Beinn na Sroine
DALMALLY
Ben Lui
Km
0 1 2 3 4
LOCH AWE
MAP 17
GLEN LOCHY TO GLEN ETIVE [3a], APPIN[3b]

## SECTION 3

# *North-west Argyll, Appin and Glencoe*

**Beinn na Sroine** (Offended Hill);
*636m*
*OS Sheet 50; GR 233289*
*3km/440m/1½–2½hrs*
*Map 17*

---

Other than grand summit views, this hill has few redeeming features, being little more than the last undulation on the long grassy ridge stretching south-westwards from the Corbett of Beinn Udlaidh on the north side of Glen Lochy. The name 'Offended Hill' could well be imagined to refer to its relative lack of visitors – Beinn na Sroine is not a frequently climbed hill.

The shortest route to the summit begins on the A85 road through Glen Lochy at the edge of a forestry plantation (GR 246287). A faint and patchy path follows the forest edge up the hill some 100m to the left but peters out higher up. Beyond is a fairly direct line which can be taken on a rising traverse to the west. Pass a minor top with a small cairn before reaching the main summit, which is a clutter of man-made equipment, including a collapsed radio mast, a wind generator, a metal shed and a trig point. On a clear day the Ben Cruachan range is seen to advantage and the view to the south is dominated by the intimidating mass of Ben Lui. Return by the same route.

The hill could also be climbed from Glen Orchy to the north but this route is marginally longer. For those with greater aspirations, it is perfectly possible to follow the long north-easterly ridge for 6km to Beinn Udlaidh. The forest plantation crossing the ridge has a good track which follows the ridge line (not marked on the OS map).

**Beinn Donachain** (Hill of Badness);
*650m*
*OS Sheet 50; GR 198316*
*11km/590m/4–6hrs*
*Map 17*

---

Beinn Donachain occupies a strategic position between Glen Orchy and Glen Strae and could be climbed from either glen, the second option being preferable if wishing also to include an ascent of Beinn Mhic-Mhonaidh, a Corbett lying about 3km to the north. The Glen Orchy approach is shorter with a pleasant wooded start and is described here.

A small pedestrian suspension bridge crosses the River Orchy at GR 232305 and conveniently located next to it is a large parking and picnic area which provides an ideal starting point. In an effort to deter parties of picnickers and day-trippers from crossing the river, the bridge contains a metal gate which is often padlocked. This can be easily climbed or the river waded if preferred. Once on the opposite bank, follow a delightful path to the left which meanders its way through natural forest, staying close to the river for about 1km before turning off to the right and emerging from the trees.

A fairly distinct stalkers' path leads up and across the open hillside from this area before doubling back to the right and passing directly below the conspicuous Creag Ghlas, a large crag higher up. Stay on this stalkers' path until just beyond the crag. From here leave the path and climb directly up on a steep incline of heather and grass initially before levelling off in the vicinity of Cruach nan Nighean. At this point it is possible to look down on lonely Lochan Coire Thoraidh, nestling peacefully within a fairly recent forestry plantation. Circle round the northern side of Heart Loch, another magical spot, and enjoy splendid views south-east to the Ben Lui group.

The final rise to the summit of Beinn Donachain lies just beyond another small lochan and the battered remains of an old fence have to be crossed before reaching the large expanse of the summit plateau. A tiny cairn on the first high point is not the actual summit which is about 100m further on, with the cairn lying on the line of a long since eroded drystane dyke.

The Ben Cruachan range is seen to advantage from here, while to the north the Corbett of Beinn Mhic-Mhonaidh dominates the skyline. Quite how this hill received its detrimental label, 'Hill of Badness', is probably unknown, but the views from the summit certainly do not reflect such a disparaging description. Return by the route of ascent.

**Meall Garbh** (Rough Hill); *701m*
*OS Sheet 50; GR 168367*
*15km/1,200m/6–8hrs*
*Map 17*

Meall Garbh is a fairly remote Graham lying to the south of Glen Kinglass, which connects Loch Etive to Victoria Bridge. A first glance at the map would

*Ben Cruachan from the summit of Beinn Donachain*

indicate an extremely long approach from Victoria Bridge as the only logical route, but Glen Strae to the south offers the closest approach, albeit with considerable loss and gain in height.

It is possible to drive up Glen Strae for about 1½km and park just before a gate. The same distance beyond the gate a hill path goes off north following the west bank of the Allt Dhoirrean. This continues up and over the Lairig Dhoirean before descending north, then west, into Glen Kinglass. Take this path as far as the Lairig Dhoirean, where there is a small lochan and various cairns. From here it is possible to make a slightly rising traverse for 1km to reach the col between Beinn Lurachan and Meall Beithe. A direct ascent of Meall Beithe is now to be tackled before a 250m drop to the col at GR 173362. A final climb of 300m to the north-west has to be made to reach the small cairn on the summit of Meall Garbh. The view across wild Glen Kinglass to the peaks of the Ben Starav range is quite stunning. Also visible is the even more remote Graham of Beinn nan Lus.

The return route can be pleasantly varied by returning to the col at GR 173362, then skirting round the eastern slopes of Meall Beithe and making an ascent of Beinn Lurachan by its easy north-east ridge. Beinn Lurachan is a fine hill in its own right and is the highest point of the whole trip at 715m. Its well-defined south-west ridge makes a delightful descent which leads back to the hill path and Glen Strae.

**Beinn nan Lus** (Hill of the Herbs); *709m*
*OS Sheet 50; GR 130375*
*40km/810m/6½–9½hrs (bike)*
*Map 17*

Lying east of Loch Etive and north of Glen Kinglass, Beinn nan Lus is one of the most inaccessible Grahams in Scotland. Its situation, south of the Ben Starav group of Munros, would suggest an ascent in combination with some of these, but this would involve a significant detour and loss in height. If a bike is available the best route uses the Land Rover track along the east side of Loch Etive, followed by the track through Glen Kinglass. This is the approach described below.

Begin at Inverawe, near Taynuilt, where the track can be followed through mixed forest for about 3km before winding its way along the lochside. There are some steep climbs as the track contours around two headlands, but the vista northwards of the long finger of Loch Etive probing into fine mountains is ample compensation. Cross the bridge over the River Kinglass and turn immediately right to begin the delightful run through the beautifully wooded Glen Kinglass with its profuse display of oak, hazel and birch. Like numerous other Highland glens, Glen Kinglass once supported a viable community and the remains of old furnaces and charcoal beds can still be seen. It is hard to believe that an iron foundry once existed in such a remote spot. A few kilometres along the glen a

*The route to Beinn nan Lus along Loch Etive side*

cairn stands on a small knoll to the left of the track and is a memorial to Lady Wyfold, the estate owner who died in 1976.

Shortly beyond is Narrachan bothy, which is a possible overnight stopping point. At this point, the extensive southern slopes of Beinn nan Lus rise steeply upwards in tiers of smooth crags and it is not advisable to make an ascent from here, besides the fact that the area around Narrachan is ecologically fairly sensitive with much varied birdlife. Continue for 2–3km beyond Narrachan and begin the ascent roughly south of the actual summit where the slopes are less steep and the crags less numerous. Alternatively, continue to the mouth of the Allt Hallater and ascend the hill by the easy east shoulder.

The summit of Beinn nan Lus is a mass of outcrops and the actual summit consists of a small cairn on an extensive platform of rock. Views from this seldom-visited perch are quite grand and the Ben Starav group is very prominent to the north. To the south, across Glen Kinglass, Beinn Eunaich is the conspicuous pointed summit, while Ben Cruachan's saw-toothed tops are just visible to the south-west. The safest means of descent is the long, easy-angled east shoulder. Return to Inverawe by the same route.

An approach to Beinn nan Lus can also be made from the east at Victoria Bridge, but this is also very long, involving a round trip of about 35km. Although a path exists to the east of Glenkinglass Lodge, it is certainly not a

Land Rover track and not ideal for a bike. Finally, note that the Graham of Meall Garbh lying to the south of Glen Kinglass could be combined with Beinn nan Lus, but this would add 2 to 3hrs to the already heavy schedule given above.

**Meall Tairbh** (Advantage Hill); *665m*
*OS Sheet 50; GR 251375*
*13km/630m/4–6hrs*
*Map 17*

Meall Tairbh and its slightly lower twin of Ben Inverveigh lie south-west of the Inveroran Hotel on the West Highland Way; and, if climbed together from the hotel, they give an extremely satisfying circuit round Coir' Orain, with the corrie separating the pair. Despite its lower altitude, Ben Inverveigh is the more popular hill, being topographically a more shapely peak, but both offer unparalleled views of the Stob Ghabhar range to the north.

Begin at the hotel and follow the route of the West Highland Way south-east into Mam Carraigh, a broad pass on the lower north ridge of Ben Inverveigh. Another track cuts off to the south at this point and follows the wide, heathery north ridge of the hill. This is not shown on the OS map but should be followed to its termination just short of a small, wind-powered generator and transmitter perched on a little false summit. From here it is a pleasant ridge wander of nearly 2km, passing a small lochan to reach the cairn at the summit of the hill. Ben Inverveigh falls short of Graham status by only 6m of relative height – there is a 144m drop to the col below Meall Tairbh – but in no way does this detract from its status as a fine hill and a superb viewpoint.

Continue along the ridge south-west of the summit and gradually drop down to the very hummocky col containing Lochan Coir' Orain. This col would be confusing in misty conditions as it is a maze of knolls and peat hags. An easy 160m climb through deep heather leads from the col to the summit of the oddly named Meall Tairbh, from where the corries and ridges of the massive Stob Ghabhar range of Munros to the north are seen to perfection. Beinn Dorain and the other Bridge of Orchy Munros to the east are also prominent from this fine vantage point. Descend Meall Tairbh by its long, broad and easy-angled north ridge, then go north-east to the Allt Orain, where the going becomes disconcertingly boggy and tussocky until the road is reached at the hotel.

**Beinn Suidhe** (Sitting Hill); *676m*
*OS Sheet 50; GR 211400*
*16km/500m/5–7hrs*
*Map 17*

Beinn Suidhe is the north-easterly outpost of a chain of small hills lying to the north-east of Beinn Eunaich, between Glen Strae and Glen Kinglass. It lies to the south of the extensive Stob Ghabhar group of Munros and is somewhat dwarfed by them, but its magnificent vantage point far outweighs its lowly stature. Cars can be parked on the A8005 road just south of Victoria Bridge, which is the usual starting point for Stob Ghabhar and the surrounding Munros.

Cross the bridge and turn left following the track north of the river. Just beyond the small climbing hut at GR 256425, take the left fork which follows the river and crosses a smaller stream further on by a footbridge. At a ford, continue by the bank of the river until the small suspension bridge, which has rather loose slats, is reached at GR 233418. Cross this and turn right along the obvious path on the south side of the river.

Beinn Suidhe rises up to the left from here and looks impressively steep and craggy in its upper stages. A deer fence can be crossed by a stile a little further on and this leads to open hillside. Another fence higher up can also be crossed by a stile and this emerges onto a fairly flat boggy platform before the obvious steep and craggy section. Climb this along a leftward slanting line on easy grass runnels, and thereafter by a succession of similar features which avoid the main crags. Finally reach the north-western top of Beinn Suidhe at GR 216408 which is a fine viewpoint, especially northwards to the wild and remote corries of the Stob Ghabhar range. The actual summit lies less than a kilometre distant along a knobbly ridge, and commands unusual views of the Ben Starav range to the north-west.

The observant climber may have noticed a new forestry track crossing the plantation south of the Abhainn Shira, and this provides a convenient return route (not marked on the 1989 OS map). To reach this, retrace your steps to the flat area below the crags and then head due east to cross the Allt Suil na Curra and the edge of the forestry plantation. The track starts some 100m from the edge and can be followed in a general easterly direction before swinging round in a large dog-leg. Just beyond this point, it passes a monument to the renowned Gaelic poet Duncan Ban MacIntyre (1724–1812), the composer of the multi-versed 'In Praise of Beinn Dorain'. The track meets the A8005 road a few hundred metres south of the starting point.

**Beinn Bhreac** (Speckled Hill); *726m*
**Beinn Molurgainn** (origin uncertain); *690m*
**Beinn Mheadhonach** (Middle Hill); *715m*
*OS Sheet 50; GR 008408, 019400, 019369*
*15km/1,220m/6½–8½hrs*
*Map 17*

---

These three relatively unfrequented hills lying between Loch Creran and Loch Etive involve rough walking over complex convoluted terrain, which in misty conditions would involve some tricky navigation. They are best reserved for a fine day, however, as the combination of sea and mountain views is quite spectacular. They are best tackled from the highest point on the B845 road through Gleann Salach to the west, which is on OS Sheet 49. It should be noted at this point that the Beinn Bhreac mentioned above refers to the north-east top of the Beinn Bhreac shown on OS Sheet 49 (GR 993400). The name actually refers to the lower summit (708m) on Sheet 49, but as the higher summit is nameless on the map, the Beinn Bhreac label has been extended to include the Graham. Both are included in the round anyway!

From the road, gain the broad hummocky south shoulder of the lower Beinn Bhreac which is followed north for about 2½km rising gradually then more steeply to the large cairn at the summit of this first top. Fine views can be enjoyed to the west of Lismore and Mull, while to the south and east Ben Cruachan and the Etive hills form a magnificent backdrop. Head north-east from the summit, dropping slightly to reach the col below the true Graham which still lies a full kilometre further on across a flat ridge of close-cropped heather and smooth slabs. The summit has a small cairn with good views to the Corbett of Creach Bheinn lying only 2km to the north-east.

The next summit of Beinn Molurgainn can be reached by continuing east along the well-defined east ridge of Beinn Bhreac over some easy rock steps, then gradually descending south-east to the wide col below the summit. Only 151m of height separates this col from

*Near the summit of Beinn Mheadhonach*

the top and Beinn Molurgainn just manages to scrape through to the Graham status by 1m of relative height. Climb easy grass slopes to the summit cairn on the south-western extremity of the hill.

The final summit of the day, Beinn Mheadhonach, lies exactly south of Beinn Molurgainn and is a shade over 3km distant as the crow flies. Behind this bald statement, however, is a tangled web of tricky terrain involving much ascent and descent with significant detouring. This section is interesting though, with several idyllic little lochans providing welcome rest spots. After a fairly steep grassy descent, a series of minor summits, knolls and lochans is followed south to the vicinity of Lochan Bealach Carra, which nestles serenely beneath the steep northern slopes of Beinn Mheadhonach.

The highest col lies 500m east of this lochan just below the minor top of Meall Biorach, and from here a fairly well-defined craggy ridge can be followed. This ridge contains much bare rock, but most of it is too broken and easy angled to provide worthwhile scrambling. The summit area of Beinn Mheadhonach is split by several deep fissures and this should be noted in misty conditions. The first fissure is about 10m deep and sheer-sided for much of its length. Beyond this, cross a smaller fissure to reach the substantial summit cairn. Grand views can be enjoyed from this point down the length of Loch Etive and the Ben Starav group stands out well. Far to the west the Connell bridge is just visible.

Descend by following the west ridge of the mountain to a minor top, then dropping down north-west on steep grassy slopes to the upper edge of the natural forest which lines the River Esragan. The river should be crossed at this point, which may be tricky in spate conditions. Once over the river, follow a grassy track through a gate and up to the remains of some old shielings. Turn off left above the ruins and follow a vague path which contours along the hillside north of the river. This path is not shown on the map and is very indistinct in places. It leads to the B845 road and the starting point.

To shorten the above round, Beinn Mheadhonach could be left for a separate expedition, climbed by the descent route just mentioned, or possibly by way of the track on the north side of Loch Etive.

**Sgorr a' Choise** (Foot-shaped Peak); *663m*
**Meall Mor** (Big Hill); *676m*
*OS Sheet 41; GR 084551, 106559*
*11km/910m/4½–6hrs*
*Map 18*

---

These two hills, lying south of Ballachulish, fill the gap between the Beinn a' Bheither Munros to the west and the Bidean nam Bian massif to the east. Although rather dominated by these and other higher and more popular neighbours, they provide an excellent day's hillwalking with views out of all proportion to their meagre

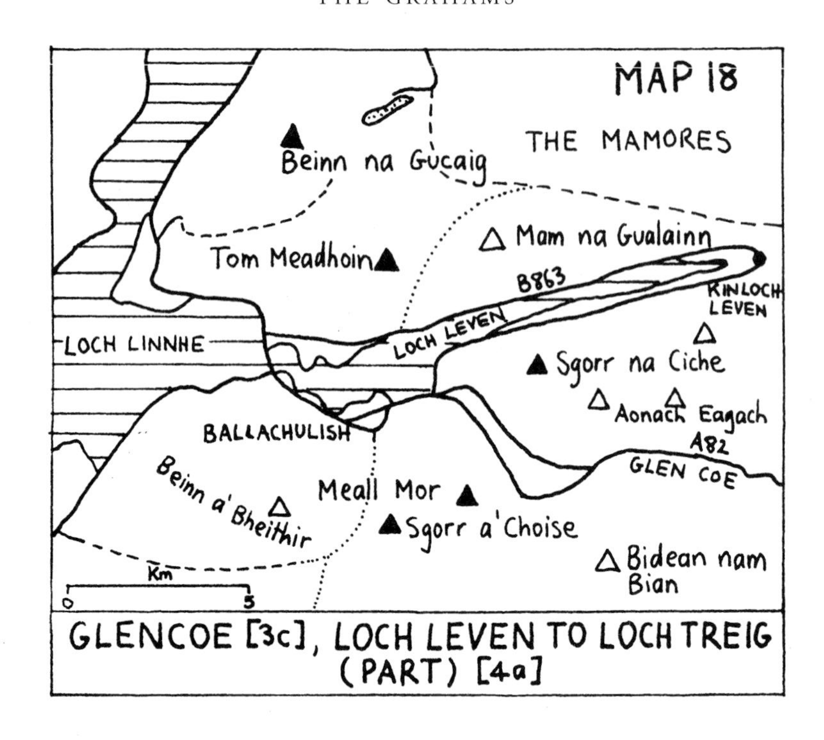

*Sgorr a' Choise from Meall Mor*

stature. In particular, Sgorr a' Choise is a grand pyramid whose elegant profile is seen to advantage from Ballachulish, which provides the ideal starting point.

Take the road which leads south past the primary school in Ballachulish and its continuation along the path following the west bank of the River Laroch. After about 2½km cross the river and climb up steep sides of heather and rock to gain the narrow south-west ridge of Sgorr a' Choise. Follow the line of this knobbly ridge on quartzite outcrops along the vague traces of a path to the airy summit which has a small cairn. The top provides a bird's-eye view of Ballachulish and is a fine vantage point for the Beinn a' Bheither ridge to the west.

To continue to Meall Mor, descend the south-east ridge of the hill over a minor top then go east to the col below Meall Mor. Ascend easy grassy slopes for about 300m of height gain to reach the large cairn which is perched near the edge of a long craggy escarpment. The summit of this hill gives a classic view of Glen Coe, its U-shaped valley being extremely prominent.

A large area of sitka forest lies between this hill and Ballachulish and the easiest way through this is to follow the wide curving ridge to the col at GR 095572, where an old drystane dyke can be followed through a rough break in the trees. From the col climb steadily, negotiating some tree cover before emerging near the transmission mast at GR 096577 (unmarked on the OS map). From here follow the edge of the forestry west down the hill to the old disused quarry at Ballachulish.

Both these hills could also be climbed from the track starting on the A82 road just south-west of Signal Rock which avoids any forestry. However, this option does involve some backtracking.

**Sgorr na Ciche** (Peak of the Breast) or Pap of Glencoe; *742m*
*OS Sheet 41; GR 125594*
*5km/720m/2½–4hrs*
*Map 18*

---

The eastern extremity of Glencoe is marked by the prominent peak of Buachaille Etive Mor. The counterpart at the western end of the glen is the smaller but no less prominent Sgorr na Ciche, more usually known as the Pap of Glencoe. The rugged symmetrical cone is well seen from the A82 road near Ballachulish across the waters of Loch Leven. It forms the true western termination of the contorted ridge along the north side of Glencoe, which includes the celebrated Aonach Eagach. In fact, the Pap of Glencoe is sometimes included as a pleasant, less serious finale to the traverse of Aonach Eagach. The route described is an ascent of Sgorr na Ciche only and is an ideal trip for an afternoon or summer evening.

Begin on the minor road between Glencoe village and the Clachaig Inn, where a farm track starts near the edge of the forest only about a kilometre from the village. Parking can often be a problem in this area. Follow the track and take the right fork across the burn, which subsequently crosses another burn before reducing to a path going up the south-east side of the obvious gully leading to the col between the Pap of Glencoe and Sgorr nam Fiannaidh. From the col, the summit is easily reached by a short climb on scree and large blocks. The summit is a truly wonderful viewpoint and the scene looking up the narrow ribbon of Loch Leven backed by the Mamore range is particularly fine. It is probably best to descend by the route of ascent but a circuit can be made by dropping west and picking up the path which follows the break through the forest and reaches the road about 700m north-west of the starting point.

The mountain can also be climbed from the B863 Kinlochleven road by the north-east ridge where there is a path with a cairn in the upper reaches. If suitable transport can be arranged, a traverse of the peak is also worth considering.

# SECTION 4

# *Loch Leven to Loch Ericht*



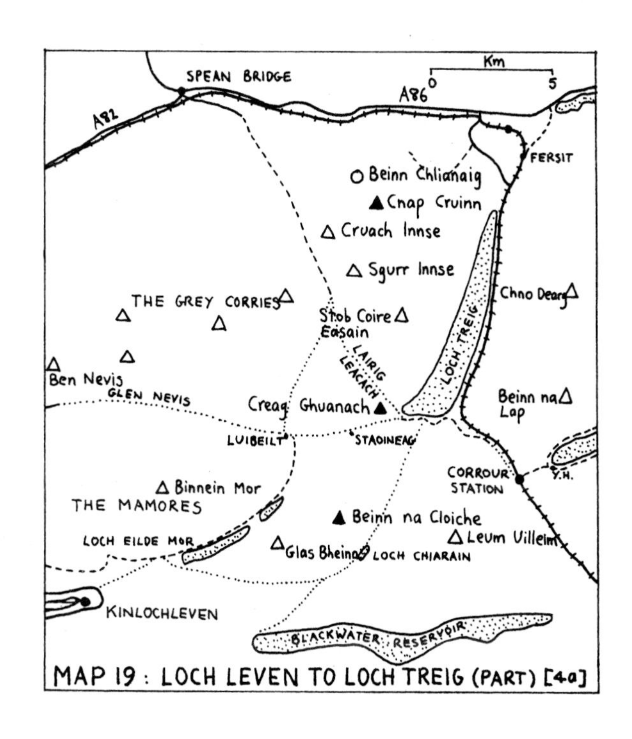

MAP 19 : LOCH LEVEN TO LOCH TREIG (PART) [4a]

**Tom Meadhoin** (Middle Mound); *621m*
**Beinn na Gucaig** (Bell-shaped Hill); *616m*
*OS Sheet 41; GR 087621, 062653*
*19km/1,100m/5–7hrs*
*Map 18*

These two hills lie to the north of Loch Leven and east of Loch Linnhe in a seldom-frequented corner of Lochaber penetrated by Gleann Righ, at the mouth of which is Inchree, just south of the Corran Ferry. Compared to the surrounding giants of the Glencoe peaks, the Mamores and Ben Nevis, they pale into insignificance, but this is part of their charm, and on a day when one wishes to escape the crowds and simply enjoy the views and some solitary wandering, these two hills are an ideal objective. The route to be described traverses both Grahams in a complete circuit of Gleann Righ, but each hill can be climbed separately from different starting points if so wished.

About a kilometre south of the Corran Ferry take the minor road to Inchree which leads to a forestry carpark and picnic area. Vehicles must be left here and either the forest track or a marked forest trail by a waterfall can be taken. Both routes eventually lead up Gleann Righ by the track to the north of the river. At GR 064628 a footbridge crosses the river to the cottage at Sallachail and any one of the choice of streams through the forest may be followed, as all lead south to the broad west ridge of Tom Meadhoin.

The summit of Tom Meadhoin is reached after first traversing a subsidiary top about a kilometre to the south-west. The summit panorama is, not surprisingly, quite stunning, with Beinn a' Bheithir and Bidean nam Bian stealing the scene to the south while to the north-east the Mamore chain clamours for attention. The summit of Ben Nevis is just visible above the Mamores.

The route continues along the north ridge of Tom Meadhoin to drop sharply to the col below Doire Ban. This next peak can be avoided by a western traverse to reach the corner of the forestry plantation, from whence an easy 300m of descent leads to the head of Gleann Righ. This provides a suitable resting spot before the long climb of 400m up to the summit of Beinn na Gucaig. During the ascent there are noteworthy views of Ben Nevis with Lochan Lunn Da Bhra forming an excellent foreground.

The long south-west ridge of Beinn na Gucaig is not quite as tempting a descent route as it appears on the map, being fairly heavy going through deep heather with numerous ditches and much tussocky ground. Nevertheless, on an early winter evening or late summer evening it is marvellous to meander down this long ridge and gaze out along the length of Loch Linnhe to the islands of Lismore and Mull, with the sun slowly sinking in the sky beyond them. This is one reason for doing the round in an anti-clockwise direction; so that a West Highland sunset can be

*The Mamores from Tom Meadhoin*

savoured from a high ridge late in the day. The ridge drops naturally down to the Gleann Righ track, and turns right to lead back to the carpark.

If you are climbing these two Grahams as 'separates', then Tom Meadhoin is best tackled from Callert House at the start of the Lairigmor track on the old B863 road to Kinlochleven. Note that this is the usual starting point for the Corbett of Mam na Gualainn and the two could conveniently be tackled together from this point.

The shortest route to Beinn na Gucaig is from Lundavra at Lochan Lunn Da Bhra to the north-east and involves a switchback drive along the fairly unfrequented minor road starting at GR 098737 in Fort William.

**Creag Ghuanach** (Stately Crag); *621m*
**Beinn na Cloiche** (origin uncertain); *646m*
*OS Sheet 41; GR 299690, 284648*
*28km/800m/7½–9hrs*
*Map 19*

---

Both these hills occupy the heart of a remote and little-frequented pocket of the Highlands between the Blackwater Reservoir and the southern end of the long fiord-like Loch Treig. They are surrounded on all sides by Munros and Corbetts and, not surprisingly, give superb vantage points. Creag Ghuanach in particular is a fine craggy little hill, bristling with character, with a commanding position above the south-western end of Loch Treig.

*Creag Ghuanach from Loch Treig*

Were it not for the splendid West Highland railway line which puts both of these hills within reasonable walking distance of Corrour station, they would almost certainly require an overnight stop. However, with an assortment of suitable bothies and idyllic wild camping spots some would see this as no great hardship. The youth hostel at Loch Ossian is also another possibility. The route about to be described begins and ends at Corrour station, and at the time of writing there is a nine-hour 'window' between morning and evening trains. Fit walkers should comfortably manage both peaks within this time but some may prefer to tackle them as two separate excursions.

From Corrour, cross the railway line and take the often boggy path which follows the railway line in a north-westerly direction. After about 2km to the railway bridge, the path becomes a good track leading down to the southern shore of Loch Treig. By this point the prominent craggy profile of Creag Ghuanach is unmistakable and once round the next headland the deserted Creaguaineach Lodge, which sits snugly at its base, comes into view.

Follow the track to the lodge, crossing the Abhainn Rath by a large footbridge. The area around Creaguaineach Lodge is as remote and delectable a spot as one could wish for if one is a lover of Highland solitude. The only sound apart from the odd snipe or curlew is the distant rumbling of a train

*The Mamores from Tom Meadhoin*

savoured from a high ridge late in the day. The ridge drops naturally down to the Gleann Righ track, and turns right to lead back to the carpark.

If you are climbing these two Grahams as 'separates', then Tom Meadhoin is best tackled from Callert House at the start of the Lairigmor track on the old B863 road to Kinlochleven. Note that this is the usual starting point for the Corbett of Mam na Gualainn and the two could conveniently be tackled together from this point.

The shortest route to Beinn na Gucaig is from Lundavra at Lochan Lunn Da Bhra to the north-east and involves a switchback drive along the fairly unfrequented minor road starting at GR 098737 in Fort William.

**Creag Ghuanach** (Stately Crag); *621m*
**Beinn na Cloiche** (origin uncertain); *646m*
*OS Sheet 41; GR 299690, 284648*
*28km/800m/7½–9hrs*
*Map 19*

---

Both these hills occupy the heart of a remote and little-frequented pocket of the Highlands between the Blackwater Reservoir and the southern end of the long fiord-like Loch Treig. They are surrounded on all sides by Munros and Corbetts and, not surprisingly, give superb vantage points. Creag Ghuanach in particular is a fine craggy little hill, bristling with character, with a commanding position above the south-western end of Loch Treig.

*Creag Ghuanach from Loch Treig*

Were it not for the splendid West Highland railway line which puts both of these hills within reasonable walking distance of Corrour station, they would almost certainly require an overnight stop. However, with an assortment of suitable bothies and idyllic wild camping spots some would see this as no great hardship. The youth hostel at Loch Ossian is also another possibility. The route about to be described begins and ends at Corrour station, and at the time of writing there is a nine-hour 'window' between morning and evening trains. Fit walkers should comfortably manage both peaks within this time but some may prefer to tackle them as two separate excursions.

From Corrour, cross the railway line and take the often boggy path which follows the railway line in a north-westerly direction. After about 2km to the railway bridge, the path becomes a good track leading down to the southern shore of Loch Treig. By this point the prominent craggy profile of Creag Ghuanach is unmistakable and once round the next headland the deserted Creaguaineach Lodge, which sits snugly at its base, comes into view.

Follow the track to the lodge, crossing the Abhainn Rath by a large footbridge. The area around Creaguaineach Lodge is as remote and delectable a spot as one could wish for if one is a lover of Highland solitude. The only sound apart from the odd snipe or curlew is the distant rumbling of a train on the West Highland line as it continues its way along the eastern edge of the long ribbon of Loch Treig.

The most sporting ascent of Creag Ghuanach is by its craggy eastern face and for those with a good head for heights this is the most satisfying approach. The route is characterised by wide grassy promontories interspersed with steep outcrops containing numerous grassy ledges and heathery gullies. A variety of lines is possible but will require a certain degree of confidence on this type of terrain. The rocky outcrops are not amenable to scrambling, being too steep and without natural footholds or handholds, and are lethal when wet. Easier routes can be found by following the path on the north bank of the Abhainn Rath for just over a kilometre and making the ascent from there. Alternatively, take the path leading north from the lodge which passes Easan Dubh and skirts round the north side of the hill, and make the ascent from there. The cairn at the summit is situated on the more westerly of two knolls and would be a fine place to linger on a summer's evening. The 'Steep Crag' of Creagan a' Chaise is prominent across the glen to the north-east and leads on to the twin Munros of 'This Yin' and 'That Yin' as Hamish Brown comically calls them. The scene to the west is totally dominated by the Mamore and Grey Corries ranges.

The south-west ridge of Creag Ghuanach makes for an easy grassy descent to the Abhainn Rath which will have to be crossed before continuing to the second Graham of the day. In spate conditions this will cause wet feet and it may be easier to go upstream beyond the outflow of the Allt Gleann na Giubhsachan. Beinn na Cloiche is the highest point of a well-defined ridge whose base begins at Loch na Staoineig. This secluded hill loch is easily reached by following the obvious stream course to its north. Ascend the ridge easily over several minor tops to the summit where a small crag and cairn overlook a tiny lochan. The Corbett of Glas Bheinn is prominent to the south-west and is of similar character to Beinn na Cloiche.

It is still a long way back to Corrour station from here and at least 3½ hours should be allowed for the return. This is best effected by descending to the path in Gleann Iolairean, and following it to Loch Treig and the track used in the approach.

## **Cnap Cruinn** (Round Lump);
*742m*
*OS Sheet 41; GR 302774*
*13km/540m/2½–4hrs*
*Map 19*

---

The relatively unexciting English translation of this admittedly relatively featureless hill does not provide much inspiration for its ascent. Nevertheless, its fine situation in Glen Spean, north-east of the Grey Corries range, makes for superlative summit views. It could be included along with the ascent of the twin Corbetts of Cruach Innse and Sgurr Innse lying to the south-west. The name, 'Cnap Cruinn', is not given on the 1:50,000 OS map although the neighbouring lower top of Beinn Chlianaig (721m), which lies just over 1km to the north-west, is noted.

The most convenient starting point is at Inverlair which can be reached by taking the Fersit road from the main A86 through Glen Spean. Just opposite a large white house, a forest track begins. It crosses a field before going through a second gate to the main forestry area. It is a pleasant walk along this track with good views opening out to the long ridge leading up on to the twin Munros of Stob a' Choire Mheadhoin and Stob Coire Easain.

After a big bend to the north-west, you will reach of the edge of the forest at GR 319781. This point is about 4km from the start, and the track should be left here to head for the fairly steep eastern flank of Cnap Cruinn. Now cross the boggy, tussocky ground initially before reaching the steep section.

The cairn which is obvious against the skyline and which is marked on the map is the point to aim for. The actual summit is only about 150m beyond this, and consists of a small cairn on a rocky rib. On a clear day the ascent will be repaid by grand views south and south-west to the 1,000m-plus Munros of the Grey Corries range. The afore-mentioned Corbetts also stand out well. Return by the same route.

**Binnein Shuas** (Upper Peak); *747m*
**Binnein Shios** (Downward Peak); *667m*
*OS Sheets 34, 42; GR 463826, 492857*
*17km/780m/5–7hrs*
*Map 20*

---

These twin peaks lie on a strip of land between Loch Laggan and Lochan na h-Earba and are outstanding viewpoints for the length of Glen Spean and the surrounding mountains. The fact that they are essentially hemmed in by the Creag Meagaidh range to the north-west and the Ben Alder range to the south does little to detract from their prominent status, and they are every bit as worth climbing as their Munro neighbours. Binnein Shuas in particular is a fine craggy hill with much character, and contains a mass of pegmatite on its east face which has been given the name of the Ardverikie Wall, and which boasts several sustained rock climbs. Cars can be parked at a large lay-by just east of the bridge over the River Spean at GR 433830. This is the usual starting point for the Creag Pitridh group of Munros.

Cross the bridge and follow the track which leads to the southern end of Lochan na h-Earba. But well before this, strike off to the left to gain the broad, grassy south-west ridge of Binnein Shuas. Higher up, some crags offer limited pockets of scrambling, but these can be treacherous in wet conditions. The summit is topped by a small cairn and offers fine views in all directions but particularly of the second Graham of

*Ben Nevis from Beinn na Gucaig* (Section 4a)

*Binnein Shios from Binnein Shuas* (Section 4b)

*Creag Dhubh* (Section 9b)

*Beinn Mheadhoin from Loch a'Choire* (Section 10Aa)

*Sgurr a'Chaorainn from Strontian glen* (Section 10Ab)

*An Stac from Gleann Cul an Staca* (Section 10Ba)

*Meall Onfhaidh from Aodann Chleireig* (Section 10Ba)

*The view east from Glas-charn* (Section 10Ba)

Binnein Shios, framed dramatically between Loch Laggan and Lochan na h-Earba.

Leave the summit in a north-easterly direction and descend into a huge trough-like depression which essentially splits the mountain into two parts. Anyone familiar with the summit of Sgurr na Stri on Skye will notice a resemblance. Binnein Shuas is surrounded by steep crags and care should be taken in locating a correct descent route. Once established in the 'trough' the most obvious route down is to follow the depression and descend by a stream course, which by-passes the main crags.

On reaching easier ground, it is possible to contour round to the left to reach the bealach between the two peaks. It is also possible to climb the other side

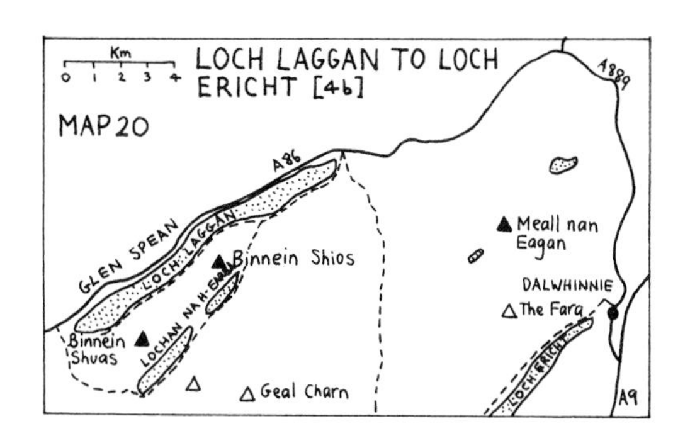


of the 'trough' and pick a way down through the crags on the north-eastern side of the hill, but note that good route-finding is essential here. The bealach is at a height of 390m and still leaves nearly 300m of ascent and 2½km distance between it and the second peak. The going is tough on pathless tussocky grass with several false summits before the true summit is finally reached. Again the views

*The view from Loch Laggan to Binnein Shios*

are quite outstanding, with Binnein Shuas's turn to be framed between the two lochs.

The quickest return route is to descend the south-west ridge, and gradually veering off to the north to reach the tree-line above Loch Laggan. Below the bealach, extensive felling has cleared a way to the track which hugs the south shore of the loch. Reach the track and follow it south-west through delightful stands of oak, larch and birch, with the ever-present Loch Laggan creating some peaceful scenes of forest, water and mountain. Not surprisingly, autumn is the best season to tackle these twin gems, although other seasons also have their own delights. One kilometre beyond the end of the loch take the right-hand fork, which leads back to the starting point.

**Meall nan Eagan** (Hill of the Possible?); *658m*
*OS Sheet 42; GR 596874*
*12km/330m/3–5hrs*
*Maps 20, 22*

This rather retiring hill lies 3km directly north of the Fara, a Corbett west of Dalwhinnie and north of Loch Ericht. It is not well seen from the road and remains partially hidden behind the featureless mass of Carn na Ceardaich to the east. Much of this area has recently been planted with new forestry and to some extent forest roads have made access easier.

Driving north out of Dalwhinnie, on the long straight section of road, two forestry tracks lead out west in the general direction of the hill, the first following the line of the Allt an t-Sluic and the second further up the road marked with a 'General Woodland' sign. The best way to tackle the hill combines both these tracks in a pleasant circuit. Take the second track which contours round the north side of Carn na Ceardaich before terminating there. Go through a metal gate and contour round to reach the featureless col between Meall nan Eagan and Carn na Ceardaich. Ascend the east ridge of the hill which is covered by heather and odd rocky outcrops all the while following a line of old fence posts. The cairn at the summit is small and perched on a crag at the base of a rusty fence post. There you can enjoy fine views of Loch Caoldair, a popular fishing loch nestling below the rocky bluff of Creag Doire na h-Achlaise. Also prominent is the impressively rocky Dirc Mhor, a gorge cutting through the northern spur of the Fara which is not visible from the Fara itself.

Return to the col and descend to the track which follows the north bank of the Allt an t-Sluic back to the road. A short road walk north leads back to the start of the walk. A longer circuit of the above hill and the Fara could also be attempted which could include an exploration of the Dirc Mhor.

# SECTION 5/6

## *The Southern Grampians*



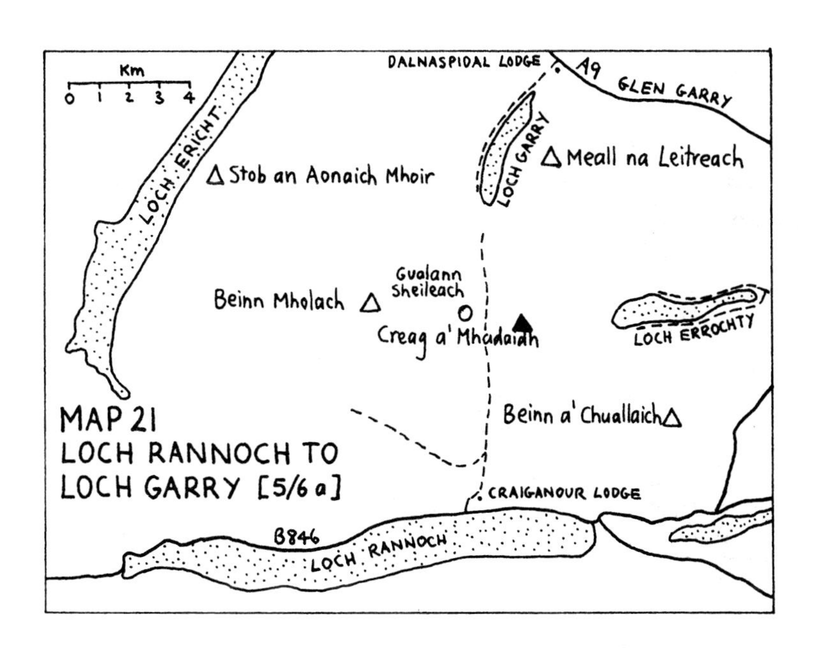

**Creag a' Mhadaidh** (Rock of the Fox); *612m*
*OS Sheet 42; GR 634650*
*18km/390m/4–5½hrs*
*Map 21*

---

This isolated and unfrequented hill lies in the heart of one of the most desolate areas of the Central Highlands. Creag a' Mhadaidh is situated well north of Loch Rannoch and west of Loch Errochty and involves a fairly long approach from any starting point. The most convenient route begins on the B846 road on the north side of Loch Rannoch at the bridge (GR 611591) where a track can be followed past Craiganour Lodge. After a short section through natural woodland, you will reach open hillside where the track follows the east bank of the Allt a' Chreagain Odhair. Continue on the track climbing up slowly until the flat col is reached between Gualann Sheileach and Creag a' Mhadaidh. At this point strike off to the east and ascend easy heathery slopes to the broad summit where there is a reasonably sized cairn. This area gives fine views of Schiehallion and the summit of this little hill is no exception. The view east across Loch Errochty is also worth mentioning. Return by the same route.

The ascent of this hill could be included in a long-distance through route between Loch Rannoch and Dalnaspidal Lodge on the A9 road, and a mountain bike may also be useful. An approach from the east at Trinafour via the south Loch Errochty track is also possible but marginally longer.

**Creag Ruadh** (Red Peak); *658m*
*OS Sheet 42; GR 685882*
*9km/310m/2–3hrs*
*Map 22*

---

Creag Ruadh appears as a rounded heathery dome from the A9 road at Dalwhinnie and it lies 3km west of its

*The view east from Creag a' Mhadaidh*

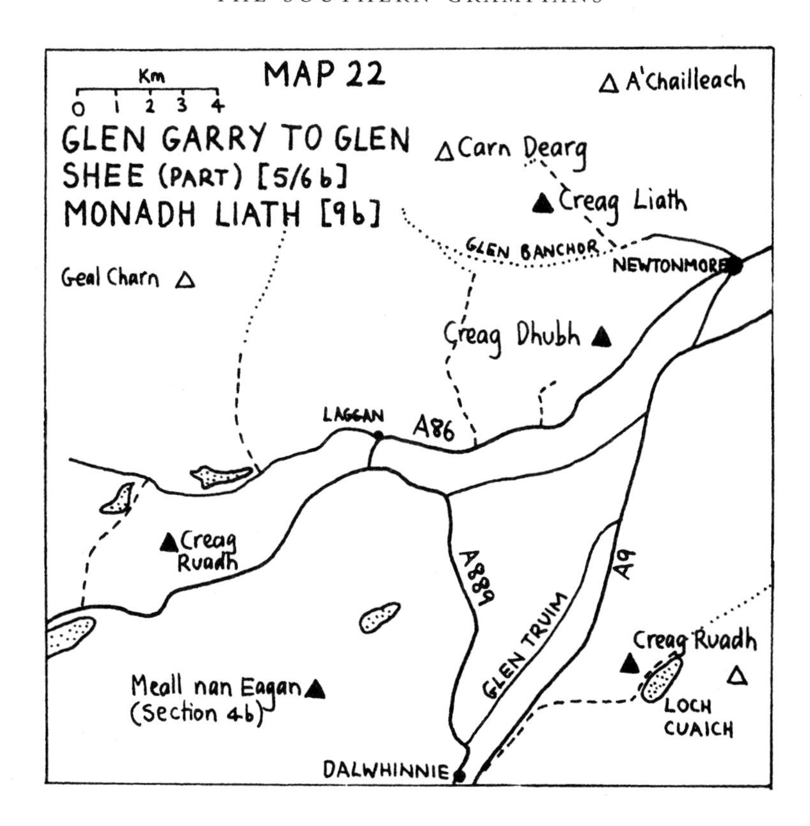


bulky Munro neighbour Meall Chuaich. It throws out a long north-easterly ridge which drops steeply to the shores of Loch Cuaich nestling snugly between it and the Munro. The two hills could easily be combined in a single walk but the following describes only the ascent of Creag Ruadh.

Begin at Cuaich on the A9 road, which is the usual starting point for the ascent of Meall Chuaich. Take the short track which leads to the aqueduct and follow this to the bridge less than 2km further on. Cross the Allt Cuaich and ascend the featureless south-west flank of the hill on heather and grass. The summit contains two small cairns and provides good views of Meall Chuaich. Return by the same route. Alternatively, follow the line of the north-east ridge to the col below Druim nan Sac and descend steeply to the north end of Loch Cuaich. The track on the north shore of the loch can then be used to return to the starting point.

**Blath Bhalg** (Womb of Bloom?); *641m*
*OS Sheet 43; GR 019611*
*7km/280m/2–3hrs*
*Map 23*

---

Blath Bhalg is situated south of the A924 Pitlochry to Rattray road and can

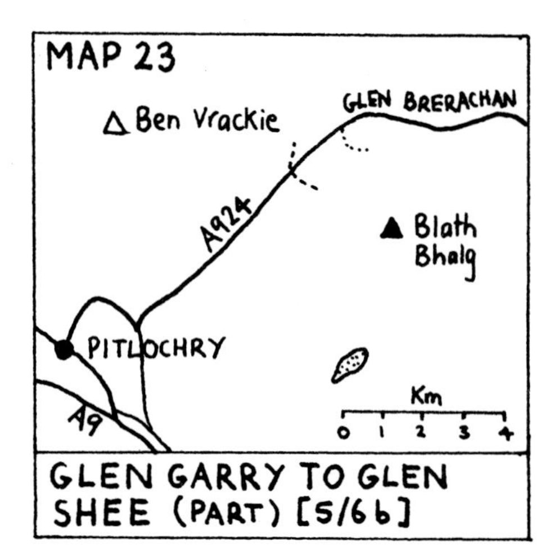


easily be climbed from the high point on this road at nearly 380m. Although it is a rather featureless heathery dome, it is ideal for a short afternoon or evening leg-stretcher, and it gives fine views of the more popular Ben Vrackie only a few kilometres distant. Cars can be parked at the highest point on the road at GR 992620 where a path leads off to the south-east. A forestry track also begins on the other side of the road. Note that neither of these are shown on the 1984 OS map.

Follow the path up to the shoulder of the hill and stay on the broad ridge which curves round before climbing sharply to two small tops. The main summit is less than half a kilometre further on at the junction of three fences where there is a small cairn. Grand views can be enjoyed of Ben Vrackie, Schiehallion, Beinn a' Ghlo and the Glen Shee Munros. The descent can be varied by dropping down the northerly slopes to a small hut at GR 012624 and following a marked path back to the road opposite Dalnacarn. A kilometre and half of road leads back to the start point.

## SECTION 7

# *The South-east Grampians*

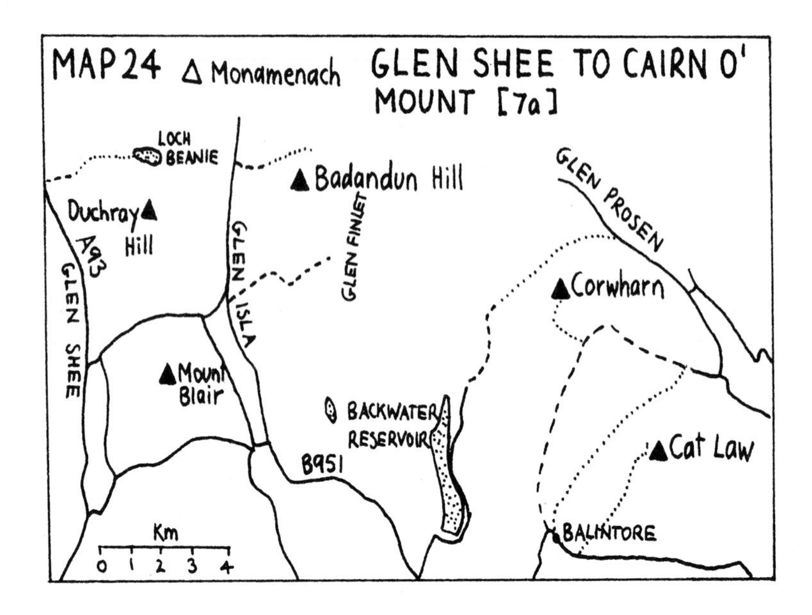


**Mount Blair** (Hill of the Plain); *744m*
**Duchray Hill** (origin unknown); *702m*
*OS Sheet 43; GR 167629, 161672*
*11km/720m/3½–5hrs*
*Map 24*

---

The prominent cone of Mount Blair stands strikingly between Glen Shee and Glen Isla and is well seen during the drive up to the Spittal of Glen Shee from the south. Duchray Hill (or Mealna Letter) lies 4km to the north of Mount Blair across the B951 road connecting Glen Shee to Glen Isla, and is a less-frequented summit but with superior views. Both can easily be climbed together from the high point on the B951 road with a return to a vehicle between hills if so wished.

At GR 163647 leave the road and climb south across grass initially. After crossing a fence higher up, the grass gives way to heather and a good track leads up the northern spur of the hill to the massive summit cairn and triangulation pillar. Mount Blair has much history connected with it and a suicide's grave is reputed to be under the prehistoric cairn. Contrasting views are available at the top, with the high rolling mountains to the north and the Lowlands to the south and east. Vary the descent by heading north-east for 1km to a small subsidiary top then dropping down its north-western spur to the road.

Duchray Hill can be reached by first descending north slightly to cross a burn then climbing the easy grassy south flank of the hill to the corner of the forest at GR 157658. From here, a well-built stone wall leads over Cairn Derig to the summit via the south-west ridge.

The views to the north from here are particularly fine. Either return by the same route or follow the ridge round clockwise and descend by the Duchray burn, which can be rather boggy in places.

The Corbett of Monamenach lies about 4km north of Duchray Hill and these could be climbed in the same excursion using either the Glen Beanie path from Glen Isla or the path to Loch Beanie from Glen Shee.

**Badandun Hill** (Place of the Fort); *740m*
*OS Sheet 44; GR 207678*
*9km/500m/2½–4hrs*
*Map 24*

---

This rarely climbed hill lies to the east of Glen Isla and west of Glen Finlet. It rather awkwardly sits on the western edge of OS Sheet 44; and since the most convenient approach is from the west, requires OS Sheet 43 in order to see the full route.

Begin on the Glen Isla road just opposite Fergus Farm where a track crosses the river and turns right into the

*The summit of Mount Blair*

*Cat Law from Corwharn*

farm by a pleasant wooded area. Turn left to follow the track which goes through the forest and out onto open heather hillside on the left bank of a stream. Beyond a small building the track degenerates into a path which after a kilometre begins to ascend the south-western flank of Craig Lair. Either continue on the path to the pleasant craggy summit of this hill or make a direct line for the wide col between it and Badandun Hill. From the col ascend the curving north-east ridge to the flat heathery summit which has a triangulation pillar. The quickest route of descent is to head directly west down the steep but easy heather slopes to the Glen Isla track and Fergus.

**Cat Law**; *671m*
**Corwharn**; *611m*
*OS Sheet 44; GR 319611, 288651*
*18km/750m/5–7hrs*
*Map 24*

---

These two rounded, heathery hills are characteristic of most hills in the Angus glens, with broad, sprawling ridges dropping to steep-sided glens. They lie south of Glen Prosen, and both can be tackled together from Wester Lednathie Farm in Glen Uig. Glen Uig is motorable to a point just short of Wester Lednathie, where a sign indicates that only authorised vehicles may proceed beyond this point. Limited parking space is available at the end of a track.

Continue on foot to Wester Lednathie and take a left fork down a track and across the river. A path indicated on the OS map following the spur to Monthrey is the objective, but is not obvious on the lower cultivated part of the hill. Climb up through a field and go through a gate where the path begins to establish itself at the edge of the forest. Beyond the trees the path is excellent and continues easily to Monthrey, a shoulder lying some 1½km north-west of Cat Law. Traces of a path lead up the wide north-west spur of the hill to its flat summit which is riddled with peat hags. The summit has a triangulation pillar and two large cairns nearby.

Return to Monthrey and pick up another path which heads north-west to the small top of Cormaud. Continue west on the same path along the broad heathery ridge before dropping down to Glen Quharity just north of the delightfully named Clinking Cauldron. Cross the burn and turn right along a grassy track for about a kilometre to reach the beginning of a path climbing up to Corwharn. This path starts just before a fence and gate across the main track. An ascent of about 250m leads to the summit, which lies just beyond a fence and has a prominent 'pencil' cairn which can be seen for miles around. To the north, the Glen Cova Munros line the horizon while the cone of Mount Blair is very obvious to the west.

Rather than descending by the same path, a variation can be made by following the line of the fence down the south-eastern spur of the hill to the col below the Hill of Adenaich. At this point pick up a track which climbs slightly before descending the south-east spur of this hill to reach the main track at the floor of Glen Uig. This descent track is not shown on the OS map. The return to Wester Lednathie follows the Glen Uig track and is a pleasant stroll through a picturesque and secluded glen which is a fine end to a satisfying circuit.

If climbing these two Grahams on separate excursions, then Cat Law is best tackled from the south-west at Knowehead of Auldallan (OS Sheet 53) where a path goes almost all the way to the summit in less than 4km. The quickest approach to Corwharn is from Cormuir in Glen Prosen, from which a path reaches the col north-west of the summit. The Glen Uig approach, however, is more aesthetically pleasing.

## Hunt Hill; *705m*

*OS Sheet 44; GR 380805*
*19km/460m/5–7hrs*
*Map 25*

At the head of Glen Esk the River Esk splits into two main tributaries, the Water of Mark and the Water of Lee. Both these rivers flow through dramatic steep-sided glens rising to rounded heathery heights. One of the most imposing of these is Hunt Hill at the head of Glen Lee, whose precipitous east face drops sharply for 250m to the floor of the glen. The mountains surrounding Glen Lee are all of this nature and, in particular, Craig Maskeldie forms a prominent rocky profile dominating the whole glen. A complete circuit of all these summits is a marvellous expedition, but the following is a description of the ascent of Hunt Hill only.

Begin at the large parking area at the end of the public road in Glen Esk and follow the track to Loch Lee which passes the remains of Invermark Castle. This castle dates from about 1526 and was used to defend the then vital pass between Glen Esk and Deeside. Some of the original slates from the roof of the castle can now be seen on the roof of the boathouse halfway along the north shore of Loch Lee. Continue pleasantly along the north shore where the rocky spur of Craig Maskeldie begins to impose its presence – and could almost be one of the Three Sisters of Glencoe.

Some 2km beyond the end of the loch, cross a wooden footbridge and follow the path which winds its way under the steep rocky eastern slopes of Hunt Hill. This leads into an impressive boulder-strewn corrie where the Falls of Unich make an interesting spectacle. The path rises up steeply at the head of the corrie and should be followed to GR 383794, where it is possible to head north above the eastern crags and climb the hill's broad heathery southern slopes to the flat summit where there is a small cairn. On this last section the view east to Craig Maskeldie and the U-shaped trough of Glen Lee is quite magnificent.

*Craig Maskeldie and Loch Lee from Hunt Hill*

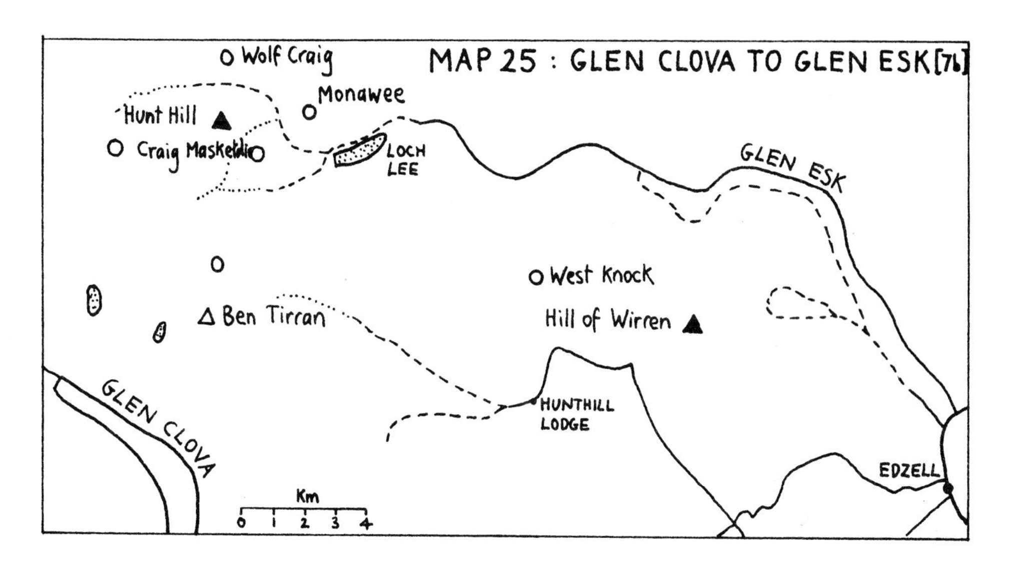


The view north to the most easterly Munro of Mount Keen is also worth mentioning.

The descent can be varied by dropping down the easy northern slopes of the hill to the Glen Lee track and then following this down to the floor of the glen and the ascent route. It should be mentioned that there is much scrambling potential on the eastern crags of Hunt Hill and this would be worth some exploration.

An alternative route, which includes Craig Maskeldie, climbs the obvious spur beginning at Inchgrundle by a track, and winds round the rim of the hanging corrie containing Carlochy to the fine summit of Craig Maskeldie. Drop down the south-western slopes to reach the ascent route described earlier. To the north of Glen Lee, Wolf Craig and Monawee could also be included to give a fine high-level circuit. Wolf Craig is actually 10m higher than Hunt Hill but is not a separate Graham as it does not possess the necessary 150m drop between it and its distant Munro neighbour of Mount Keen.

## Hill of Wirren; *678m*

*OS Sheet 44; GR 522739*
*7km/500m/2–3hrs*
*Map 25*

This sprawling flat-topped hill lies south of Glen Esk and throws out spurs and ridges in all directions, giving it the appearance of a spider when seen from above or on a map. Oddly enough, two hills to its north-west are both higher than the Hill of Wirren, but neither are Grahams as they do not have the necessary relative drop between them and the Corbett of Ben Tirran lying to their west.

The shortest route to the summit begins in the south at the small rickety suspension bridge (GR 510713) which crosses the West Water in the unnamed glen leading to Hunthill Lodge. Cross this bridge and climb the broad heathery spur which steepens higher up with some boulder hopping. Reach a broad, flat area of deep heather and peat hags which is scattered with the remains of a crashed aircraft. The triangulation pillar is a good half-kilometre away to the north and would be tricky to locate in misty conditions as the summit plateau is featureless. However, in clear weather there are fine views of Mount Keen (the most easterly Munro), Mount Battock and Lochnagar. The descent can be varied by dropping down the west spur of the hill past some cairns and shooting butts to Auchowrie and following the road back to the start.

Hill of Wirren is an ideal hill to traverse completely if transport problems can be solved, and a track beginning in Glen Esk to the north climbs by the Burn of Beag to a height of 500m which provides a useful ascent or descent route. Other tracks to the east also climb quite high up the various ridges and corries.

## SECTION 8

# *The Cairngorms and Buchan*

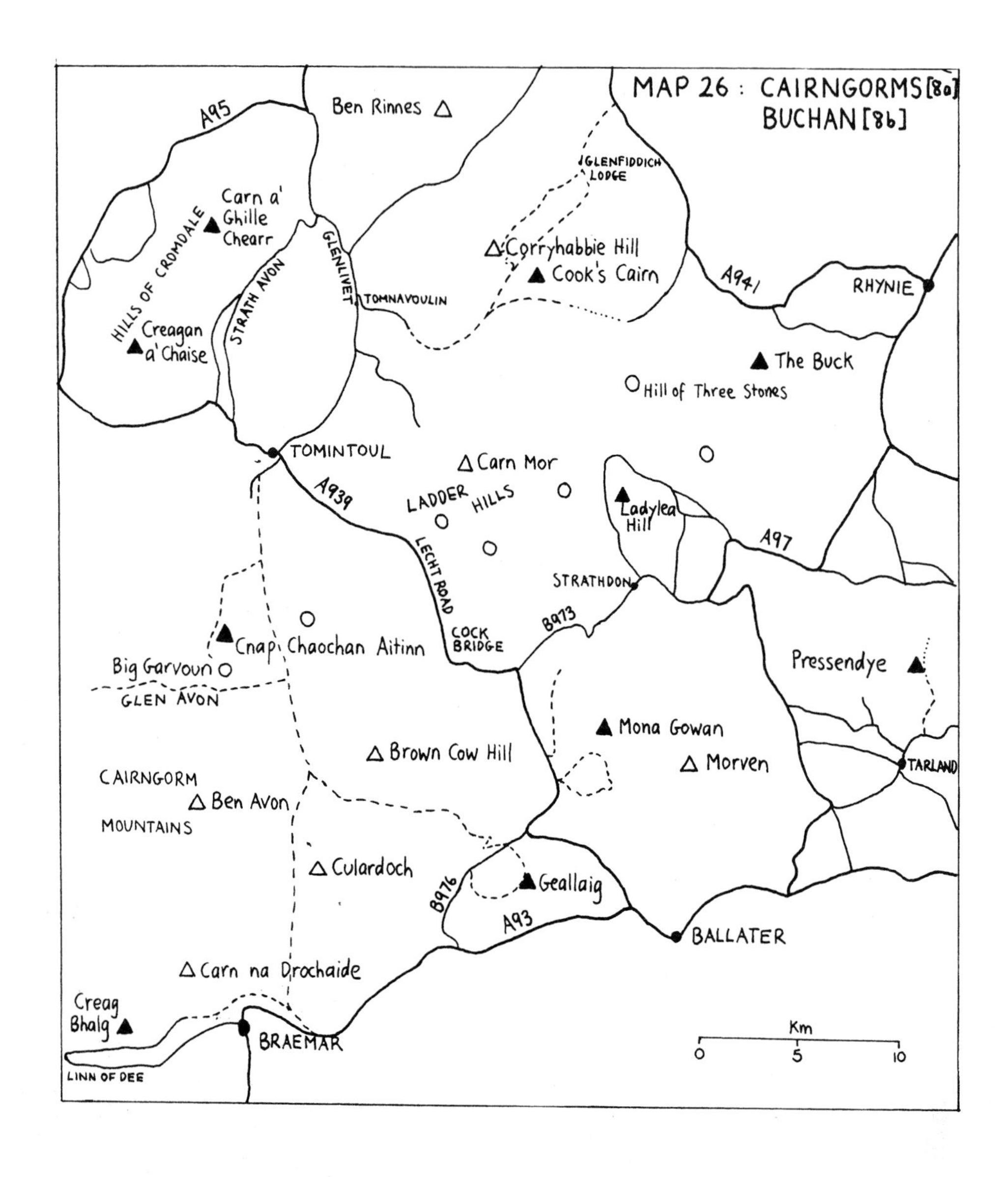
MAP 26 : CAIRNGORMS [80]
BUCHAN [86]
Ben Rinnes
A95
GLENFIDDICH LODGE
Carn a' Ghille Chearr
HILLS OF CROMDALE
GLENLIVET
STRATH AVON
Corryhabbie Hill
Cook's Cairn
A941
RHYNIE
TOMNAVOULIN
Creagan a'Chaise
The Buck
Hill of Three Stones
TOMINTOUL
Carn Mor
A939
LADDER HILLS
Ladylea Hill
A97
LECHT ROAD
STRATHDON
B973
Cnap Chaochan Aitinn
COCK BRIDGE
Pressendye
Big Garvoun
GLEN AVON
Mona Gowan
Brown Cow Hill
Morven
TARLAND
CAIRNGORM MOUNTAINS
Ben Avon
Culardoch
Geallaig
B976
A93
BALLATER
Carn na Drochaide
Creag Bhalg
BRAEMAR
LINN OF DEE
Km
0
5
10

**Creag Bhalg** (Womb Hill); *668m*
*OS Sheet 43; GR 091912*
*5km/320m/1–2hrs*
*Map 26*

Creag Bhalg is one of only two Grahams which can truly be said to be part of the Cairngorms. In reality it is little more than one of several foothills of the sprawling mass of Munro giants to the north and north-west. On the pleasant drive west from Braemar, and following the peaceful, meandering River Dee, is Creag Bhalg which rises as a heather-clad whale-back on the opposite side of the glen. Its steeper eastern face is tree-lined and drops sharply to the Linn of Quoich. If you are based in Braemar with little time to spare, then Creag Bhalg is an ideal hill to gain a greater appreciation of the main Cairngorm scenery to the north-west.

About 2km east of the Linn of Dee, on the north side of the glen, a track heads north-east from the road through fairly open Scots pine forest. Follow this for 1km and take the second track which forks off to the left heading in a roughly north-westerly direction. Cross a deer fence by a stile with wide wooden steps, and almost immediately after this turn off right on a vague path which leads more or less directly to the summit. Near the top there is a stone

*Creag Bhalg from the south-east*

shelter, while further to the right are two twin cairns about 30m apart. The right-hand one of these is the actual summit. On a clear day the view north-west to Ben Macdui and the Lairig Ghru is well worth the ascent of this modest little hill. Return by the route of ascent.

For those with time at their disposal, numerous longer variations are possible, perhaps including a visit to the remote glaciated lochs at Clais Fhearnaig and a return by either Glen Lui or Glen Quoich.

**Cnap Chaochan Aitinn** (Lump of the Juniper Stream); *715m*
*OS Sheet 36; GR 145099*
*22km/400m/2½–3½hrs (bike)*
*Map 26*

---

Between the extensive high mountain plateau of Ben Avon and Tomintoul to the north lies a little-frequented area of rolling heathery hills and secluded steep-sided glens. The River Avon and Glen Avon form the dominant geographical features of this region, with the river flowing east from the remote mountain sanctuary of Loch Avon in the heart of the Cairngorms, then north to Tomintoul. Cnap Chaochan Aitinn is a rather featureless lump forming the highest point of the undulating ridge north of Glen Loin, but despite this, its ascent provides a fine appreciation of the surrounding area. It is one of only two hills described in this book where a cycle track leads right to the summit and a bike is recommended.

Begin just south of Tomintoul at GR164175 where a carpark marks the beginning of the track which follows the River Avon south. Queen Victoria passed this way on her travels and there is a viewpoint near the carpark looking south down the beautifully wooded Glen Avon. The very prominent conical hill in the distance is Liath Bheinn. It too has a track leading almost to the summit, but although over 2,000ft high it does not have the required 150m of re-ascent to be classed as a Graham. Cnap Chaochan Aitinn is further round to the right and not visible from this point.

Follow the track south which becomes a tarred road beyond the bridge near Delavorar. After 3½km, cross a wooden hump-backed bridge over the Avon and climb south-west past the deserted farm cottage of Wester Gaulrig. The track continues through a field and a section of birch wood before crossing a small stream. Beyond this point, climb steadily, roughly south-wards, over Carn an t-Sleibhe where the track swings south-eastwards onto the little top of Geal Charn. Shortly before this point a second track leads south to the col north-west of Cnap Chaochan Aitinn, although it is not shown on earlier editions of OS maps. Follow this track to the col where a smaller track leads in a few hundred metres to the flat summit which is marked by a cairn with a quartzite top. On a clear day, the finest views are to the south, over Big Garvoun to the wild northern corries of Ben Avon. If a bike has been used, the return journey is the highlight of the trip with a grand, mostly downhill, run to the start point which should only take about 30–40 minutes.

If suitable transport can be arranged, a fine way to ascend this hill would be to combine it with a long, cross-country run between Tomintoul and Invercauld Bridge east of Braemar, via Loch Builg. This route is often known as the Bealach Dearg. If time permits, it is worth making a detour to visit 'The Castle', a strange rock pyramid forming part of the canyon-like walls of the Water of Ailnack. This is situated at GR 123108, about 2½km west-north-west of the Graham.

**Geallaig** (White Hill); *743m*
*OS Sheets 37, 44; GR 297981*
*6km/380m/1½–2½hrs*
*Map 26*

This high, heathery hill, misquoted as 'Geallaig Hill' on the OS map, stands 5km north-east of Balmoral and is a fine viewpoint. Its ascent is extremely easy as a track can be followed all the way to the summit, and the start is at an altitude of over 350m. The beginning of the track is on the B976 road north of Crathie, just opposite a cottage at GR 281000. Note that a second track begins about 2km before this, at an altitude of 480m, but involves a slightly longer walk. An ideal circuit would be to combine both routes as both tracks are in effect a single loop, but this would involve some walking on the road.

Follow the track easily up the north-western slopes of the hill. At the summit plateau, the track divides, with the left fork going by the cairn and the right fork continuing down to meet the B976 road in the loop already mentioned. The summit triangulation pillar is surrounded by a large ringed drystane dyke. The above statistics are based on a return by the route of ascent.

A more ambitious descent is to continue on east beyond the cairn over Creag na Creiche and Carn Dearg and follow the south-eastern slopes of this hill through natural pine forest to the Bridge of Gairn. This is a much longer proposition and would require a kind driver or a second car.

**Mona Gowan** (Goat Moor); *749m*
*OS Sheet 37; GR 336058*
*10km/370m/3–4hrs*
*Map 26*

Mona Gowan is the highest of a chain of hills strung out on a broad heathery ridge north-west of the Corbett of Morven. The ascent of these hills combined with Morven would provide a long and interesting expedition beginning at Glen Fenzie on the A939 road. But the route described below does not include Morven.

Begin on the A939 road just north of the Glen Fenzie track and follow the track which climbs north almost to the summit of Scraulac, which is the most western top of the chain of hills mentioned above. From here, head east along the broad ridge over Cairnagour Hill, following a line of fence posts to the third top of Mona Gowan. The summit has a huge well-built cairn which was constructed for the jubilee of Queen Victoria. Spacious views can be enjoyed here, with Morven particularly prominent. East of Mona Gowan lies an interesting rocky gorge called the Slacks of Glencarvie, which you would come to if you were continuing on to climb Morven.

Descend the easy south ridge of Mona Gowan to meet the track at the col which crosses a stream and leads to the ruin of Glenfenzie and the road. A short walk north along the road then leads back to the starting point. Note that cars are probably best left at Glenfenzie as there is not much parking space at the start of the walk.

Mona Gowan can also be approached from the north by a handful of possible routes, the shortest of which starts near Fleuchats, which is probably the shortest route to the summit. A good track finishes just short of the top.

**Ladylea Hill**; *610m*
*OS Sheet 37; GR 343168*
*2km/280m/1hr*
*Map 26*

---

Ladylea Hill has the claim to fame of being the smallest Graham and was only recently promoted from 609m to 610m. It is also the easiest to climb, taking less than an hour up and down by the shortest route.

Cross the road-bridge at Strathdon and drive up the minor road on the left signposted Glenbuchat Lodge. About 500m past the entrance to Invernettie Farm, just beyond a small plantation, park the car and begin by crossing a fence into a field usually occupied by sheep. Head directly up the field and go through a gate higher up to reach open heather hillside. Follow a line of stone shooting butts which lead to the broad summit plateau and a small cairn and post.

The summit views are not exceptional, but the rounded dome of The Buck (another Graham) is plainly visible to the north-east. Descend by the same route, or, to make more of a round, follow the ridge south-east to Clashenteple Hill before descending to Invernettie farm.

**Pressendye**; *620m*
*OS Sheet 37; GR 490089*
*6km/370m/2–3hrs*
*Map 26*

---

Pressendye is the highest of an arc of hills lying north and east of the fertile undulating bowl of Cromar. It is also the most easterly Graham north of the River Dee. From most aspects it appears as a broad heather whale-back, and it throws out a long western ridge known as the Maalie'waat by locals. An approach can be made from most directions and the ideal route would combine two in a complete traverse of the hill.

The approach described begins at Pett Farm to the south of the hill. Leave the B9119 road at the road to Pett Farm (signposted as 'The Petts') and drive to the farm where cars may be left. Follow the track north from here and fork right twice to keep to the edge of the forest. The OS map shows a second track breaking off to the left after about a kilometre. There are in fact about three of these, which resemble fire-breaks more than tracks. The last one leads up through the forest and to another track. Take this and go left at the top. This eventually leads to a fairly recent wide forestry track which winds round the south-western flank of Pittenderich. Follow this wide track until it leaves the trees and reaches a fence. Beyond this point the track deteriorates significantly but can be followed directly to the summit. Note that this is not marked on the OS map.

The summit area consists of a trig-point on the left and a large cairn and stone shelter on the right separated by a fence. On a clear day the most prominent landmark is the Corbett of Morven lying to the south-west. If a return by the same route is not necessary, it is possible to follow a path along the crest of the Maalie'waat to Lazy Well over the intermediate top of Broom Hill. Alternatively, reach the col between Pressendye and Broom Hill and descend by a path through Black Howe to Boig Farm, which also provides another possible route of ascent. The above time and distance information is based on a return to Pett Farm by the route of ascent.

## The Buck; *721m*

*OS Sheet 37; GR 412233*
*4km/310m/1–2hrs*
*Map 26*

---

This hill is known to locals as the Buck o' the Cabrach, Cabrach being a small hamlet north-west of the hill. It offers fine views of wild and undulating grouse moors to the west, culminating in the braes of Glenlivet and the Glen Fiddich Forest – real whisky country.

The shortest approach is from the B9002 road north of the hill at GR 422252. Follow a fence over initially very boggy ground called Dry Know (!) where a path begins on the left-hand side of the fence. This leads directly to the summit with a significantly steep incline for the second kilometre. The trig-point is perched on a craggy tor with the remains of an old drystane dyke passing below.

Descend by the same route, or traverse across to Scad Hill and follow a track east for 2½km before making a dog-leg by another path back to the starting point. For those with more time and flexible transport, longer traverses of The Buck can easily be worked out with a map and some imagination.

**Cook's Cairn;** *755m*
*OS Sheet 37; GR 302278*
*23km/480m/3–5hrs (bike)*
*Map 26*

This demoted Corbett lies in the heart of the heather-clad high ground between Tominotul and Dufftown, which is peppered with familiar names such as Glenlivet, Glenfiddich, Tomnavoulin and other famous malts. It is a remote hill to reach from any direction, but the existence of numerous tracks through the glens make access with a mountain bike the obvious solution. Two hours should be added to the above time if a bike is not available. The hill lies very close to the Corbett of Corryhabbie Hill and the two could easily be combined if so wished.

Begin at the Allanreid parking area south-east of Tomnavoulin which is on OS Sheet 36 and which marks the end of the minor road running north of the River Livet. Follow the track from here, taking a less distinct fork right after a short distance which crosses a minor stream and follows the course of the river. (The left fork goes up to Achdregnie Farm.) After going through a couple of gates, the grassy track reaches a wooden pedestrian bridge across the Livet. Cross this and continue along the rough track on the south side of the river. The track varies between gravel, grass and mud, with several sections of water. This, together with the odd gate, makes dismounting unavoidable.

About 3km up the glen the track fords a river which may be difficult to cross in spate conditions. Just north of this river go through a metal gate and climb steadily to reach the sad empty Suie, a fine two-storey house surrounded by an immaculate drystane wall but long since abandoned. Beyond this is an equally fine but smaller dwelling-house, also deserted.

Shortly beyond, take a right-hand fork which makes a gradual rising traverse of the western flank of Carn na Bruar, a top lying south-west of Cook's Cairn. In its lower reaches, this track has been badly eroded by flooding, and cycling here is almost impossible. Further up, the track improves and it should be followed all the way to the wide bealach between Cook's Cairn and Carn na Bruar. Another minor track breaks off here and continues for the last 1½km up the south-western spur, going almost directly to the summit. The small cairn at the summit lies some 50m off to the left of the track at the highest point. Note that this latter track is not indicated on the map.

The summit views are not spectacular but there is a fine feeling of spaciousness at this remote outpost. To the north-west, Corryhabbie Hill is the obvious ridge across the glen, while the Corbett of Ben Rinnes is strikingly prominent beyond. The distant Cairngorms also jostle for attention. Return by the route of ascent unless a through route has been planned, which may end at numerous possible points on the A941 Rhynie to Dufftown road.

A slightly closer approach to the hill begins at Aldivalloch to the east but

*Cook's Cairn from Glenlivet*

involves a certain amount of ascent and re-ascent. For those without access to a bike this is probably the best option. If Corryhabbie Hill is to be included as well, the Glenlivet approach is the most efficient route. An approach from the north is also possible.

**Carn a Ghille Chearr** (Hill of the Wronged Boy); *710m*
**Creagan a' Chaise** (Steep Rock); *722m*
*OS Sheet 36; GR 139298, 104241*
*20km/640m/4½–6½hrs*
*Map 26*

---

These two hills are the highest points of a long broad ridge known collectively as the Hills of Cromdale. This ridge runs from south-west to north-east and forms an obvious divide between Strath Avon and Strathspey. The distance between the two Grahams is nearly 8km, a part of which has to be retraced if returning to the point of departure. This observation, along with the fact that much of the ridge involves walking on blanket bog and peat, may deter the walker from ascending both these hills together. Having said this, the more well-drained parts of the ridge higher up offer easier walking on short grass and moss and the following route describes a traverse of the ridge.

Two convenient starting points, neither having any advantage over the other, are Balnalon in Strath Avon or Wester Rynaballoch in Strathspey. From both these points paths lead directly onto the ridge some 2½km south-west of Carn a Ghille Chearr. In both cases, the path is actually a track for a good part of the way but degenerates into little more than a sheep track through the heather at the latter stages, which shows how little used these paths are. From this point, continue over the minor top of Carn Eachie to the flat featureless summit of Carn a Ghille Chearr, where there is a triangulation pillar. To the south, the Cairngorms are visible while the Corbett of Ben Rinnes is very prominent to the north-east.

Retrace your steps and follow the broad ridge south-west on tussocky, boggy terrain which alternates with easier lichen-covered higher ground. Two obvious tops are passed, the second having a cairn – and at this point the ridge narrows and improves somewhat, finally curving south to arrive at the summit of Creagan a' Chaise. The huge cairn was constructed in 1887 to commemorate the jubilee of Queen Victoria and there is a similar one on Mona Gowan in this section.

A return to Balnalon can be made by descending north-east to reach the track on the north side of Milton burn which leads to the road 1½km from the start point. If the Strathspey start has been used, retrace your steps along the ridge to the subsidiary top (which has a cairn) before descending north-west to Clach nam Piobair or Stone of the Pipers. This is a large boulder where pipers played to encourage a force of Highlanders who fought King William's troops in 1690 at the Battle of Cromdale. A track leads from this area to the road just west of Wester Rynaballoch.

If you are tackling those Grahams separately, Creagan a' Chaise could easily be climbed by either of the routes of descent described above. However, a more interesting route begins at Lynebreck on the A939 road to the south-west, where the ridge over Sgor Gaoithe, Carn na Cloiche and Carn Tuairneir can be followed to the summit. Carn a Ghille Chearr is best tackled by the route of ascent already mentioned.

SECTION 9

# *Glen Roy to the Monadhliath and Strathspey*

**Creag Dhubh** (Black Rock); *658m*
*OS Sheet 34, 41; GR 322824*
*7km/510m/2–3½hrs*
*Map 27*

---

This rounded heathery hill, situated south and east of Glen Roy, has few distinguishing features other than fine views of its loftier neighbours. It is easily accessible from the A86 road to the south, but as this involves rather a steep and laborious climb the best approach is from Bohenie to the west, which can be reached by a 3km drive up the single-track road on the east side of the River Roy.

Just beyond a stream, a vague path follows the north bank into some trees. Cross the stream and turn to the immediate left where a path continues up to the edge of the forest at a gate and deer fence. From here the path follows the line of fence roughly south-east, but the going is boggy and the path is not at all obvious. After a kilometre, you will reach a well-constructed path which contours round the west flank of Creag Dhubh. Follow this north for a few hundred metres before striking off up the vague west ridge, which is a succession of shoulders and minor dips. In less than 2km, you will reach the summit, which has a triangulation pillar and cairn.

On a clear day, the Grey Corries stand out well to the south, while the Creag Meagaidh range dominates the view to the east. Beinn Teallach, a fairly recent addition to Munro's Tables, is the obvious mountain to the north-east. Return by the route of ascent.

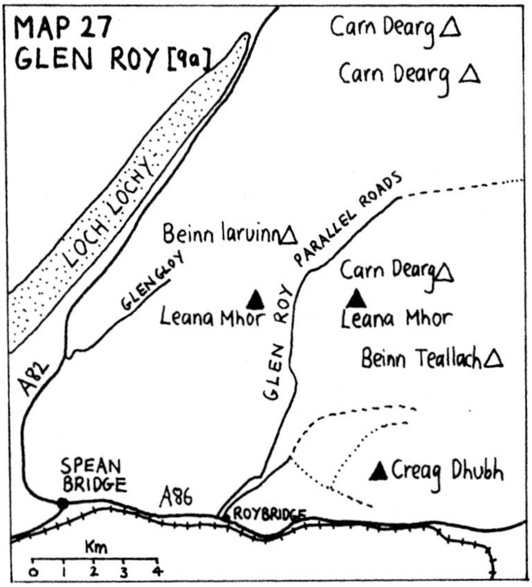

**Leana Mhor** (Big Meadow) (east of Glen Roy); *676m*
*OS Sheet 34, 41; GR 317879*
*10km/550m/3–4½hrs*
*Map 27*

---

The hills forming the sides of Glen Roy are characterised by very steep lower slopes gradually rounding off to flat plateau-like summits. Leana Mhor, on the east side of Glen Roy, is no exception, as is its namesake exactly due west on the opposite side of the glen, which is also a Graham, and described next. Whoever named the hills around Glen Roy had a lack of imagination as there are three Corbetts all called Carn Dearg and two Grahams called Leana Mhor.

Begin at a point about 4½km up the single-track road which goes up Glen Roy. Look for a large boulder on the right-hand side of the road marking the beginning of a track leading down to the River Roy. This is marked as 'Stone' on the OS map. There is a small lay-by just beyond the boulder and cars should be parked here. Follow the track which zigzags steeply through trees down to a disused footbridge. Both ends of this bridge are fenced off but the bridge itself is in reasonable condition bar the odd missing wooden slat. Cross the bridge and follow the track for about 100m before striking off up the hillside to reach a deer fence which can be negotiated by a gate further up.

As height is gained, cross the famous 'parallel roads' of Glen Roy. These linear features which traverse the sides of the glen are ancient shore lines of natural lochs formed during the Ice Age. Reach a broad grassy shoulder at a height of 400m before climbing a steeper section for 150m leading to the summit plateau. The actual summit is still over a kilometre distant and should not be confused with an intermediate top of 650m which has a larger cairn than the actual top! The finest views are south to the Grey Corries range and north-west beyond the Corbett of Beinn Iaruinn to the Munros on the western side of Loch Lochy. Return by the route of ascent.

It would be possible to combine the ascent of Leana Mhor with the Corbett of Carn Dearg to the north-west via the bealach at GR 323873, but this would involve a fairly lengthy addition. If this option was being considered the bridge over the Roy at GR 331909 would be the most advantageous starting point.

*Glen Roy and Leana Mhor (west)*

**Leana Mhor** (Big Meadow) (west of Glen Roy); *684m*
*OS Sheets 34, 41; GR 284878*
*6km/480m/2–3hrs*
*Map 27*

---

This is the higher of Glen Roy's twin Leana Mhors, albeit only by 7m. It is of similar character to its eastern partner, but considerably easier to ascend with a shorter itinerary. Both could be easily climbed in a day.

Begin on the Glen Roy road at GR 296867 where a well-constructed track follows a stream course up to the col between Leana Mhor and Beinn a' Mhonicag. Leave the track at this point and ascend the steep southerly flank of Leana Mhor. Just short of the summit, you will pass an obvious shoulder. The summit cairn is an excellent viewpoint.

Leana Mhor could be ascended in conjunction with the Corbett of Beinn Iaruinn to the north via the bealach at GR 284886. The ridge between Leana Mhor and its south-western outlier of Coire Ceirsle Hill is 4½km-long. In good snow cover this would make a grand ski tour which could be extended to include Beinn Iaruinn.

**Creag Ruadh** (Red Hill); *622m*
*OS Sheet 35; GR 558913*
*7km/330m/2–3hrs*
*Map 22*

---

This little hill lies south-west of the main Monadhliath range and has fine views down the length of Loch Laggan and of the Monadhliath to the north and north-east. It can be most easily climbed from the minor road to the start of the Corrieyairack Pass at Sherrabeg, south of the River Spey. From here, ascend the north-east ridge of the hill which is squeezed between two forestry plantations. A deer fence and all-terrain vehicle track follow the ridge initially, while higher up the ridge narrows with the odd crag providing some interest. Cross the deer fence to reach Loch na Lairige, an idyllic spot less than 500m from the summit. The top consists of a trig-point and a cairn about 50m away which gives a superb vantage point for Loch Laggan and the twin Grahams of Binnein Shuas and Binnein Shios. The Creag Meagaidh and Ben Alder groups are also seen to advantage from this viewpoint.

The descent can be varied by heading west to Glen Shirra and following the track to Glenshero Lodge and the road, from where it is about 1½km back to the starting point.

**Creag Dhubh** (Black Hill); *756m*
**Creag Liath** (Grey Rock); *743m*
*OS Sheet 35; GR 678972, 663007*
*19km/930m/6–8hrs*
*Map 22*

---

Creag Dhubh and Creag Liath lie west of Newtonmore on the southern fringe of the extensive Monadliath range. Creag Dhubh's distinctive pointed profile is well seen from the A889 road between Dalwhinnie and Laggan and gives the impression of being a much higher mountain than it actually is. Both hills can be ascended on separate excursions but the route described below is a continuous traverse of both hills, making for a satisfying day.

Begin on the A86 road at GR 664947 where a track leads north up the open hillside for about 1½km before deteriorating at a boggy area in the vicinity of the south-west ridge of Creag Dhubh. A fence can be followed round to the foot of the ridge and a path hugs the line of the fairly narrow ridge all the way to the summit. A small dip in the ridge is passed during the ascent and the summit area contains two cairns, the second larger one being on the true top. On a clear day the views are quite extensive, and the next objective, Creag Liath, is very prominent across the wide Strath of Glen Banchor to the north.

Continue north-east along the ridge crest, descending to a flat area after about 1km. From here descend directly down the heathery hillside for about 300m to reach the River Calder, which is a main tributary of the Spey, and runs through Glen Banchor. The bridge across the Calder, marked at GR 677988, unfortunately only goes halfway across the river to a small island, the second half having been long since washed away. In fairly dry conditions, the river can probably be negotiated by boulder hopping; but in spate conditions, the walker must be prepared for a cold and wet wade across!

Once on the opposite bank, follow a rough track through various gates to the farm at Glen Balloch. Cross the bridge and take the track which forks off left up the north side of the Allt Fionndrigh. This track should be followed for about 2km (or further if so desired) before crossing the Allt Fionndrigh and making a steep ascent on heather and rock to reach the summit of Creag Liath. Alternatively, the track can be followed until it crosses the north ridge of the hill from where a less steep approach to the summit can be made. The Munro of Carn Dearg is particularly prominent from the summit, its long undulating south ridge plainly visible across the brooding emptiness of

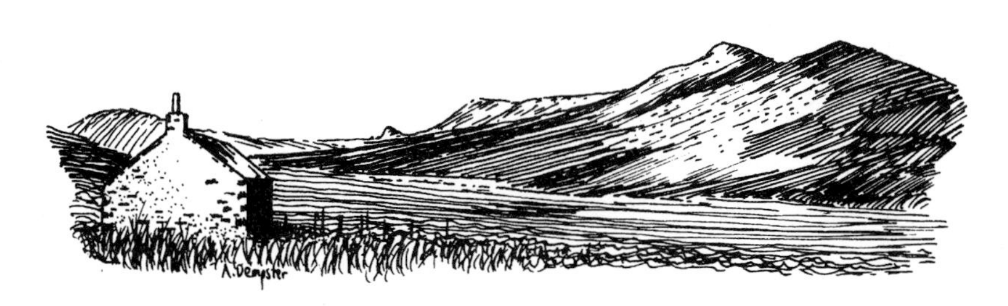


*Creag Liath from the bothy in Glen Banchor*

Gleann Ballach. Another Munro, A'Chailleach, is also visible to the north-east.

Descend Creag Liath by its easy south ridge and cross the Allt Ballach below the ruin of Dalballoch. From here a rough path leads west along the north bank of the River Calder and the building shown at GR 648984 is the next objective. The bridge marked just north of this building does not exist, but by heading another 200m upstream, wet feet can be avoided by the use of a fairly recent 'log and slats' bridge. The building on the other side is a small bothy which is a welcome retreat in poor weather. From the bothy a good Land Rover track runs south through Strath an Eilich to the vicinity of Cluny Castle and the A86 road. This track makes a delightful, relaxing end to the day's tussle but it should be noted that a further 2km of walking on a road is still required to reach the starting point.

If you are tackling Creag Liath separately then an approach from Newtonmore would be the most logical starting point; beginning at the end of the public road at GR 693997.

**Carn na h-Easgainn** (Hill of the Eels); *618m*
*OS Sheet 27; GR 744320*
*10km/340m/2–4hrs*
*Map 28*

This hill is the highest point of a rather featureless tract of moorland lying west of the A9 near Loch Moy about 20km south of Inverness. It is unlikely to be climbed as part of any 'drive there and back' intention but possibly as part of a journey north or south with a few hours to kill *en route.*

Park about 2km north of the Little Chef restaurant at Tomatin where an 'old road' lay-by gives access under the railway to a track south of the Allt a' Chuil. Follow this track for 2 to 3km until you have passed some old wooden sheds on the right. The hill visible to the north at this point is Carn na Loinne and should not be confused with Carn na h-Easgainn, which lies about 2km to the north-west along a broad heathery ridge. Leave the track and take the rough line of this ridge across numerous peat hags to the flat summit with a trig point. The views are fairly nondescript but there is a delightful sense of remoteness and solitude. The Kessock Bridge is visible to the north. Return by the same route.

**Carn Glas-choire** (Cairn of the Grey Corrie); *659m*
*OS Sheets 35, 36; GR 891291*
*13km/380m/3–4hrs*
*Map 28*

This rather featureless hill is the highest point of a vast area of grouse moor lying north and east of the A9 at Carrbridge. It is best approached from the south-east where a track can be followed to within striking distance of the summit.

Begin at the B9007 road to Forres at the start of the track sign posted

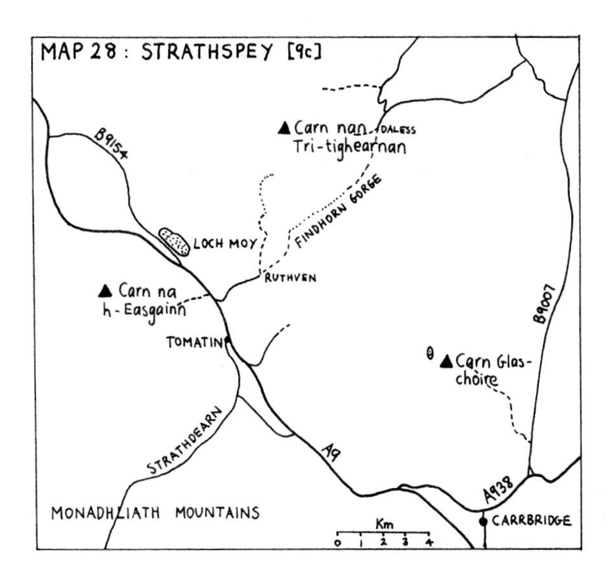


Auchterteang. There is just room for a car to be parked here but it may be wiser to find a larger space at another point. Follow the track to the recently vacated farmhouse at Auchterteang, where a locked metal gate is met with the rather abrupt sign: 'Cawdor Estate – Private Grouse Moor'. Assuming that it is outwith the grouse-shooting season or grouse are not being shot that day, it is quite permissible to continue.

About 2km beyond, you will pass a well-built wooden shelter with a corrugated iron roof used by estate workers (*not* a bothy!). A short distance further on, take a fork off to the right and continue round a spur until the track ends beyond the point shown on the map. The summit lies about 500m to the west and consists of a trig point and a fairly substantial cairn. On a clear day the finest view is south to the sprawling mass of the high Cairngorms, while to the north the Moray Firth is visible. There is a wonderful sense of space and solitude on this hill and it is unlikely that any other walkers will be around.

Return by the route of ascent or vary this by traversing the high ground east to Creag na h-lolaire (Crag of the Eagle) which is not as craggy as the map indicates. The main track lies south of this crag.

## **Carn nan Tri-tighearnan** (Hill of the Three Lairds); *614m*

*OS Sheet 27; GR 823390*
*9km/370m/2–3hrs*
*Map 28*

---

This hill is not so much a hill as the highest point of an extensive plateau rising north of the River Findhorn and east of the A9 at Loch Moy. This plateau, despite its relatively low rainfall, has poor drainage owing to the absence

*Carn Glas-choire from the south-east*

of steep slopes, and as a result is prolific in peat hags and wet bogs – walkers beware! Along with the usual heather and sphagnum moss, there also exists the fairly unusual Cladonia or 'reindeer moss' lichen. Carn nan Tri-tighearnan is a remote and featureless hill and ideal for those who love wild empty moorland and no other walkers.

The shortest approach to the hill is from the east at Daless, about a mile past Drynachan Lodge in the steep-sided Findhorn valley. At the end of the public road at Daless, a track winds its way up the hillside south of the Allt Breac, crossing it higher up. Soon after this point the track ends, and from here climb the steep heathery slopes of Carn an Uillt Bhric, the eastern spur of Carn nan Tri-tighearnan. From the trig point at the summit of this eastern spur, the actual summit lies exactly due west and is 1½km away. During this 1½km of undulating heather and peat hags, there is a rise of only 16m in height! The feeling at the summit is truly one of being in the middle of a vast rolling moorland (for a 'hill' is not really the correct name for this remote outpost).

It is also possible to reach the summit from Ruthven in the south just off the A9 but this involves a much longer walk with the bulk of it on trackless, boggy and peat hag terrain.

*The view north-east from Carnan Cruithneachd* (Section 11a)

*The summit of An Cruachan (possibly the remotest hill in Scotland)* (Section 12c)

*The view west from Beinn na Muice* (Section 12c)

*Beinn Alligin from Beinn na h-Easglaise* (Section 13c)

*Looking to the Fisherfield Forest from Groban* (Section 14a)

*Beinn nan Ramh from Loch Fannich* (Section 14b)

*Loch Lurgainn and Cul Beag from Stac Pollaidh* (Section 16a)

*Sgorr Tuath, Stac Pollaidh and Suilven from Beinn an Eoin* (Section 16a)

## SECTION 10A

# *Morvern, Sunart and Ardgour, and Moidart*

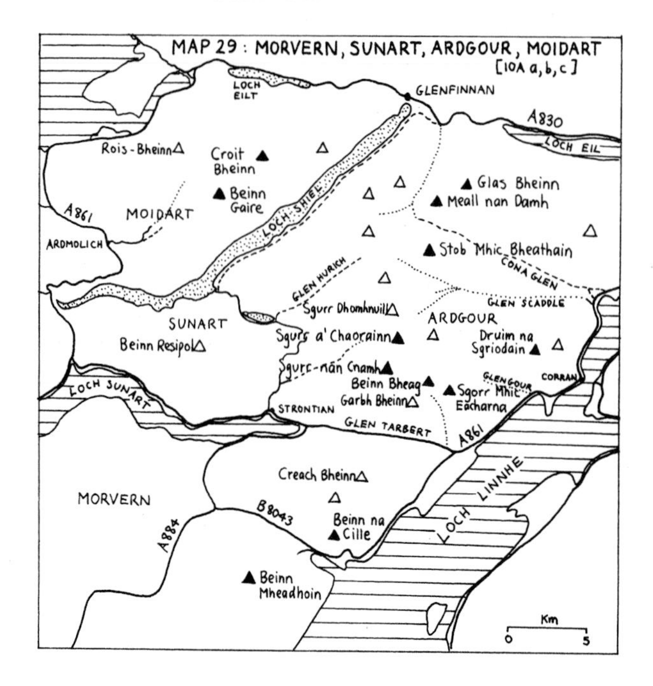


**Beinn na Cille** (Hill of the Church); *652m*
*OS Sheet 49; GR 854542*
*6km/600m/3–4hrs*
*Map 29*

---

There is a huge horseshoe-shaped ridge enclosing Glen Galmadale and facing Loch Linnhe which also contains two Corbetts and the above Graham. The complete traverse of this ridge is a marvellous day's hillwalking and is well documented in other sources. It is unlikely that Beinn na Cille would be climbed for its own sake, and it is normally included in the round of the glen. However, the following describes a shorter variation which only covers the Graham.

Begin on the B8043 road at the start of the south ridge of Beinn na Cille just before a forestry plantation. From here it is an easy climb up the ridge which is covered by grass interspersed with granite outcrops flattening out somewhat at around 500m. The ridge narrows for the last 100m to the cairn at the summit which, at the time of writing, was littered with large wooden posts. The view south and east across Loch Linnhe to Lismore island and the peaks beyond is quite stunning on a clear day.

To vary the descent, drop north to the col below Fuar Bheinn, then follow the stream east down to Glen Galmadale, where a track leads back to the road. It is then only a kilometre's walk back to the starting point.

An alternative horseshoe can be accomplished other than the round of Glen Galmadale by climbing Fuar Bheinn, then following the north-west ridge round onto Glas Bheinn (623m) and descending into Coire Ghardail. This is a relatively unfrequented and shorter alternative to the round of Glen Galmadale. If a car is parked at the forestry track end at GR 837536 then little or no roadwalking is required.

**Beinn Mheadhoin** (Middle Hill); *739m*
*OS Sheet 49; GR 799514*
*12km/920m/4–6hrs*
*Map 29*

This extensive sprawling mountian lies south-west of the Beinn na Cille group and on the southern side of Loch a' Choire. Its north-eastern aspect displays an array of fine corries separated by narrow spurs backed by a curving summit ridge. Numerous routes of varying duration are possible, although a circuit of Coire Ban, the main corrie, is a satisfying objective which in itself offers an excellent appreciation of the topography.

Begin at the B8043 road just west of the bridge near Tigh Ghardail. Cross the river, which may be a problem in spate conditions, and ascend the steep tussocky slopes for about 200m to a level shoulder. The steeper, craggier slopes of Sgurr Shalachain rise up from here, but the summit of this subsidiary top is easily gained by the left-hand (east) ridge. This is the first main top of the round, and Beinn Mheadhoin's summit is well seen beyond the deep bowl of Coire Ban. From here it is a delightful ridge walk on a wide grassy

*Looking north-east from the summit of Beinn Mheadhoin*

ridge with pockets of sound rock to add a spring to the step.

The next high point is Meall na Greine at 604m and about 1½km from the first top. Continue on to another small top before dropping down to Bealach a' Choire Bhain, the final col before Beinn Mheadhoin. An initial steep slope followed by easier grassy terrain leads in a kilometre to the substantial cairn and triangulation pillar at the summit.

The mountains of Mull are plainly visible to the south-west on a clear day, while to the north-west the Mamores and Glencoe peaks pepper the skyline beyond Loch Linnhe. Closer at hand, and to the north, Beinn Resipol, Sgurr Dhomhnuill and Garbh Bheinn all proclaim their individual profiles. On a less aesthetic note, the Glen Sanda 'Glory Hole' quarry and associated buildings can be seen and heard 2km away along the ridge to the south-east, and detracts somewhat from the peaceful ambience.

Descend the east-north-east ridge which is done easily at first until the short steep step which has to be negotiated and which forms the narrowest part of the ridge. The normal sound granite of Beinn Mheadhoin is superseded here by crumbling shale and great care should be exercised on this section. Beyond this point, the ridge resumes its grassy undulating character, though a series of steep gullies drop sharply on the left into Coire Ban. At the foot of the ridge follow the right-hand edge of the plantation until the Old Mill is reached. Continue along the left bank of the river and reach a gate on the right-hand side of a small plantation of trees just beyond a field. Go through the gate and cross a field leading to the farmhouse at N. Corry. Turn right here and follow the road up to some white cottages. Just beyond these cottages a grassy path leads up into the trees and this should be taken. Just after going through a gate on this track, turn immediately right, where a second path winds its way steeply up through the trees to arrive on the B8043 road. A 1km road walk leads back to the start point.

A full traverse of the Beul Choire nan Each ridge to the south-east makes for a longer day but is spoiled to some extent by the quarry workings.

**Druim na Sgriodain** (Ridge of the Stony Ravine); *734m*
*OS Sheet 40; GR 978656*
*10km/810m/4–5hrs*
*Map 29*

---

This hill, shown as Meall Dearg Choire nam Muc on the 1:50,000 map, is the highest point of a curving ridge which encloses Coire Dubh on the Ardgour side of the Corran Ferry. The hill is overshadowed by its more shapely and prominent neighbour, Sgurr na h-Eanchainne (Peak of the Brains), whose conspicuous profile is seen to advantage from Corran, rising steeply from sea level to its sharp summit. Although slightly lower (730m) than the actual

*Looking across to Ardgour from the Corran Ferry*

Graham, it commands superior views in every way and should not be omitted from any itinerary. The route to be described is basically an anti-clockwise circuit of Coire Dubh and therefore ascends Sgurr na h-Eanchainne first.

If you are not already based in Ardgour it should be noted that it is possible to use the Corran ferry free of charge as a passenger and to leave a vehicle at Corran. The above distance/time information is based on a start and finish at the Corran Ferry. Follow the A861 road north for about 2km to the point where the obvious south-east ridge of Sgurr na h-Eanchainne meets the road at Cille Mhaodhainn. Climb this ridge which is quite steep until it begins to level off at a shoulder after about 450m of ascent. Cross the head of a wide gully and begin the final few hundred metres of again fairly steep climbing to the airy summit which boasts a trig point and cairn. The views in all directions are quite superb, particularly north-east up the Great Glen to Loch Lochy and beyond, with Ben Nevis providing a worthy backdrop. The wide and remote heartland of Ardgour beckons to the west and the ridge walk to come is a small sample of the character of this rugged and beautiful region of Scotland.

Leave the summit and follow the ridge in a general westerly direction, dropping to Lochan a Choire Dhuibh before ascending a minor top. From here the summit of Druim na Sgriodain lies little more than 500m away behind a series of small lochans. The small cairn is a grand place to linger on a warm day with the feeling of being on a remote and seldom-frequented summit.

The return route follows the ridge south to hug the south-western rim of Coire Dubh and offers some glorious vantage points during the descent. After a final descent from a cairn on a prominent shoulder it is possible to traverse into the lower reaches of Coire Dubh, where you will see a large television mast and building below the level of the Maclean's Towel waterfall. From here, take a direct route over a series of small hillocks to the road, at which point it is about 1km back to the Corran Ferry. The Ardgour Hotel provides welcome refreshment if the ferry is not yet at the jetty!

**Sgorr Mhic Eacharna** (origin uncertain); *650m*
**Beinn Bheag** (Little Hill); *736m*
*OS Sheet 40; GR 928630, 914635*
*13km/900m/4½–6hrs*
*Map 29*

---

These two rugged hills are to some extent overshadowed by their magnificent neighbour, Garbh Bheinn, which is one of the finest Corbetts in the Western Highlands. Garbh Bheinn itself is an extremely popular mountain, especially with rock climbers and scramblers, and these two Grahams are often overlooked even by hillwalkers. A glance at the map shows all three summits to lie on a horseshoe ridge surrounding Coire an Iubhair and the ideal expedition is to traverse them all in a single outing. If this is the intended objective then an anti-clockwise circuit is a good idea as some interesting scrambling can then be enjoyed on the north ridge of Garbh Bheinn. The route described does not include Garbh Bheinn but could easily be extended to do so.

Begin at the parking area at the mouth of Coire an Iubhair (just off Sheet 40) and follow the good path up the glen for about 500m. Those familiar with the film *Rob Roy* may recognise the view up this glen as that appearing at the end of the film when Rob Roy returns home. His house was specially constructed on the floor of the glen but has since been removed. The obvious pointed hill on the skyline is Beinn Bheag, and Garbh Bheinn is not visible from here. Strike off to the right at almost any point and climb the steep grassy slopes for nearly 400m to reach the broad south ridge of Sgorr Mhic Eacharna, named Druim an Iubhair on the map. Follow this ridge easily to the north, passing a small lochan *en route.* A final steep face leads to the rocky but relatively flat summit where stunning views can be enjoyed of the rocky ramparts of Garbh Bheinn's east face. The Great Ridge is clearly visible on the left with Great Gully to its right. Another lochan lies just north of the summit, which may be found refreshing in hot weather (but not to drink from!).

Descend west to a grassy col and make the 250m ascent to the summit of Beinn Bheag where more glorious views present themselves. In particular the

*Beinn Bheag from Coire an-Iubhair*

*Sgurr a' Chaorainn and Sgurr nan Cnamh from Strontian glen*

view north across wild Glen Gour to the rugged interior of Ardgour is impressive. Head west from the summit along the well-defined ridge and make another slight ascent before descending to the col at the head of Coire an Iubhair. Note that this descent is quite steep and in the latter stages an easy grassy gully with some old iron fence posts should be followed. This leads down to the col which contains a small lochan, and is a beautifully wild spot to rest and perhaps bathe the feet.

The descent route descends the corrie to the east, picking up the path on the north side of the river after about 1½ km. This leads directly back to the start of the route. For those attempting Garbh Bheinn, the lochan is only the halfway point and the ascent of the north ridge of this peak is the next objective. Crags to the left of an obvious weakness provide an entertaining scramble but easier lines are possible.

**Sgurr a' Chaorainn** (Peak of the Rowan); *761m*
**Sgurr nan Cnamh** (Peak of Chew); *701m*
*OS Sheet 40; GR 895662, 886643*
*20km/1,370m/8–11hrs*
*Map 29*

---

At the head of Glen Strontian and Glen Gour a cluster of fine craggy peaks typify the area's charm and general remoteness. Sgurr a' Chaorainn and Sgurr nan Cnamh lie on each side of the bealach separating the two glens with further Corbetts and Grahams situated in a wider arc beyond. The two peaks could be approached from either glen but Glen Strontian has the advantage of an excellent nature trail leading far up the glen. The two Grahams, together with the 'Lesser Corbett' of Sgurr na h-Ighinn, make a natural round of Glen Strontian; but the vast drop between the two could constitute a case for two separate expeditions.

Begin at the small parking/picnic area at GR 830634 and follow the nature trail/track for over 3km through delightful natural woodland of oak and birch. At the edge of the forest, cross a wooden footbridge and continue along the upper path for just over 1km to some disused mine workings. Cross the river at this point and ascend the hummocky slopes of Druim Leac a' Sgiathain, which forms the west ridge of Sgurr na h-Ighinn. Once established on this ridge, there are fine views of Sgurr Dhomhnuill, a Corbett lying off to the left and the highest peak in Ardgour. It is possible to include this peak in the round by climbing Sgurr na h-Ighinn and then making a northerly diversion with little drop in height.

However, if continuing directly to Sgurr a' Chaorainn it is best to contour round the southern flank of Sgurr na h-Ighinn just below a girdle of crags at around the 600m mark and then to drop steeply down to the col below Sgurr a' Chaorainn. From here the hill can be ascended easily on grass and sound rock. Just below the summit you will pass a tiny lochan nestling between the crags. The true summit is the most easterly of two high points and has a small cairn. Sgurr a' Chaorainn has the honour of being the second highest Graham, beaten only by Beinn Talaidh on Mull, which was previously a Corbett! Less than 3km to the east and separated by a 560m col is Beinn na h-Uamha, which, at 762m, is the smallest Corbett. So the ridge leading off to the east connects the lowest Corbett with the second highest Graham – quite a unique ridge!

Across the glen to the south lies Sgurr nan Cnamh and to reach it requires much descent and re-ascent. Begin by dropping south from the summit where an obvious shoulder continues on to the subsidiary top of Sgurr na Laire. Before reaching this top descend south, avoiding the crags which lie directly below the summit of Sgurr na Laire. Finally reach the bealach a short distance south-east of Lochan a'Chothruim, at a height of 200m. The ascent of Sgurr nan Cnamh can be made by crossing the stream which tumbles steeply down from near the summit, before gaining the obvious rocky spur to the east. This leads to a small knoll from where it is only a short 70m climb to the summit. On a clear day unusual views of Garbh Bheinn's remote northern flanks can be enjoyed.

The descent is north-west along the complex terrain which forms the north-west ridge of the mountain and which drops steeply into Upper Glen Strontian. At Sgurr a' Bhuic descend steeply and cross the river to reach the lower path. This leads naturally past a ruin and drystane dyke to a track which connects with the original nature trail at GR 849648.

## **Stob Mhic Bheathain** (origin uncertain); *721m*

*OS Sheet 40; GR 914713*
*28km/650m/5–8hrs (bike)*
*Map 29*

This hill is the remotest Graham in Ardgour and as such will require a firm level of commitment to climb. It forms part of the undulating ridge on the southern side of Upper Cona Glen; this glen is the most convenient approach route. Unfortunately, the local estate owners have seen fit to prohibit cycling along the Land Rover track in the glen, but a diplomatic telephone call in suitably humble tones may loosen their resolve.

From the A861 road at GR 022686 take the Cona Glen track which follows the north side of the river. Cona Glen is one of the most picturesque of Scottish glens and this soon becomes apparent in just a few kilometres. After an initial section of natural woodland containing oak, birch and other native trees, the glen begins to open out with numerous stands of Scots pine and birch forming a charming foreground to the wild mountains beyond. A private bothy is on the right (Corrlarach), and just over 2km beyond a prominent knoll to the right of the track – a remnant of the last Ice Age. Stob Mhic Bheathain rises directly up from this point on the south side of the glen and the ascent of the north-east ridge presents no problems, apart from possibly the river crossing which could be tricky in spate conditions. Higher up, any crags are easily avoided and the cairn at the summit is situated on the more easterly of two obvious high points about 150m apart. The finest view is to the south and south-west where several prominent Corbetts, including Sgurr Dhomhnuill, immediately arrest the eye. This is Ardgour at its wildest and most rugged.

For those with plenty of time available it is quite feasible to follow the crest of the ridge north-west over Stob a' Chuir and Meall Mor to the remote Corbett of Stob a Bealach an Sgriodain. This ridge is probably one of the most unfrequented ridges in the whole of Scotland. The shorter alternative is to descend slightly north of west, following a line of old iron fence posts to the col below the next small top. Climb this top, then descend by its north-east ridge which has a fairly constant gradient all the way down. This makes a satisfying horseshoe route. Return by the track along Cona Glen.

This Graham could also be climbed from the head of Glen Scaddle to the south but this would involve relentless steep slopes and it is not so pleasant or varied an ascent as the one just described. However, the head of Glen Scaddle is an ideal camping base for the ascent of the three Corbetts to the south and west, and Stob Mhic Bheathain

*Looking up Cona Glen to Stob Mhic Bheathain*

could well be included as a separate excursion.

**Meall nan Damh** (Hill of the Stag); *723m*
**Glas Bheinn** (Grey Hill); *636m*
*OS Sheet 40; GR 919745, 938758*
*15km/900m/5–7hrs*
*Map 29*

These two splendid hills lying north of Cona Glen and south-east of Glenfinnan are somewhat overshadowed by their more illustrious Corbett neighbours to the west. Meall nan Damh especially has much individual character, however, and is a twin-topped peak throwing out a long, rugged, north-east ridge. Together they provide a satisfying round with some delightful ridge walking.

Begin at the big bend in the A830 road shortly after the road goes under the railway line, and park at the start of the track which leaves the road at this point. Follow the track and cross the bridge before turning left along the track which leads to the cottage named Callop on the map. Leave the track at the point where it bends right to Callop and follow a footpath which winds its way along the west bank of the Allt na Cruaiche. After 2km, the path reaches the end of the wooded section and makes an obvious turn to the west. This is the signal to leave the path, cross the Allt na Cruaiche and gain the foot of the long north-east ridge of Meall nan

*On the Meall nan Damh–Glas Bheinn ridge*

Damh. This section is beautifully forested with many natural Scots pine trees and the views to the rugged north-east ridge of Sgorr Craobh a' Chaorainn are particularly fine.

Once established on the ridge, follow its undulating crest for about 2km to the slightly lower west top of Meall nan Damh, so named as the corrie to the east often holds many deer. An easy kilometre's ridge walk leads east to the hill's true summit where the cairn is situated slightly further on and lower than the actual top. This summit is almost directly north of the very remote Graham of Stob Mhic Bheathain lying only 3km away across the deep and lonely Cona Glen. The whole area of Ardgour to the south contains many wild Corbetts and Grahams and is a haven for lovers of solitude.

Glas Bheinn can be reached by continuing east along the ridge for 500m before dropping north to the col at 480m below the easy slopes of the hill. Climb the remaining 105m or so to the summit, which has both a trig-point and a cairn (the highest point) lying a short distance to the north-west. It will no doubt be apparent that a large area of forestry plantation lies between this hill and the starting point but suitable use of fire-breaks will avoid any bushwhacking! Further down the hill to the north it pays to stop for a moment and check the best fire-beaks to use. An obvious one follows the Allt Tarsuinn to a long ride running north-east, which in turn leads to a break ending just south of Callop. All this is visible from above – on a clear day! Once out of the forest, cross the river and regain the path back to the starting point.

**Beinn Gaire** (Laughing Hill); *666m*
**Croit Bheinn** (Croft Hill); *663m*
*OS Sheet 40; GR 781748, 810773*
*22km/870m/7–9hrs*
*Map 29*

---

The rugged and remote country to the west of the long arm of Loch Shiel contains some outstanding peaks and ridges, with the Rois-Bheinn group being the most well known and most climbed. Between this group and Loch Shiel lie Beinn Gaire and Croit Bheinn, the latter a very distinctive conical hill somewhat overshadowed by its higher Corbett neighbours and rarely climbed because of its remoteness. Beinn Gaire is the highest point of a rolling mass of high ground and is not as prominent as Croit Bheinn although it is a few metres higher. Both hills can be approached via Glen Moidart to the south-west but their combined traverse makes for a long hard day.

From the A861 road at Ardmolich drive up Glen Moidart for 3km to the end of the public road at a small carpark. The Glen Moidart track begins about 50m back along the road and follows the south side of the glen. The track directly ahead leads to Glen Moidart House and other private houses. Take the former track past the picturesque Loch nan Lochan where fine views can be enjoyed northwards to the Rois-Bheinn range. After 2km, a track forks off to the right and this should be taken up to the unnamed hill loch in Glen Forslan. Note that this track is unmarked on earlier editions of OS maps.

Cross the small dam at the western end of the loch and cross a fence from whence a short climb leads to the crest of the Sron Dubh an Eilich, the steep south-western ridge of Beinn Gaire. Climb this easy ridge of grass and rocky outcrops, crossing an obvious depression at around 450m. The summit of the mountain can be reached from here by bearing round to the left, thereby avoiding the steeper section directly ahead. The terrain from here to the summit is quite complex with many hidden troughs and lochans and would be tricky to navigate in misty conditions. Even the summit itself contains two confusing tops, the north-easterly one being the higher. The summit offers a grandstand view of the Rois-Bheinn ridge across Glen Moidart. Beinn Resipol is also prominent to the south.

To reach Croit Bheinn, continue north-east along the wide undulating ridge which drops steeply northwards to Upper Glen Moidart and Glen Gluitanen. After about 3km of gradual descent and several minor bumps, you will reach Bealach a' Choire Mhoir which sits directly below the southern slopes of Croit Bheinn. A short climb of some 200m is livened up by a ring of crags which girdle the summit, and the cairn has quite an airy feel. A short distance east of the cairn, two prominent standing stones are perched on the edge of the precipitous slopes which drop down to lonely Glen Aladale. Croit Bheinn is dominated by a grand northerly arc of Corbetts and other subsidiary tops and these serve to enhance its isolated position.

The return to the start is in some ways the hardest part of the expedition and much rough walking is required. From the summit, drop south-west and then west into Glen Gluitanen where a very tussocky pathless descent can be made to the Bealach na Lice. At this point, however, the river flows through a narrow gorge and can only be negotiated by some judicious route planning which will involve boulder-hopping and tricky down-climbing. If the river is in spate the only practical alternative is to climb high to avoid the gorge. Once in Upper Glen Moidart, follow the north side of the river on very boggy ground, keeping well to the right of the river to avoid the boggiest areas. Shortly beyond an obvious knoll, the old ruin of Assary comes into view and more boggy ground is crossed until, thankfully, a reasonable path is reached. Follow this path for almost 3km and turn off left along a signposted path which crosses a footbridge to join the track used on the approach.

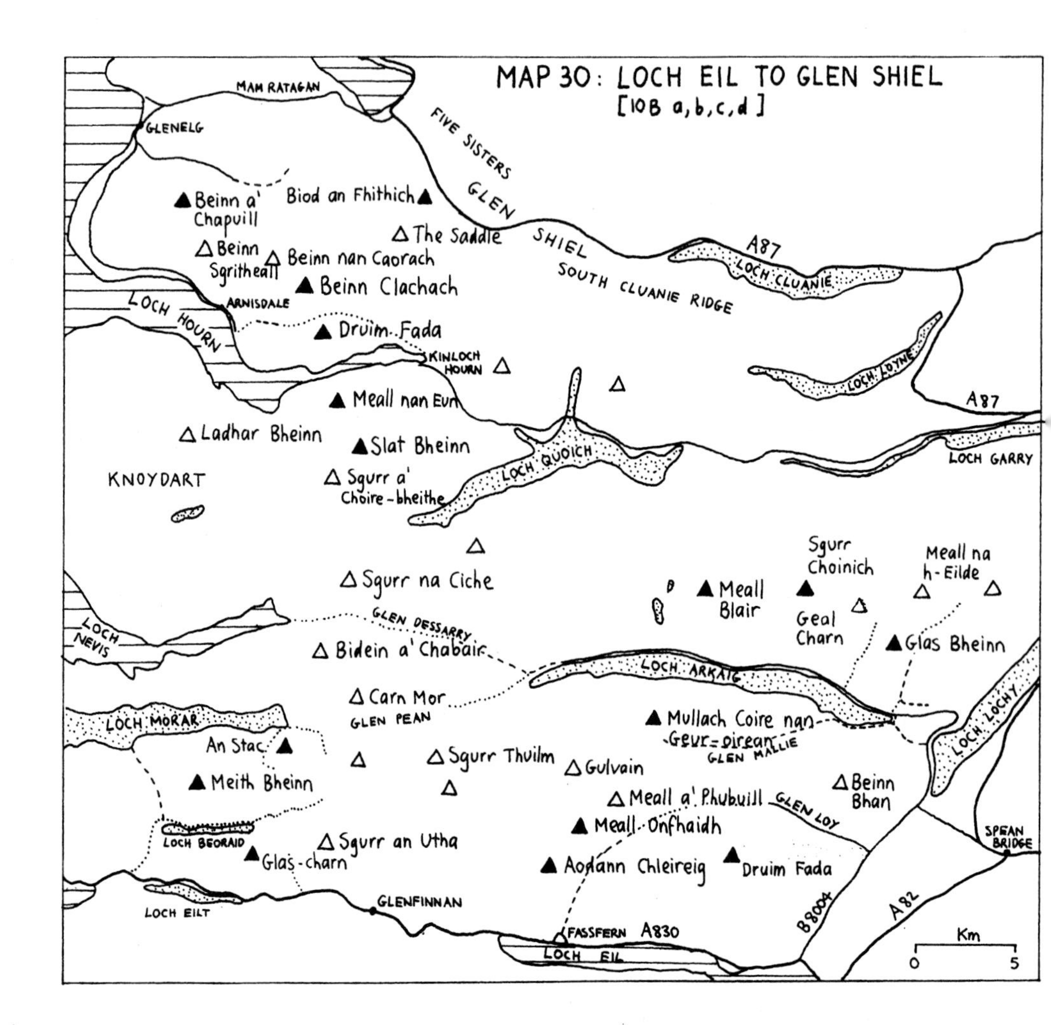
MAP 30: LOCH EIL TO GLEN SHIEL
[10B a,b,c,d]
MAM RATAGAN
GLENELG
FIVE SISTERS
GLEN
SHIEL
Beinn a' Chapuill
Biod an Fhithich
The Saddle
Beinn Sgritheall
Beinn nan Caorach
Beinn Clachach
SOUTH CLUANIE RIDGE
A87
LOCH CLUANIE
LOCH HOURN
ARNISDALE
Druim Fada
KINLOCH HOURN
LOCH LOYNE
Meall nan Eun
A87
Ladhar Bheinn
Slat Bheinn
LOCH QUOICH
LOCH GARRY
KNOYDART
Sgurr a' Choire-bheithe
Sgurr na Ciche
Sgurr Choinich
Meall na h-Eilde
Meall Blair
Geal Charn
Glas Bheinn
LOCH NEVIS
GLEN DESSARRY
Bidein a' Chabair
LOCH ARKAIG
Carn Mor
GLEN PEAN
LOCH MORAR
Mullach Coire nan Geur-oirean
GLEN MALLIE
LOCH LOCHY
An Stac
Sgurr Thuilm
Gulvain
Meith Bheinn
Beinn Bhan
Meall a' Phubuill
GLEN LOY
Meall Onfhaidh
SPEAN BRIDGE
LOCH BEORAID
Sgurr an Utha
Glas-charn
Aodann Chleireig
Druim Fada
LOCH EILT
GLENFINNAN
B8004
A82
FASSFERN
A830
LOCH EIL
Km
0
5

## SECTION 10B

# *Loch Eil to Glen Shiel*

**Druim Fada** (Long Ridge); *744m*
*OS Sheet 41; GR 087824*
*8km/640m/2½–3½hrs*
*Map 30*

---

Between Loch Eil and Loch Arkaig is an area of rounded hills and pleasant broad ridges. The most easterly of these is the long ridge of Druim Fada which runs from east to west and contains Stob a' Ghrianain as its highest point. The quickest and most scenic ascent begins in Glen Loy to the north.

Either cross the footbridge or ford the River Loy and follow the track to Puiteachan. The forest south of here is a fine remnant of the old Caledonian forest and has some magnificent examples of Scots pine and larch. Follow the stream up through the trees or alternatively bypass the forest completely on its west side. Once beyond the tree-line make for the north ridge between Coire Dubh and Coire Odhar, where a large cairn is prominent on the skyline. The actual summit has a much smaller cairn lying further up to the right (south-west) of this large cairn.

Once on the summit the views to the south and south-east are magnificent. The obvious landmark is Ben Nevis rising above the urban sprawl of Fort William while further east the peaks of the Mamore ridge jostle for attention. The more remote hills of the north and west are also seen to advantage from this fine viewpoint.

In good conditions, Druim Fada can be followed west to Point 729, but a shorter alternative makes a circuit of Coire Dubh and descends by the broad spur to its west. The above distance/time information is based on this route. In either case it is an easy descent north to Glen Loy and the path which runs along the north side of the River Loy. This leads east to Achnanellan and the starting point.

If transport is not a problem, Druim Fada can be traversed in its entirety to Coille Mhor at the western end before dropping steeply to the forestry track in Gleann Suileag. This track leads south to Fassfern and the main A830 Fort William to Mallaig road. From Coille Mhor it is of course possible to descend north to the Glen Loy path which is a continuation of the track already mentioned.

**Meall Onfhaidh** (Hill of Fury); *681m*
**Aodann Chleireig** (Clergyman's Face); *663m*
*OS Sheets 41, 40; GR 010840, 994825*
*17km/970m/5–7hrs*
*Map 30*

---

These two hills are the last south-westerly high points of a long ridge forming the north and west sides of Glen Loy and Gleann Suileag respectively. The Corbett of Beinn Bhan is the easterly high point while a second Corbett, Meall a' Phubuill, lies just a few kilometres north of Meall Onfhaidh. A complete traverse of this grassy undulating ridge would be a long and demanding expedition and the route

*The summit of Meall Onfhaidh*

described below attempts only the two Grahams, though Meall a' Phubuill could be included. Note that Aodann Chleireig lies rather annoyingly just off OS Sheet 41 and consulting OS Sheet 40 shows this Graham to have the attendant satellite top of Beinn an t-Sneachda to the south-west, the true termination of the ridge mentioned previously.

The obvious starting point is Fassfern to the south where a right of way leads northwards through Gleann Suileag then curves east through Glen Loy. Bonnie Prince Charlie came this way *en route* to Invergarry after his optimistic raising of the standard at Glenfinnan. Walk up the forestry track on the east bank of the river, ignoring several other tracks branching off. An opening in the forestry a few kilometres up gives fine views of Meall Onfhaidh while Meall a' Phubuill dominates the scene to the north. After emerging from the forest the track gradually descends to the river, and shortly before the deserted cottage of Glensulaig a bridge crosses the river where a hill path leads up to the wide bealach between Meall Onfhaidh and Meall a' Phuibuill. Leave the main track in the glen and ascend this hill path to a small wooden bridge crossing the Allt Fionn Doire. Head west to gain the broad east ridge of Meall Onfhaidh which gradually curves round to the summit along a ridge to the north-west. During the ascent and from the summit cairn the twin-topped Munro of Gulvain steals the limelight to the north and this is possibly one of the finest viewpoints of this Munro.

Aodann Chleireig is easily reached by descending west then south-west to the bealach at 350m. From here, a 300m ascent with a steep section near the top leads to the cairn at the summit. This Graham has quite an extensive summit area with several false tops and numerous lochans, and could be confusing in a mist. Views of Gulvain are again quite spectacular with its vast western corrie separating it from the Corbett of Braigh nan Uamhachan.

The easiest descent is via the long, easy-angled south-east ridge known as Druim Beag. Alternatively, it is possible to continue round the ridge to visit the subsidiary top of Beinn an t-Sneachda and this round of Coire Chur would be a good proposition if Meall Onfhaidh was being omitted. Lower down the Druim Beag ridge, go through a gap in the forestry and follow the left plantation down to pick up a grass track which leads through ferns, gorse bushes and small trees to Fassfern and the starting point.

**Mullach Coire nan Geur-oirean**
(Summit of the Hollow of the Sharp Edge); *727m*
*OS Sheet 41; GR 049892*
*30km/700m/5–7hrs (bike)*
*Map 30*

---

This remote hill is the second highest summit of a long ridge running east from the Munro of Gulvain (the highest point) to the shores of Loch Arkaig, some 15km away. The route described begins at the eastern end of the loch and assumes the use of a bike. Cars can be parked at the Eas Chia-aig carpark just before the bridge at the western end of the 'Dark Mile'.

Take the minor track signposted 'Achnacarry' and fork right after the wooden bridge to follow the fairly rough track which switchbacks its way along the south shore of Loch Arkaig for 4km to the bothy at Inver Mallie. Go over the bridge and continue along the track as it winds its way through a pleasant wooded section by the north bank of the River Mallie. Glen Mallie is a beautifully wild glen with many natural Caledonian pine trees still standing, though further up the glen these gradually fade away.

At some point before the ruin labelled 'Glenmallie' on the map it is best to leave the track (which deteriorates significantly beyond the ruin) and strike off up the hillside to reach Druim na Giubhsaich, the broad ridge lying east of the summit. Follow this ridge past several small lochans and a final rise to the spacious summit of Mullach Coire nan Geur-oirean with its tiny cairn. Enjoy a grand view of Gulvain and the Corbett of Meall a' Phubuill on the opposite side of the glen.

A return can be made either by retracing your steps along the ridge or dropping directly south down steep slopes to reach the end of the track. This is then followed back to the starting point.

**Glas-charn** (Green Cairn); *633m*
*OS Sheet 40; GR 846837*
*9km/480m/2½–4hrs*
*Map 30*

---

This accessible little hill has few distinguishing features, being little more than the highest point of a complex upland area of knolls and lochans lying between Loch Eilt and Loch Beoraid. It could be included with an ascent of the neighbouring easterly Corbett, Sgurr an Utha, but on its own provides a pleasant half day's hillwalk with fine summit views.

Begin on the A830 road 3km west of Glenfinnan where a track starts just east of the bridge over the Allt Feith a' Chatha. Note that an area of new forestry exists on the north side of the road which is not shown on the second series OS map. You will come upon a locked gate which, initially, should be avoided. Use the stile further along the fence instead. Follow the track upwards for about 500m where it makes a turn east to ascend the spur on the south side of the Allt an Utha. This section of the track is not indicated on the second series map but is useful for gaining access to the Corbett of Sgurr an Utha. Leave the track at the point where it turns east and cross the Allt an Utha by a wooden footbridge. The path from herein is indistinct, but follow the course of the Allt Feith a' Chatha.

Somewhere below the craggy western slopes of Sidhean Mor, leave the path and head west to gain the easy eastern flank of Glas-charn which can be ascended by a variety of lines. The summit area boasts a profusion of false summits and would be a problem in misty conditions. The actual summit is a prominent little crag topped by a small cairn and is an excellent viewpoint for the beautifully wild surroundings. The north side of Glas-charn drops in continuously steep slopes to the dark waters of Loch Beoraid which is unfortunately not quite visible from the summit. However, by moving across to a neighbouring crag, the loch can be seen. Return by the route of ascent unless you are also planning to climb Sgurr an Utha.

**Meith Bheinn** (Sappy Hill); *710m*
**An Stac** (The Stack); *718m*
*OS Sheet 40; GR 821872, 866889*
*28km/1,830m/9–13hrs*
*Map 30*

---

These two wild and inaccessible hills are set in some of the grandest scenery in the Western Highlands. Together they make a formidable challenge for the fit walker, and An Stac in particular can be regarded as one of the remotest Grahams. They are both situated north of the A830 Fort William to Mallaig road and south of Loch Morar, the deepest loch in Scotland. The above statistics are based on a day's walk from the western end of Loch Eilt, but a more sensible option would be to spread the load over a few days by the judicious use of a tent. There is also a bothy north of An Stac on the south shore of Loch

Morar which may be found useful.

At the western end of Loch Eilt a path begins at the point where the railway crosses a bridge. Follow this uphill by the Allt na Criche to a wide boggy col before dropping steeply through natural woodland and open hillside to the small hydro-electric generator and bridge at the outflow of Loch Beoraid. This loch has a beautifully wild setting and is almost Coruisk-like in the view from its western end. Cross the bridge and continue north along the track for about 500m before striking off to the right up the steep and relentless western slopes of Meith Bheinn. After about 450m of ascent the angle lessens and the character of the hill changes to a series of rocky bluffs and small lochans which would be very confusing in a mist. The actual summit is well to the east and consists of a (detached) triangulation pillar and a small cairn. The next objective, An Stac, is well seen from here but is still almost 5km away to the east as the crow flies.

Descend Meith Bheinn by its complex rocky north-east ridge where there is a feeling of really entering into the heart of wild remote country. Eventually, after about 3km you will reach the pleasant secluded hollow of Gleann Cul an Staca where a delightful stream makes an idyllic lunch spot. From this point the west ridge of An Stac rises up in tiers of sound rock providing some entertaining scrambling if the best crags are hunted out.

Ascend the ridge to the flattish summit area where a false summit is passed before reaching the true top to the north-east. This could also be confusing in a mist; but it is wise to keep this mountain for a clear day as the views are marvellous – in particular the view down the length of Glen Pean to the east, with Loch Arkaig just visible. This provides another possible approach to An Stac which stands at the head of this glen; and there is a genuine feeling of absolute remoteness standing on this summit with mountains pressing in on all sides. Do remember, however, that if you are attempting these hills in a single day, it is still a long, long way back.

Descend An Stac by the route of ascent before crossing the stream and climbing west for about 200m to reach the broad, grassy bealach to the north of Meith Bheinn. Pass a few small lochans and you will eventually reach a path which descends by the Allt Slaite Coire to the track just south of Meoble. Follow the track south which will lead back to the route used on the walk in. A possible variation on the return route is to climb up to Lochan a' Bhrodainn after descending the west ridge of An Stac and heading directly for Loch Beoraid where a path can be followed along its north shore to the hydro-generator and bridge. This second option involves much the same distance and a very steep descent to Loch Beoraid, but is more scenic.

*The view east along Glen Pean from the summit of An Stac*

*Glas Bheinn from near Bunarkaig*

**Glas Bheinn** (Green Hill); *732m*
*OS Sheet 34; GR 171919*
*14km/690m/3½–5hrs*
*Map 30*

---

The north side of Loch Arkaig is blessed with some fine Corbetts and Grahams, each with its own individual character. Glas Bheinn, at the eastern end of the loch is no exception and offers exceptional views down Loch Arkaig to the wilds of Morar and the far west. North of Glas Bheinn is an arc of high tops including two Corbetts which could conceivably be combined with the ascent of Glas Bheinn in a long day, although the following description gives an interesting circular route traversing the Graham only.

Begin at the carpark at the western end of Mile Dorcha (Dark Mile) where a fine waterfall tumbles out of Gleann Cia-aig. Follow a steep path upwards through the forest to meet a forestry track higher up. This can be followed north through Gleann Cia-aig which soon opens out to give a grand view of the peaks at the head of the glen. The prominent pointed summit on the right is Meall an Tagraidh (Hill of the Pleading) where Bonnie Prince Charlie took refuge for several days and nights. Cameron of Clunes generously kept him sane by taking up whisky, bread and cheese, and accompanying him by day lying at the summit wrapped in plaids – in the rain!

Meall an Tagraidh is one of countless hills in Scotland which refuses to slot neatly into a predetermined list. It is a subsidiary top of the neighbouring Corbett, Meall na h-Eilde, which is separated by a high bealach – too high in fact for it to be a separate Graham. It falls just short of the 2,500ft mark and could be described as a 'Lesser Graham' according to the unofficial definition mentioned in the introduction.

Within less than 2km the forestry track gives way to a footpath which descends to the river and emerges from the trees over a kilometre further on. If not in spate conditions the river can be crossed here; but otherwise continue on the path and cross the small wooden footbridge at GR 188928. The bridge marked on earlier editions of the OS map south of this bridge has long since been washed away.

Cross the Allt Tarsuinn at a suitable point and begin the ascent of easy grassy slopes. After 1km of distance and 300m of ascent, you will reach the minor top at GR 177928 which marks the start of the pleasant curving north ridge of Glas Bheinn which leads directly to the fairly substantial summit cairn. During the ascent, you can enjoy unusual views east to the two Munros on the west side of Loch Lochy. Once on the summit, it is the view to the west which holds the attention, with the long dark ribbon of Loch Arkaig leading the eye to a tangle of rugged peaks.

Descend south initially before gradually curving south-west on steeper ground to eventually reach the path on the east bank of the Allt Dubh. Follow this old stalkers' path down to the road just west of Achnasaul from where a

*Looking north from the summit of Sgurr Choinich*

pleasant 2½km of road leads back to the starting point.

The quickest way to ascend Glas Bheinn would be via the path used in the descent but this does not really do justice to the hill. If the Corbett of Geal Charn is to be included then this path would be the logical route of ascent. Note that the previous route description can easily be reversed.

**Sgurr Choinich** (Peak of the Moss); *749m*
*OS Sheet 34; GR 127949*
*8km/700m/2½–4hrs*
*Map 30*

---

Sgurr Choinich, the central and highest of the three Grahams which rise on the north side of Loch Arkaig, is seldom climbed. Its finest features face north; nonetheless, this is not the direction from which it would normally be approached. The narrow north-east ridge and steep craggy northern corrie are completely hidden from the south and even the summit of the mountain is not visible from the road along the north side of Loch Arkaig. However, the southerly approach is described, as it is significantly shorter. The finest way to tackle the mountain would be a complete traverse from north to south but this would obviously incur transport problems.

Sgurr Choinich throws out a long, broad spur to the south, from where the ascent is tedious but is the most direct route to the summit. Cars can be parked near a bridge between two forestry plantations. A vague path follows the edge of the western one. Beyond the trees, seemingly interminable hummocky slopes continue upwards with the rounded summit dome not appearing until a considerable gain in height; although by this time, extensive views west to the peaks of Knoydart will have somewhat relieved the monotonous nature of the terrain. Finally, after 4km from the road, you will reach a line of metal fence posts and the fairly substantial summit cairn. The view north and west is very fine indeed with the Loch Quoich and Glen Shiel Munros dominating the skyline. To the south the hulking profile of Ben Nevis is unmistakable.

Descend by the same route in considerably less time than the ascent!

**Meall Blair** (Hill of the Clearing); *656m*
*OS Sheet 33; GR 077950*
*8km/590m/2–4hrs*
*Map 30*

This hill is the most westerly of the three Grahams lying north of Loch Arkaig and displays some similar characteristics to Sgurr Choinich. The southern aspect is of long monotonous slopes dropping down to Loch Arkaig while the northern slopes are steeper and craggier.

The most direct approach is from the south at a point about 500m past the cottage of Caonich on the Loch Arkaig road. From here a rough all-terrain vehicle track winds its way up to the vicinity of Loch Blair. Follow this track before striking off up the broad grassy south-west ridge which will give increasingly fine views of more alluring mountains to the west. You will reach an initial false summit. Now cross a wide depression leading to a second false summit. The actual summit lies a few hundred metres beyond with a triangulation pillar and small cairn. Return by the route of ascent.

**Meall nan Eun** (Hill of the Birds); *667m*
**Slat Bheinn** (Rod Hill); *700m*
*OS Sheet 33; GR 903052, 910027*
*23km/1,600m/7–10hrs*

These two hills are tucked away in the relatively inaccessible mountainous wilderness between Loch Hourn and Loch Quoich. Immediately west lies the fabled 'Rough Bounds of Knoydart' and the whole area (effectively the bottom half of OS Sheet 33) is a hillwalker's and backpacker's paradise, with a multitude of wild rocky peaks and stalkers' paths. Meall nan Eun rises on the south side of fiord-like Loch Hourn and is fairly easily reached from the excellent coastal path following the lochside. Slat Bheinn, however, cannot be reached without much rough walking or a vast descent and re-ascent from Meall nan Eun. As the above statistics indicate, the ascent of both these hills in a day is a long, hard undertaking for fit and determined walkers only. The bothy at Barrisdale may be found useful for those planning an overnight stay.

From the end of the public road at Kinloch Hourn, follow the coastal path to a high point just under a kilometre past Skiary. From here strike off to the left in a south-westerly direction ascending initially heathery hillside. At a height of around 400m, the terrain begins to level off into a grassy but boggy circular hanging corrie. Continue south-west onto an obvious subsidiary ridge which goes over a small top before continuing easily to the east top of Meall nan Eun. A pleasant ridge walk leads to a small lochan before the steep rise to the summit where there is a small cairn. Better views can be obtained from another high point about 500m further west which is only marginally lower than the actual top. Particularly prominent is the Munro of Ladhar Bheinn rising gracefully above Loch Hourn and Barrisdale Bay.

The next objective of Slat Bheinn involves a descent of over 500m into Glen Barrisdale and this is best achieved by first descending to Lochan Coire Chaolais Bhig, which is beautifully situated in the wild bealach between Meal nan Eun and the rocky subsidiary top of An Caisteal (The Castle). Care should be taken on this descent as there are numerous crags directly south of the western top of Meall nan Eun. From the lochan it is an easy grassy descent south-east to Glen Barrisdale where a welcome stop can be made at the river before the next long ascent. An obvious north-facing spur provides the easiest line of ascent initially and thereafter a variety of lines on excellent rough, rocky outcrops and grassy runnels leads to the summit area of Slat Bheinn which is split by a wide fissure. Cross the fissure and make the short climb to the substantial cairn at the summit. The prominent cone of Sgurr a' Choire-bheithe (a Corbett) is well seen to the south-west – and is even more remote than Slat Bheinn.

Descend by approximately the same route to Glen Barrisdale before the final 350m ascent north on steep grass and heather to reach the wide bealach between Meall nan Eun and Sgurr Sgiath Airigh. This leads easily into the circular hanging corrie used on the approach from whence the coastal path is soon reached.

Meall nan Eun could quite easily be ascended on its own or in combination with the Corbett of Sgurr nan Eugallt. In fact, the traverse of the whole ridge from Sron Lice na Fearna to Carn Mairi would make a fine expedition though it is not without logistical transportation problems. Slat Bheinn can also be climbed as a separate expedition by leaving the road north of Loch Quoich at GR 985036 and by following the lochside round to the outflow of the Abhainn Chosaidh and picking up the path on its north side.

**Druim Fada** (Long Ridge); *713m*
*OS Sheet 33; GR 894083*
*14km/850m/5–7hrs*
*Map 30*

---

The long contorted ridge of Druim Fada is very prominent on the motorist's approach to the picturesque village of Arnisdale on the north shore of Loch Hourn. Situated on the south side of Glen Arnisdale, Druim Fada presents a rugged, twisted spine, 6km long, whose steep, wooded southern slopes rise up directly from upper Loch Hourn. The highest point, a magnificent vantage point, is unnamed on the OS map. This hill could be climbed in combination with Beinn Clachach to the north-west, but the massive drop between the two hills does little to favour this alternative.

Follow the Glen Arnisdale track eastwards past a cottage and cross the river by a bridge before continuing on the track along the south bank. Further on the track deteriorates somewhat and climbs steeply through a wooded section of oak, beech, birch and other natural trees. Just before the track turns and descends to cross a footbridge south of Dubh Lochain it crosses a stream flowing down from Druim Fada. To the north-east of this stream a fairly well-defined craggy ridge rises almost directly to the summit. This ridge is the north-west ridge and marks the route of ascent.

Gain the foot of the ridge just after crossing the stream by a short, steep, initially grassy scramble whilst avoiding some crags to the left. Once established on the ridge, fine views down to the twin lochans (Dubh Lochain) can be enjoyed. Follow the ridge upwards on grass and numerous pockets of sound rock. Towards the top, there is an extensive area of rocky slabs which is not quite at a steep enough angle for scrambling but is enjoyable nevertheless. The actual summit is the easternmost of two small cairns about 50m apart. The view eastwards to the head of Loch Hourn and the wild mountains beyond is exceptionally fine while the rugged Knoydart peaks beckon to the south with the Munro of Ladhar Bheinn dominating the scene to the south-west.

Although it is rough going, the traverse of Druim Fada out to the western top of Sgurr Mor and beyond is a grand romp and does justice to the mountain. However, it should be pointed out that the ridge itself is a convoluted crest of false summits, lochans and gullies which would be tricky to navigate in misty conditions. In fine weather it is a continually interesting route with the saw-toothed Cuillin of Skye forming a suitable backdrop to the west. Continue for a kilometre beyond Point 614 with its shattered triangulation pillar, before descending north down a grassy spur to the bridge over the Arnisdale River.

Druim Fada could also be climbed from Kinloch Hourn to the east where an excellent path leads up the east ridge of Carn nan Caorach, the easternmost top of the ridge. If transport is not a problem, the ideal solution is a complete traverse of the ridge beginning at

Kinloch Hourn and ending at Corran. Note that the Glen Arnisdale track leads eventually to Kinloch Hourn, part of which is used in the approach to Druim Fada from the east.

**Beinn Clachach** (Stony Hill); *643m*
*OS Sheet 33; GR 885109*
*9km/680m/3–4hrs*
*Map 30*

This wild craggy hill rises to the north of Glen Arnisdale and south-east of the Beinn Sgritheall range. It could conceivably be included in a traverse of this range without too much loss in height. The route described, however, begins near Arnisdale on the coast and is the shortest route to the summit, with the option of including the Corbett of Beinn nan Caorach.

Take the Glen Arnisdale track as far as the bridge over the river, then cut across the field on a vague path to reach an excellent stalkers' track which ascends the western slopes of Beinn Clachach and eventually into Coire Chorsalain, the corrie between Beinn Clachach and Beinn nan Caorach. Shortly after some obvious zigzags but before the track enters the corrie proper, leave the track and climb the craggy west shoulder of the mountain. This is quite steep initially, but levels off at around 400m. Beyond this point, the angle again steepens considerably in a tier of slabbed crags interspersed with

*Beinn Clachach from Glen Arnisdale*

deep heather, and care should be taken on this section. A cairn at the top of this part is not the true summit, which lies 1km beyond along a wide ridge. The actual summit boasts a tiny cairn just north of a small lochan, and on a sun-drenched day is a marvellous spot to while away a lazy hour, with the possibility of a dip in the lochan.

The easiest return route is to descend the northern spur to the bealach between Beinn Clachach and Beinn nan Caorach and follow the path west through Coire Chorsalain. However, if time is not pressing and fitness permits, the Corbett of Bheinn nan Caorach can be ascended from the bealach by its prominent east ridge. This latter peak provides excellent views and is easily descended on its south-western flank. This gives a satisfying round of Coire Chorsalain.

Beinn Clachach can also be climbed from Kinloch Hourn to the east via Glean Dubh Lochain, but this is an altogether much longer proposition.

**Beinn a' Chapuill** (Hill of the Horse); *759m*
*OS Sheet 33; GR 835148*
*12km/710m/4–6hrs*
*Map 30*

Beinn a' Chapuill is essentially the northern outlier of the isolated Munro of Beinn Sgritheall and as such could well be included in a traverse of this Munro. It is, however, a distinctive peak in its own right and throws out a long and narrow eastern ridge which provides a suitable means of ascent. The actual named summit on the map at a height of 742m is not the true summit which lies nearly a kilometre to the south-east.

Begin at the end of the public road in Gleann Beag at Balvraid where a track can be followed north of the river to a small suspension bridge at Strath a' Chomair. Cross the bridge and gain the foot of the east ridge which is 3km long and rises gradually at first, but becomes steeper around the 450m contour. The route is steep and is characterised by grass and a little rock, but with precipitous crags on the north (right) side.

The summit of the mountain is an extensive area of knolls and lochans but the highest point is conveniently placed to the left of the first small lochan, on a knoll where there is also a cairn. Note that the summit of this hill can be very confusing in mist. From the top, grand views can be had of the wild and rocky northern aspect of Beinn Sgritheall, which makes an ideal next objective given time and inclination.

However, the described route descends the hill by the route of ascent to regain the track in Gleann Beag. Note that it is not advisable to make a shortcut by attempting to leave the ridge early and crossing the river lower down, as the river flows through a deep wooded gorge at this point which, from past experience, is fairly suicidal! The ideal longer expedition from Balvraid would be a continuous traverse of Beinn a' Chapuill, Beinn Sgritheall and Beinn na h-Eaglaise, and descending by Druim nan Bo – a Munro, a Corbett and a Graham in one outing; but this would make for a long day.

**Biod an Fhithich** (Point of the Raven); *644 m*
*OS Sheet 33; GR 950147*
*6km/600m/2–3hrs*
*Map 30*

This little hill on the west side of Glen Shiel is completely dominated by the striking Munro known as The Saddle to its south-west, and by the Five Sisters of Kintail across the glen to the north-east. Not surprisingly, it gives unrivalled views of both these ranges but in particular of The Saddle and its fabled Forcan Ridge, which is seen in profile. Biod an Fhithich is unlikely to be climbed purely for its own sake but rather as a precursor to an ascent of The Saddle and its associated tops. In fact, one of the finest high-level horseshoe circuits in Scotland begins at Shiel Bridge, ascends the long A'Mhuing Ridge onto Biod an Fhithich, traverses The Saddle and its six Tops via the Forcan Ridge, and descends to Loch Coire nan Crogachan from where a path can be followed back to the starting point. The Corbett of Sgurr Mhic Bharraich could also be thrown in for good measure! The route described below, however, is a basic ascent and descent of the peak from Glen Shiel.

Begin at the point on the road where a good stalkers' path climbs the eastern slopes of Meallan Odhar and traverses right to reach the col between Biod an Fhithich and Meallan Odhar. This is the usual start for the ascent of The Saddle. Take the path to this col and then ascend Biod an Fhithich easily by its south ridge, giving a further height gain of about 150m. The narrow summit has a small cairn and, as already mentioned, is a superb viewpoint. The hill also receives few visitors as it is just off the main 'trade route' to The Saddle, and this is a part of its charm.

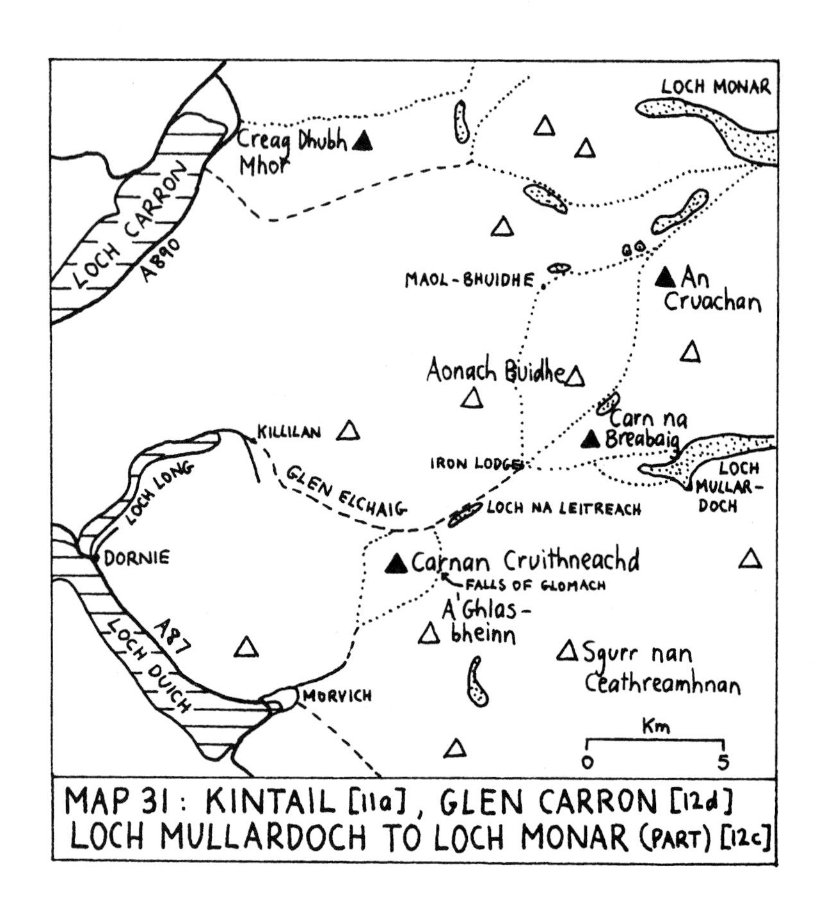


MAP 31: KINTAIL [11a], GLEN CARRON [12d] LOCH MULLARDOCH TO LOCH MONAR (PART) [12c]

# SECTION 11

# *Kintail and Glen Affric to Loch Ness*

**Carnan Cruithneachd** (Wheat Cairn); *729m*
*OS Sheets 25, 33; GR 994258*
*9km/680m/4–5hrs*
*Map 31*

---

This retiring but shapely mountain is a hidden gem whose modest height compared to surrounding Munros and Corbetts is out of all proportion to its magnificent position and character. It stands 2km west of the much-visited Falls of Glomach and could easily be combined with a visit to the falls to make a memorable Highland day. In just 1km, its northern slopes drop sharply for over 2,000ft to Glen Elchaig, where the pointed profile of the mountain is seen to its best advantage, especially from the vicinity of Loch na Leitreach.

The normal walking route to the Falls of Glomach begins at a parking area a few kilometres up Strath Croe and this provides an ideal starting point for this hill. Once established on the forestry track leading from the parking area, a left fork should be taken at GR 984230 which eventually ascends through the forest to a gate at GR 983241. From there, a good path leads northwards to the broad bealach between Carnan Cruithneachd and Beinn Bhreac. By this point, the rocky profile of the hill will be seen to good advantage and some scrambling opportunities are available on countless crags. A line to the left offers the best scrambling and a large crag near the first false summit gives a superb climb by its left-hand edge. Feral goats and deer are common on this hill, and with a bit of luck both may be spotted. The actual summit consists of a small cairn perched on the edge of a grassy/mossy mound and is an absolutely stunning viewpoint. The glorious vista up Glen Elchaig to Loch na Leitreach and the remote mountains beyond is perhaps the finest view, but all directions offer marvellous panoramas and it is quite a wrench to have to leave this magnificent stance.

Rather than return the same way it makes sense to descend the eastern ridge of the hill for a short distance before making a beeline south-east to reach the main Glomach Falls path at the Bealach na Sroine. If a visit to the falls is to be included, then it is best to continue along the crest of the east ridge for 2km before a short, steep descent to the falls path at GR 017623. Note that the above distance/ascent/time information does not include this visit to the Falls. From the Bealach na Sroine, the path hugs the side of the steep corrie and will take you to the forest track which leads back to the carpark.

The other obvious approach route to this mountain is via Glen Elchaig, but this is a much longer proposition as cars are not allowed up this glen. However, a bike would be an obvious advantage.

*Descending Caisteal Liath on the summit ridge of Suilven* (Section 16a)

*Looking north-west from the summit of Ben Stack (the most northerly Graham)* (Section 16b)

*Cruach Choireadail and Corra-bheinn from Loch Scridain (Mull)* (Section 17c)

*Looking to Ben More from Ben Buie (Mull)* (Section 17c)

*The Cuillin from Belig (Skye)* (Section 17e)

*Beinn Dearg Mhor from Marsco (Skye)* (Section 17e)

*Clisham and Uisgnaval Mor (Harris)* (Section 17f)

*View of Carnan Cruithneachd from near Iron Lodge*

**Beinn a' Mheadhoin** (Middle Hill);
*610m*
*OS Sheet 25; GR 218255*
*5km/380m/1–2hrs*
*Map 32*

---

This hill is one of only a handful of Grahams whose height is almost exactly on the 2,000ft contour, and since the starting height is nearly 800ft, the ascent is very quick. Beinn a' Mheadhoin occupies a strategic position at the entrance to Glen Affric and stands immediately north of the loch of the same name – Loch Beinn a' Mheadhoin. Its height, position and ease of access are all conducive to a summer evening's climb, when the setting sun beyond Loch Affric and the Munro giants of the west provides a fitting climax at the summit.

Cars can be parked just before the bridge at the end of the public road at GR 215243. Follow the track which winds round the edge of a forestry plantation, the walker's trade route for the Munros of Toll Creagach and Tom a' Choinich. After about a kilometre, you will reach the end of the trees. Now break off to the right on a vague all-terrain vehicle track which, you will find, fades out during the ascent. The summit area contains a small lochan with a cairn just before it, but the cairn at the actual summit is perched on a small crag beyond the lochan and looks out over the broad eastern shoulder of the hill. The view to the west is particularly fine, especially up wild

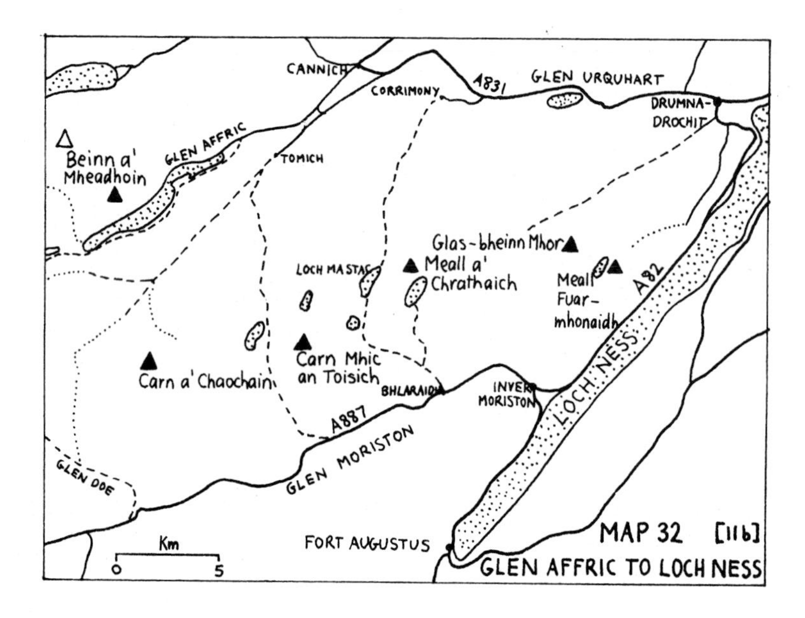


Gleann nam Fiadh, which is surrounded by a clutch of Munros, and to Loch Affric and the hills of the west. Descend by the same route.

**Carn a' Chaochain** (Cairn of the Streamlet); *706m*
*OS Sheet 34; GR 235177*
*10km/450m/3–5hrs*
*Map 32*

This is the highest of the assortment of small heathery hills lying between Glen Moriston and Glen Affric. As such, it is an excellent viewpoint for this unfrequented lochan-studded area, but more so for the Affric giants to the north-west. Any approach from Glen Moriston to the south is long and fairly tedious, and therefore the northerly approach from Guisachan Forest is described. This is a shorter approach but it will require the use of OS maps 25 and 26.

From the A831 road near Cannich, drive up the minor road to Tomich which begins at the bridge over the River Glass. From Tomich, follow the signs to Plodda Falls passing Hilton Lodge *en route.* A carpark exists for visitors to the Falls but it is possible to drive on beyond this point along the forestry track to Cougie. Just before the track bends north to cross the bridge to Cougie a fire-break heads up to the left. (The map indicates a path here but it does not appear to exist.) Follow the fire-break up to the edge of the forest at around 450m. Cross a deer fence and head directly across peaty moorland to the Bealach Feith na Gamhna, the col below the prominent north-east ridge of Carn a' Chaochain. Ascend the ridge to an obvious cairn on the skyline and continue over a second false summit to

*The Affric hills from the summit of Carn a' Chaochain*

the triangulation pillar. The true summit is 2m higher and lies almost 500m south with little drop in height.

The pyramidal summit of Sgurr nan Conbhairean stands out well to the south-west but, as already mentioned, the Affric Munros arrest the eye to the north-west. Due to the profusion of false summits, Carn a' Chaochain is not a hill to be climbed in misty conditions. A cold clear winter's day is ideal when the higher peaks adopt an Alpine splendour. Return by the route of ascent.

**Meall a' Chrathaich** (Shaking Hill?); *679m*
**Carn Mhic an Toisich** (Macintosh Hill); *678m*
*OS Sheets 26, 34; GR 360220, 310185*
*26km/720m/7–9hrs*
*Map 32*

---

These two hills are tucked away in the lochan-studded, heather-clad high ground north of Glen Moriston and south of Cannich. They are both relatively nondescript hills but their locality in such a wild and unfrequented part of the Highlands makes their ascent a challenging and rewarding expedition.

The ideal starting point for both hills is in Glen Moriston to the south at the small hamlet of Bhlaraidh, where a good track winds its way steeply up the hill through birch forest and sitka plantation. There is a locked gate at Bhlaraidh but a bike would be useful for the initial section of the track. After about 1½km, take a left fork over a bridge and follow this to open hillside past Bhlaraidh Reservoir and eventually to Loch Liath. The summit of Carn Mhic an Toisich lies about 3km west-south-west of this point along a vague heathery ridge crossing the minor top of Carn na Caorach *en route.* The summit is situated at the north-eastern end of a well-defined ridge.

Retrace your steps to the track and continue north to its termination at Loch ma Stac, which is on OS Sheet 26. From here the summit of Meall a' Chrathaich lies just over 2km away in a north-easterly direction over fairly boggy ground initially. Traverse a minor top at 630m before the final short ascent to the summit ridge which is topped by a triangulation pillar. The true wild nature of the terrain can be well appreciated from this vantage point, particularly to the north-east where myriad small lochans nestling in rugged heather moorland are a fisherman's paradise. The large loch to the south-east of the hill gives the hill its name. A return to Bhlaraidh is best effected by the route of ascent, though it is possible to reach the track which ends at the southern shore of Loch a' Chrathaich, following this back to the starting point to give a good circuit.

Meall a' Chrathaich can also be reached from Corrimony to the north, where a delightfully scenic track can be followed for 9km to near its termination at the northern end of Loch ma Stac where a large fishing/shooting lodge is situated. A small bothy at GR 358269 is useful for shelter or an overnight stay. An ideal way to tackle both hills is to begin at Corrimony and end at Bhlaraidh, although this obviously involves a kind driver. Carn Mhic an Toisich can also be climbed using the track beginning at Dundreggan some 8km south-west of Bhlaraidh on the Glen Moriston road; but this follows electricity pylons all the way and is not aesthetically pleasing.

**Meall Fuar-mhonaidh** (Hill of the Cold Slopes); *699m*
**Glas-bheinn Mhor** (Big Green Hill); *651m*
*OS Sheet 26; GR 457222, 436231*
*14km/700m/5–6hrs*
*Map 32*

---

Meall Fuar-mhonaidh and its lesser neighbour, Glas-bheinn Mhor, stand roughly halfway along the length of Loch Ness on its western side. Meall Fuar-mhonaidh is undoubtedly the finer of the two hills, being a prominent landmark of the Great Glen. On a clear day, it offers views which encompass the whole 30-mile stretch of Loch Ness. It is a long whale-backed ridge with steep crags on its north-western aspect that drop sharply to the wild waters of Loch nam Breac Dearga. Not surprisingly, it is a popular little hill both with locals and tourists, and a new access path has recently been constructed from Balbeg to the north-east of the hill.

From Drumnadrochit take the minor road just east of Borlum bridge up a series of hairpin bends initially, then levelling out onto high moorland above Loch Ness. Near Balbeg, a rough purpose-built carpark marks the beginning of the walk with numerous signposts displaying 'To the Hill' thereafter. The path, though obvious, is rather disjointed initially with plenty of gates, stiles and fences as it winds its way through a birch wood to emerge on an open heather hillside accompanied by a large white flag. By now the distinctive bulk of the hill begins to dominate the scene and its whale-back ridge is easily reached by crossing a deer fence stile which is by another large white flag. These flags may well provide useful guides in summer but in winter their colour renders them pretty useless.

The north-east ridge is followed easily on a well-worn path with a few steep rises to the top. The summit area is a confusion of four different cairns, the highest point being the cairn furthest away. A short distance away a smaller cairn provides a better view of Loch Ness and the Great Glen – a grand spot for a bite to eat and to contemplate the vista.

From the summit it is possible to descend more or less directly north-west to Loch nam Breac Dearga, but from personal experience this is probably best avoided! In wet or windy conditions the northern crags of Meall Fuar-mhonaidh are not the safest place to be. Instead, continue south-west along the crest of the ridge for about 1km before turning right and reaching the south-western end of the loch. Nestling under the looming crags, Loch nam Breac Dearga has a wild, remote atmosphere and is usually sheltered from any prevailing wind.

The summit of Glas-bheinn Mhor is only 1½km from here in a north-westerly direction. Another small lochan is passed *en route*. A cairn is perched on a small crag with the trig point about 50m beyond. It is strange that this smaller summit with more restricted views steals the trigpoint from Meall Fuar-mhonaidh.

A return route to Balbeg is best made by heading directly for the northern end of Loch nam Breac Dearga before cutting through the gap between the northern aspect of Meall Fuar-mhonaidh and an obvious knoll. A rising traverse then leads back onto the north-east ridge of the hill and the path.

If a return to the starting point is not necessary, a pleasant variation is to head north from the summit of Glas-bheinn Mhor and to cross the River Coiltie to reach the Glen Coiltie track. This can be followed for about 7km to the minor road near Clunemore. A slightly shorter alternative is to make for Loch Dubh 4km north-east of the summit, and then to follow a path to Dhivach Lodge which is in roughly the same area.

MAP 33: GLEN CANNICH [12a], STRATH-CONAN [12b], L.MULLARDOCH - L.MONAR(PART) [12c]
Sgurr a' Mhuilinn
Meallan nan Uan
Meall na Faochaig
STRATH CONAN
LOCH MEIG
A832
MARYBANK
LOCH BEANNACH-ARAIN
Carn na Coinnich
Bac an Eich
Beinn Mheadhoin
ORRIN RESERVOIR
An Sidhean
Sgurr Fhuar-thuill
Beinn a' Bha'ach Ard
LOCH MONAR
Beinn na Muice
GLEN STRATHFARRAR
STRUY
Sgorr na Diollaid
Carn Gorm
GLEN CANNICH
LOCH MULLARDOCH
CANNICH
A831
Km
0
5

# SECTION 12

# *Glen Cannich to Glen Carron*

**Carn Gorm** (Blue Hill); *677m*
*OS Sheet 26; GR 328355*
*8km/530m/3–4hrs*
*Map 33*

Standing at the entrance to Glen Cannich and Glen Strathfarrar this little hill is rather overshadowed by its more alluring Munro neighbours to the west. It could be combined with an ascent of the Corbett of Sgorr na Diollaid lying 5km west and which is on OS Sheet 25; but the route to be described is the shortest and begins in Glen Cannich.

About 4km up Glen Cannich, take the track across the bridge which goes to Craskie. Avoid the house if possible by leaving the track at the point where it bends right and cross a small stream to regain the track higher up. Above this point, go through a deer fence by a gate to reach open hillside. Climb directly up in deep heather by following the intermittent deer tracks and stalkers' paths until you are level with the top of the forest plantation to the right. At this point, a prominent tall cairn should be visible on the skyline above and to the right, and this is the next objective.

From the cairn, the subsidiary top at GR 315351 can either be traversed or bypassed on the west. Either option leads naturally down to Loch Coir' an Uillt Ghiubhais which nestles peacefully between the top mentioned and the main summit. An easy ascent of about 130m must then be made to reach the top of Carn Gorm. The summit itself is the south-western extremity of a string of tops ending at Carn Moraig about 4km to the north-east – and the complete traverse of this ridge would make a pleasant outing. Return by the route of ascent.

**Carn na Coinnich** (Cairn of the Moss); *673m*
*OS Sheet 26; GR 324510*
*10km/580m/2½–4hrs*
*Map 33*

Carn na Coinnich is the highest of a series of small hills forming a vague twisting ridge between Strathconon and Orrin Reservoir. Their relatively low height and undistinguished nature ensures that they see few visitors, but many would see this as all the more reason to pay them a visit.

The shortest approach is from Strathconon to the north from where a path leads almost all the way to the summit. Just before the public road in Strathconon across the River Meig, a track forks off west and cars can be parked in a small area on the left about 1km along the track. Continue on foot along the track and take the sharp turn left before the house, where a grassy track climbs open hillside past a forest. About 500m beyond the forest, this minor track meets another track where a left turn should be taken. This track soon degenerates into a stalkers' path which climbs the heathery hillside between the craggy north face of Creag Ghaineamhach and Meall a' Bhogair Mor. Follow this path upwards to the left of a burn and you will eventually reach a boggy area at around the 600m mark. The triangulation pillar on Carn na Coinnich is plainly visible from this point. Leave the path at any suitable place and gain the broad, mossy north ridge of the hill from where it is a pleasant walk to the final rocky cone and pillar.

The twin Corbetts of Meallan nan Uan and Sgurr a' Mhuilinn are well seen from the summit rising to the north-west. The above information is for a return by the route of ascent, but a circular variation can be made by heading north-west, then west to reach another stalkers' path which descends to near Balnacraig (on OS Sheet 25). Another track can then be followed to Dalbreac Lodge and the starting point.

**Beinn Mheadhoin** (Middle Hill); *665m*
*OS Sheet 25; GR 258477*
*9km/520m/2–4hrs*
*Map 33*

North of the big glens of Affric, Cannich and Strathfarrar is the lesser known Strathconon with a clutch of Corbetts and Grahams at its head – but no Munros. Strathconon is a long glen to drive down, being 17 miles from Marybank to Scardroy. Beinn Mheadhoin and the next Graham, Meall na Faochaig, are both easily climbed from near Inverchoran, a farm about 5km from the end of the public road. Beinn Mheadhoin has few distinguishing features other than fine views from its

*The summit of Carn na Coinnich*

rolling summit.

Walk along the private track to Inverchoran and cross the main burn by a footbridge which gives access to the Gleann Chorainn track. This is the normal route to the Corbett of Bac an Eich, which could be included with Beinn Mheadhoin in an extended outing. A few hundred metres from the farm take another minor track which steadily climbs round the north-eastern slopes of Creagan a' Chaorainn. Beinn Mheadhoin is not visible from this point but Meall na Faochaig and the Corbetts of Meallan nan Uan and Sgurr a' Mhuilinn are well seen rising up on the north side of the glen. Once round the east side of Creagan a' Chaorainn, the main objective comes into view and its steep, heathery eastern slopes are easily climbed from the track.

The summit area contains several false tops but the true top is a prominent little crag surmounted by a boulder cairn. The nearest high summit lying across Gleann Chorainn is Bac an Eich, but the finest view is undoubtedly southwards to the serpentine switchback crest of the four Munros lying north of Glen Strathfarrar. The descent could be varied by dropping down steep slopes to Gleann Chaorainn but the above information is for a return by the route of ascent.

**Meall na Faochaig** (Hill of the Shell?); *680m*
*OS Sheet 25; GR 257525*
*6km/530m/2–3hrs*
*Map 33*

---

This hill and the previous one (Beinn Mheadhoin) can easily be ascended in the same day from the start of the track to Inverchoran Farm in Strathconon. Less than 500m west of this point, a good track climbs steadily north-west for about 1km before doubling back to reach the col between Creag Iucharaidh and Meall na Faochaig. Reach this point before ascending the obvious south-eastern spur leading to the main summit ridge of the hill. The actual summit lies just over 500m to the east and has a small cairn.

The north side of the hill drops steeply down to Gleann Meinich, and the Corbett of Meallan nan Uan lies prominently beyond with the craggy bluff of Creag Ghlas adding to the wild setting. The view west on a clear day is outstanding, with Liathach and the other Torridon peaks forming a dramatic and distinctive horizon over 30km away. This hill almost begs to be climbed on a late summer's evening when the setting sun adds further to the mountainous western skyline. Descend by the route of ascent.

**Beinn na Muice** (Hill of the Pigs); *695m*
*OS Sheet 25; GR 218402*
*8km/550m/3–4hrs*
*Map 33*

This fine little hill occupies a strategic position above the eastern end of Loch Morar at the head of Glen Strathfarrar. Even with permission being given to drive up this glen to the foot of the hill, it still has a deliciously remote feel and is an incomparable viewpoint for one of the wildest parts of the Scottish Highlands. Beinn na Muice is unlikely to be climbed purely for its own sake but rather as a prelude to the string of tops to the north which connect with the Munro of Sgurr Fhuar-thuill. The complete round of the corrie containing Loch Toll a' Mhuic and returning via Creag Ghorm a' Bhealaich and its broad south ridge is a classic expedition, and is highly recommended. The route to be described below, however, is an ascent of the Graham only and traverses the summit ridge from east to west.

Munro-baggers who have traversed the four Munros to the north of Glen Strathfarrar, beginning with Sgurr Fhuar-thuill, will know that permission to drive up the glen has to be obtained from the keeper who resides at the cottage by the locked gate near Struy. The current position is that between the end of March and the end of October a permit must be obtained at the keeper's house. At all other times, access by car is by prior arrangement only, and the keeper can be contacted by telephone on (01463) 761260. The glen is also normally closed to vehicles on a Tuesday. It should also be noted that Glen Strathfarrar has a large population of deer and sensitive deer management is of prime concern. Culling can take place at any time during the winter months and access to the hills may be restricted on particular days.

Drive (or cycle) to the start of the track which follows the west bank of the Allt Toll a' Mhuic (GR 224392). Walk up this track for just over 1km until an obvious waterfall comes into view. Leave the track and gain the heathery east ridge of Beinn na Muice, which is interspersed with rocky outcrops. The dramatic rocky prow of its big brother, Sgurr na Muice, is very prominent to the north and this peak is arguably the finest in the immediate vicinity – including the four Munros. Its massive eastern face is lined with steep crags and drops magnificently to the dark brooding waters of Loch Toll a' Mhuic nestling in the heart of the corrie. Sgurr na Muice at 891m fails to reach Corbett status as it does not possess the required 150m drop between itself and the Munro Top of Sgurr na Fearstaig to the north. According to the blurb in the introduction, it would be classed as a Lesser Corbett. Whatever it is, it is certainly worth climbing!

The summit ridge of Beinn na Muice is a succession of craggy tops but the true summit has a small cairn with stunning views west along Loch Monar to a host of remote Munros and other peaks. But the admiration of this beauty is also tinged with sadness when it is remembered that Loch Monar is a man-made watery grave to many remote Highland dwellings which existed prior to the Second World War. For those contemplating the round of the corrie via Sgurr na Muice and Sgurr Fhuar-thuill the day will have hardly begun. If the aim is to climb the Graham only then the descent can be varied by continuing west along the ridge and dropping down to Monar Lodge where the road can be followed for 3km back to the starting point.

**An Cruachan** (The Stack); *706m*
**Carn na Breabaig** (Hill of the Small Peak); *678m*
*OS Sheet 25; GR 093358, 066301*
*52km/1,020m/8–12hrs (bike)*
*Map 31*

In the heart of the vast tract of mountainous terrain between Loch Mullardoch and Loch Monar lies An Cruachan, arguably the remotest of all Grahams and a true test of determination to reach from any direction. Unless the ascent is included as part of an overnight camping expedition or stay in a bothy, the only feasible approach route is Glen Elchaig to the south-west. This also makes the ascent of Carn na Breabaig at the head of the glen a viable proposition, and it can be included either on the outward or return journey from An Cruachan. The use of a bike is highly recommended from near Killilan to Iron Lodge, and the lack of it would add at least another 3 hours to an already lengthy schedule.

Cars can be parked at a recently constructed carpark just beyond the turn-off at Camus-luinie, used mainly by hillwalkers and visitors to the Falls of Glomach. Follow the excellent tarmac road through Killilan to Faddoch, where it becomes a pleasant track, leading up Glen Elchaig, with steep rugged slopes rising on both sides. The lower part of the glen is dominated by the shapely peak of Carnan Cruithneachd, another Graham described in Section 11a. Carry on to Loch na Leitreach; and, eventually, after 14km the remote outpost of Iron Lodge. Here the main track ends and three footpaths head off towards and through three separate glens. One heads north between the Corbetts of Aonach Buidhe and Faochaig to the remote MBA bothy of Maol-bhuidhe. One heads east to Loch Mullardoch, and the third heads north-west over a high pass to the intended objective of An Cruachan, whose summit is still 10km away.

Leave your bikes and follow the path north-east from Iron Lodge, forking off to the right after a few hundred metres to cross the An Crom-allt. The path climbs steadily up the north bank of the Allt na Doire Gairbhe where grand views can be enjoyed down Glen Elchaig to Carnan Cruithneachd. Carn na Breabaig rises up to the right from here and its ascent is probably best left until the return journey. At the 400m

*An Cruachan from near Loch Mhoicean*

mark the path levels off and becomes significantly boggy, as it passes by the beautifully wild Loch Mhoicean. Shortly beyond the northern end of the loch, a cairn marks the descent from the pass, and An Cruachan is seen to advantage on the skyline, although it is still 4km away.

The path from here on deteriorates significantly and beyond the point where it crosses the Allt Coire nan Each it is often little more than a vague furrow in the grass. Once established in this glen, the feeling of remoteness is absolute. No human habitation exists in any direction for at least 20km. The next step is to reach the wide col south of An Cruachan by a rising traverse from the path. From here, a stiff climb of 200m on steep slopes of grass and boulders leads to the well-constructed and prominent summit cairn. It is worth noting that An Cruachan contains some unusual rock in relation to the area and for this reason is of interest to geologists.

An Cruachan is literally surrounded on all sides by Munros and Corbetts but this only serves to accentuate the very fine views from its summit. Lurg Mhor and its companion, Bidein a' Choire Sheasgaich, rise to the north-west, while the undulating crest of the Loch Mullardoch group dominates the view to the south-east. Beyond the little subsidiary top of Beinn Bheag to the north-east, Loch Monar's 'tide marks' are backed by a jostling array of peaks and ridges.

Return by the same route, but shortly after passing the southern end of Loch Mhoicean, leave the path to cross the Allt na doire Gairbhe to gain the grassy northern slopes of Carn na Breabaig. A climb of some 270m leads to the sprawling summit area and the actual top consists of a few stones on a craggy outcrop. The descent can be varied by heading south-west down a broad grassy spur which levels off at 500m before descending steeply to the path leading from Iron Lodge to Loch Mullardoch. This zigzags down easily to Iron Lodge where your bikes can be retrieved. The run back down Glen Elchaig is a pleasant change from walking and forms a delightful end to a tiring but satisfying day.

**Creag Dubh Mhor** (Big Black Rock); *612m*
*OS Sheet 25; GR 982404*
*15km/600m/4–6hrs*
*Map 31*

This hill is the highest point of a complex area of knolls and lochans lying east of Loch Carron and west of the Loch Monar high country. It is seldom climbed but is well served by an excellent stalkers' path passing to its north *en route* to the bothy at Bearnais. The route described below uses this path on the ascent and returns by another path, making a fine circular expedition in wild unfrequented country.

Begin at the small hamlet of Achintee just south of Strathcarron. Follow the signs indicating 'Footpath' until 50m beyond the first gate. At this point, fork off to the left along an indistinct path which follows a fence and crosses a stream further on. The path climbs a heathery hillock and thereafter keeps to the south bank of the River Taodail where the odd Scots pine makes a fine foreground to An Ruadh-stac and Maol Chean-dearg rising prominently beyond Strathcarron. After almost 2km, take a left fork which crosses a stream and gradually gains height to follow another stream with a waterfall.

By this point the north-western crags of the hill will be very distinct with a grassy break to their left. Either leave the path at a suitable point and ascend this break in the cliffs or continue for another 500m before ascending the northern slopes of the hill to reach a small subsidiary top. A further short ascent leads to a false summit which is separated from the true summit by a short dip. The actual summit has a small cairn on a rocky outcrop. On a clear day there are fine views east to the remote Munro of Bidein a' Choire Sheasgaich.

The next objective is the stalkers' path which lies beyond Loch an Fheoir and which is nearly 3km from the summit. Leave the summit and head in a roughly south-westerly direction by weaving a way through the maze of small lochans which lie west of the top. This would be confusing terrain in misty conditions. Take a more or less direct line to Loch an Fheoir and reach the path beyond its western extremity. This is easily followed back to Achintee and the start point. A quicker return route is to head directly to Loch nan Creadha, avoiding the girdle of crags on their western side, and then picking up a subsidiary path which leads to the path used on the approach.

# SECTION 13

# *Applecross, Coulin and Torridon*



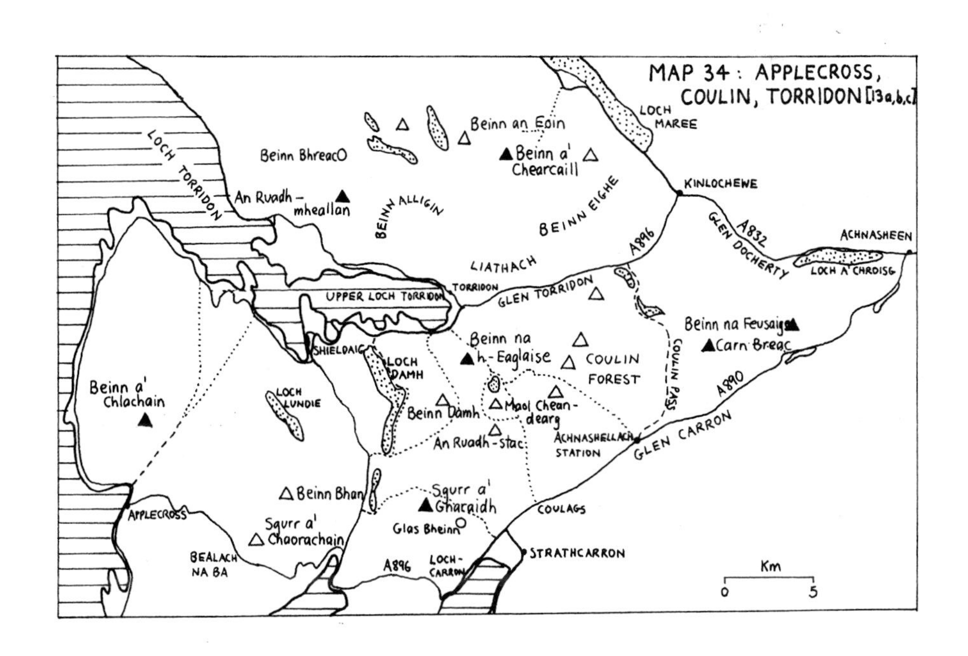

**Beinn a' Chlachain** (Hill of the Stepping-Stones); *626m*
*OS Sheet 24; GR 724490*
*12km/610m/3½–5hrs*
*Map 34*

---

This fine, flat-topped hill lies north-east of Applecross Bay and its continuously steep south-western slopes drop sharply to Srath Maol Chaluim, a pleasantly wooded glen containing the Hartfield Adventure School. The hill gives grand views of Raasay and Skye. Any ascent of the hill is either short and steep or long and gradual. The following describes a short and steep ascent followed by a long relaxing descent with seaward views.

Cars can be driven down Srath Maol Chaluim and parked near the Hartfield Adventure School. Just beyond the school, cross a field and a fence and follow the edge of the forestry plantation by a drystane wall. Beyond the forest, the angle steepens considerably and a gradual traverse upwards and to the right is the easiest line. Any crags can be avoided by grassy gullies and terraces. At a height of around 500m, the angle relents to a broad ridge of numerous knolls and lochans. Head in a roughly north-easterly direction on sandstone outcrops and boggy ground, passing several lochans *en route*, one of which is situated just below the final knoll containing the summit triangulation pillar surrounded by a ringed cairn.

The best descent is to follow the long, south-westerly ridge for over 4km, which becomes rather boggy and tussocky in the lower reaches. A good path can then be taken to Cruarg and the coastal road from where the Srath Maol Chaluim road can be followed back to the start point.

**Sgurr a' Gharaidh** (Rocky Peak of the Dyke); *732m*
*OS Sheet 24; GR 884443*
*8km/680m/3–5hrs*
*Map 34*

---

This is an exceptionally fine craggy mountain situated north of Lochcarron, and often overlooked in favour of the Applecross hills to the west and the Coulin hills to the north-east. It possesses much more bare rock than the OS map suggests and lies in the heart of some beautifully wild and complex terrain. Sgurr a' Gharaidh has much untapped scrambling potential, especially on its steep northern flanks.

The most convenient approach begins on the Lochcarron-Shieldaig road (A986) at Loch an Loin. Follow the track round the southern shore of the loch to the cottage, beyond which the track should be left via a gate. Ascend through a field and another gate to reach open heath. A fairly recent continuation of the Loch an Loin track makes a steep ascent of the hillside some distance further on but degenerates into an all-terrain vehicle track soon after this and is not recommended.

The west ridge of Sgurr a' Gharaidh soon becomes evident and is characterised by a succession of craggy promontories and knolls offering superb scrambling opportunities in the upper reaches. The rock is fairly sound with a profusion of ledges and deep holds. A drystane dyke crosses the ridge higher up and is possibly the source of the mountain's name.

Just before the final summit pyramid, you will pass a delightful little lochan, one of many in the vicinity of the hill. A final rocky ascent of about 150m leads to the flat summit area which has a substantial cairn. Better views can be obtained by moving across to the edge of the steep northern slopes which appear to be marginally higher than the cairn. During the ascent, the craggy eastern corries and buttresses of the Applecross hills would have dominated the view, but now the eye will be drawn to the east across wild country peppered with small lochans and the imposing cliff of Glas Bheinn plunging down to Bealach a' Ghlas-chnoic.

A grand but longer excursion would be to continue on east beyond Sgurr a' Gharaidh past a collection of lochans to reach the summit of Glas Bheinn which lies just off OS Sheet 24. Steep slopes could then be descended to Tullich (OS Sheet 25) and the A896 road at the head of Loch Carron. This would of course incur some transport problems. Another possibility is to make use of the stalkers' path which connects Tuillich to Loch an Loin via Bealach a' Ghlas-chnoic and this is a fine walk in its own right. The above statistics are based on a return by the route of ascent but the aforementioned path could also be used

*The final summit cone of Sgurr a' Gharaidh*

following a steep descent of the northern slopes.

**Carn Breac** (Speckled Hill); *678m*
**Beinn na Feusaige** (Bearded Hill); *625m*
*OS Sheet 25; GR 045530, 093542*
*17km/800m/4–6hrs*
*Map 34*

Both these rounded heathery hills lying to the east of the Coulin Pass are in stark contrast to their higher and more rugged neighbours to the west and south. They nevertheless provide a highly satisfying day's hillwalking when perhaps the Munros and Corbetts are immersed in cloud. Having said this, the view north-west from the summit of Carn Breac is truly dramatic and an extremely poor day does not do justice to these neglected outliers.

The best approach is from the A890 road in Glen Carron where a good stalkers' path begins at the lay-by west of Loch Sgamhain and just east of the bridge over the Allt Coire Crubaidh. Follow the path up the north side of the river which winds its way between two forestry plantations. After about 3km, you will reach a couple of old ruined shielings, and indicated on the map is a fork in the path which climbs up to the foot of the broad north-east ridge of Carn Breac. This fork can be difficult to locate but it is an easy ascent of only 100m to reach this point.

Ascend the wide north-east ridge on short heather and slabs of rock for 2km past a series of cairns and false summits. The upper section of this ridge would be very confusing in mist but the true summit is unmistakable – for there is a stone triangulation pillar surrounded on three sides by a box cairn. To the north-west the twin lochs of Coulin and Clair nestle serenely between wooded slopes and provide an ideal foreground to the Torridon giants of Beinn Eighe and Liathach. Carn Breac is certainly a grand vantage point.

Beinn na Feusaige is the lesser of the two Grahams both in terms of height and in the quality of views from its summit. To reach it requires a 6km ridge walk with an intervening hillock known as Meallan Mhic Iamhair. Retrace your steps down the north-east ridge of Carn Breac to the rather peat-ridden col below this hillock. Climb the hillock and descend eastwards to the little lochan of the same name which lies below the western flank of the final summit. Climb easily to the flat summit of Beinn na Feusaige. Again the summit area of this hill contains a confusing selection of cairns but the actual summit lies about 200m east of the tiny lochan marked on the OS map.

The quickest descent route involves retracing your steps until about halfway down the western slopes before gradually turning south-west down steep heathery slopes to reach the edge of the forest. This leads to the path used on the walk in.

**Beinn na h-Eaglaise** (Mountain of the Church); *736m*
*OS Sheet 25; GR 908523*
*9km/700m/3–4½hrs*
*Map 34*

---

This fine little mountain occupies a wonderfully scenic position in the heart of the wild Torridonian landscape. It lies south-east of Upper Loch Torridon and is surrounded by Munros and Corbetts, any of which could be included with an ascent of this Graham. The route described ascends the Graham only but involves a complete traverse of the hill.

Begin on the A896 road just above the bridge over the Allt Coire Roill where an excellent path starts at a gap in the rhododendron bushes. This path rises up through a magnificent natural pine forest to emerge above the tree-line with glorious views of Beinn Alligin opening up across Loch Torridon. Continue on the path, taking the left fork further on, and cross the Allt Coire Roill where the path makes a rising traverse along the south-western flank of Beinn na h-Eaglaise. The massive mountain directly ahead is the Munro of Maol Chean-dearg. Reach the idyllic little lochan at Drochaid Coire Roill which is the bealach between the Graham and the Corbett of Beinn Damh.

Leave the path here and climb the steep southern slopes of Beinn na h-Eaglaise for about 250m to reach a flat top south-west of the main summit. The actual summit lies about 500m away across an area of small lochans and is easily reached. The summit cairn is a truly marvellous viewpoint on a clear day and gives a fine appreciation of the topography of the Torridon peaks. The sight of Beinn Alligin's curving ridge across the waters of Loch Torridon is one which will stay in the mind for some time. The view south-east to the peaks of the Coulin forest is also very fine.

Descend by the long, curving north-west ridge which offers continually grand views of Upper Loch Torridon especially in the magical light of a West Highland summer evening when the sun is sinking low in the west. Lower down, the ridge becomes less pronounced with much deep heather. You will eventually reach the path used on the ascent; follow it to the start point. Note that this route description involves OS Sheet 24 for much of the route.

This hill could also be ascended by using the Annat path which winds round the northern side of the hill to traverse the lower eastern slopes. The wide bealach between the Graham and Maol Chean-dearg provides the start of the mountain's eastern spur.

**An Ruadh-mheallan** (The Red Hill); *672m*
*OS Sheet 19, 24; GR 836615*
*5km/420m/3hrs*
*Map 34*

---

This hill could easily be dismissed as a rather lacklustre satellite of its resplendent Munro neighbour, Beinn Alligin, the jewel of Torridon. Certainly from across Upper Loch Torridon it is the graceful sculpted lines of Beinn Alligin which command attention, with An Ruadh-mheallan dwarfed in her shadow to the west. However, despite these obvious initial observations, on closer acquaintance the hill has much to commend it and is an ideal climb when conditions on the higher tops are poor. On a clear day, the views from its summit rival those from any of the other more popular Torridon mountains.

Cars can be parked at the viewpoint on the Diabaig road just beyond Bealach na Gaoithe (Pass of the Winds). From there it is a matter of picking a rather convoluted route through a maze of knolls, crags, bogs and lochans for about 1½km before the real steepness of the hill. *En route* the largest lochan is Loch nan Tri-eileanan or Loch of the Three Islands, which is a good landmark from higher up as it is easy to become disorientated in such confusing terrain.

Pass a small lochan at 500m before the last steep 172m to the summit, which is a large sandstone plinth surmounted by a fair-sized cairn. The name 'Red Hill' is understandably an apt description. Mighty Beinn Alligin dominates the view to the east though it is not seen to best advantage as its fine corries all face the other way. The finest view is undoubtedly to the south and south-east across sparkling Loch Torridon with Beinn Damh and the peaks of the Coulin forest speckling the skyline.

The fine wilderness area to the north-east, with its two remote Corbetts of Baosbheinn and Beinn an Eoin, is a lure for lovers of seclusion, and part of this area can be sampled by continuing on to Beinn Bhreac to the north via the unnamed top at GR 859629. The time and distance given above is based on a return by the same route and an extension to include Beinn Bhreac (not a Graham incidentally) would constitute a full day's outing. The ascent of Beinn Alligin could also be included with An Ruadh-mheallan but this

*The summit of An Ruadh-mheallan*

approach does not really do justice to the mountain.

**Beinn a' Chearcaill** (Mountain of the Girdle); *725m*
*OS Sheet 19; GR 931637*
*12km/700m/3–5hrs*
*Map 34*

---

This fine little hill is situated in a relatively unfrequented corner of the wilds of Torridon and is surrounded by Munro and Corbett giants on all sides. As such, it makes a truly exceptional viewpoint particularly to Slioch, and to the magnificent triple buttress of Beinn Eighe, which lies a short distance to the south. It is strongly recommended to keep the ascent of this hidden gem for a clear sunny day when the grand views can be appreciated.

The most convenient approach begins on the A832 road south of Loch Maree where a good stalkers' track begins near a house and follows Glen Grudie below the eastern slopes of the mountain. This path is marked on the map but the start of it can be quite tricky to find. Follow the path for just over 2km until a small cairn is reached at the start of another path which climbs west into Coire Briste. This secondary path is not shown on the map and is not so well defined as the Glen Grudie stalkers' path. Follow the Coire Briste path for about 1½km to reach the wide col between Beinn a' Chearcaill and its northern outlier of A' Choineach Beag.

The summit of the Graham is still

*Looking to Beinn Eighe from the summit of Beinn a' Chearcaill*

nearly 2km to the south across a gradually rising, broad area of sandstone slabs, heather and small lochans. The whole summit area is of this nature and would create some navigational problems in misty conditions. In addition, steep craggy slopes defend the mountain on all approaches bar the north and this is another reason for only attempting the hill on a clear day. The actual summit is situated at the south-western extremity of the main hill mass and is formed of a massive plinth of sandstone about the size of a hockey pitch, with a good-sized cairn perched on the edge of an almost sheer drop.

The Torridonian architecture of the neighbouring peaks can be well appreciated from this unique vantage point, particularly of Coire Mhic Fhearchair with its triple buttress to the south, and west across wild lochan-studded Srath Lungard to Beinn an Eoin, Beinn Dearg and Beinn Alligin. On the north side of Loch Maree, mighty Slioch dominates the landscape as it has done for much of the ascent.

Descend by the route of ascent, or for a slight variation a return can be made over A' Choineach Beag before descending to the main stalkers' path by its broad north-east ridge.

## SECTION 14

# *Loch Maree to Loch Broom and Garve*

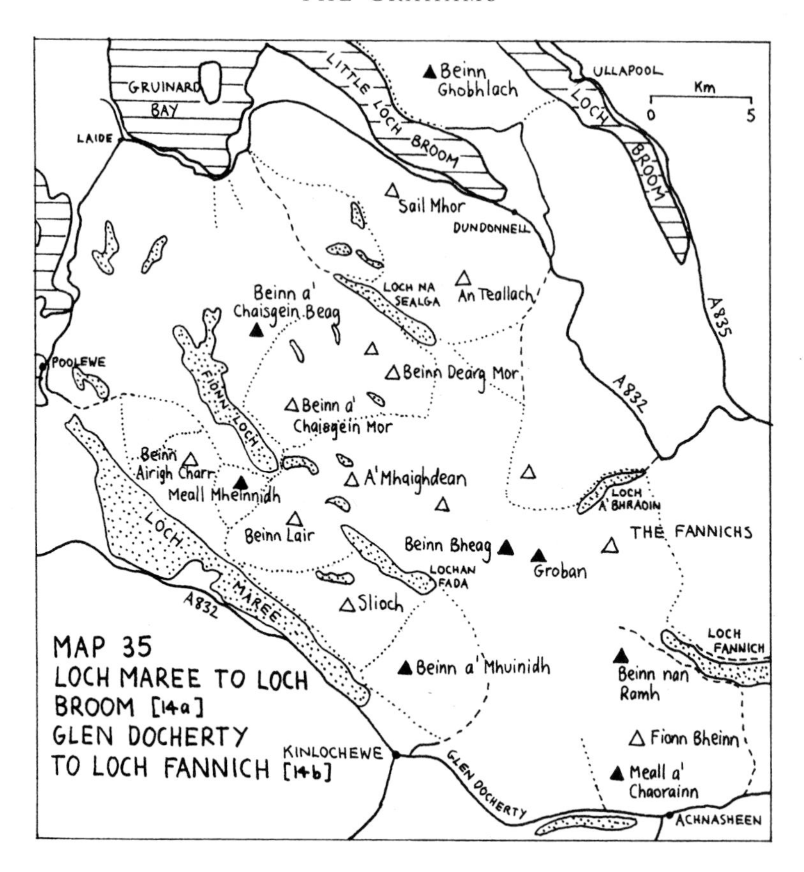


**Beinn a' Mhuinidh** (Mountain of the Heath); *692m*
*OS Sheet 19; GR 032660*
*12km/670m/4–6hrs*
*Map 35*

Somewhat overshadowed by its Munro neighbour of Slioch across Gleann Bianasdail to the north-west, this neglected little hill nevertheless provides an excellent half-day's hillwalking with marvellous views. Beinn a' Mhuinidh is an extensive tilted plateau running north-west to south-south-east with a girdle of almost continuous crags and steep slopes facing to the south-west above Kinlochewe River and to the north-west above Gleann Bianasdail. Although these crags are generally too steep for scrambling, the area around the summit possesses large continuous outcrops of excellent rough gneiss which give pockets of enjoyable scrambling.

The mountain is best climbed from Incheril, near Kinlochewe, where cars can be parked near a farm. The most sporting and scenic route to the summit plateau ascends a heathery spur to the right of the prominent waterfall at GR 024648 which tumbles for 90m over a sheer face. Follow the well-worn path along the north bank of the Kinlochewe

River for about 3km to reach the foot of the spur. Climb up easy slopes through initially deep heather and bracken by following a vague path on the southern side of the stream's course. Higher up the angle steepens and the waterfall is seen to advantage from this point. The Waterfall Buttress was one of the original rock-climbs undertaken on these crags by Glover and Inglis Clark at the end of the last century.

Weave a way through a band of small outcrops above which the angle relents to reveal an upper grassy amphitheatre backed by further cliffs and crags. Go through the obvious gap in these crags to the north-east or enjoy some scrambling on the right-hand quartzite outcrops. This leads to an area of lochans where there is a good view of the final summit pyramid lying 1km to the north and almost 300m higher. Take a fairly direct line to the summit from here, indulging in the odd pocket of super rough scrambling on exposed gneiss. Just below what appears to be the summit is an extensive easy-angled crag which provides a final entertaining scramble. The cairn at the top of this crag is not the true summit, which actually lies 250m to the north-west beyond a small lochan.

Slioch has the appearance of a huge armchair from the 'footstool' of Beinn a' Mhuinidh with its vast eastern corrie and arms of Sgurr Dubh and Sgurr an Tuill Bhain. Beinn Eighe dominates the view to the south-west. Descend the mountain by dropping down easy slopes to the south-east and then curving

*On the ascent of Beinn a' Mhuinidh*

south for nearly 4km across the lochan-strewn plateau to reach the track which follows the Abhainn Bruachaig. This can be easily followed westwards back to Incheril.

**Groban** (Point of Rock); *749m*
**Beinn Bheag** (Little Hill); *668m*
*OS Sheet 19; GR 099709, 086714*
*24km/650m/7–9hrs*
*Map 35*

Together with Meallan Chuaich to the south-east, these two rounded hills form a high-level link between the Fisherfield Forest Munros to the west and the Fannich Munros to the east. Not surprisingly, they are superb vantage points and the view west from Beinn Bheag must rank as a classic in the north-west Highlands. The two Grahams are connected by a high col, the Bealach Gorm, at a height of 470m, and, apart from the long walk in their traverse, is quite straightforward.

The most convenient starting point is from the north-east on the A832 road near Braemore junction, where a track leads in 1km to the eastern end of Loch a' Bhraoin. (This is on OS Sheet 20.) Follow this track down to the boathouse before striking west along the footpath which winds its way along the northern shore of the loch. Continue along the pleasant lochside with Groban and Beinn Bheag rising prominently at the end of the loch. After 5km you will reach the open bothy of Lochivraon. Follow the path south-west until it approaches the river. Cross the river at a suitable spot, which may be quite far upstream if it is in spate. The summit of Groban looks deceptively close from here but there is still a long grind of 2½km up tussocky heathery hillside. Towards the top, the going becomes easier and the summit area is flat and rocky with a small cairn. Beinn Bheag looks little more than a pimple from Groban and hardly worth climbing. However, it would be a shame to omit it as the views from its summit are superior to those from Groban.

From Groban, descend north-west down easy grassy terrain to the rather boggy Bealach Gorm, from whence it is only 200m of ascent to the flat summit of Beinn Bheag. There are two cairns about 100m apart, the true summit being at the most easterly one. However, the west cairn boasts the finest views. Quite the most outstanding features are the long ribbon of Lochan Fada with mighty Slioch dominating its southern side. To the north of Lochan Fada the chaotic jumble of peaks, corries and ridges form the heart of one of the most impressive wilderness areas of Scotland. Descending north from the summit of Beinn Bheag gives equally fine views north up the wild U-shaped glen containing Loch an Nid to the pinnacled ramparts of An Teallach far in the distance. Also prominent are the unusual vast sheets of unbroken quartzite on the eastern flanks of Mullach Coire Mhic Fhearchair and Sgurr Ban.

Gradually begin to descend from

*Groban and Beinn Bheag from Loch a' Bhraoin*

north to north-east down easy heathery slopes to eventually reach the path in the wide bealach between the two Grahams and the Corbett of Creag Rainich to the north. It would be perfectly feasible to include this Corbett in the expedition which would involve another 450m of ascent but with little extra distance. Turn east along the path to reach Loch a' Bhraoin and the route of the walk in.

**Meall Mheinnidh** (Grassy or Solitary Hill); *722m*
*OS Sheet 19; GR 955748*
*30km/720m/6–8hrs (bike)*
*Map 35*

On the long and remote tree-fringed north-east shore of Loch Maree rises an almost continuous ridge of four mountains: one Munro (Slioch); two Corbetts (Beinn Airigh Charr and Beinn Lair); and a Graham (Meall Mheinnidh). Apart from Slioch, the other three mountains are fairly inaccessible and the use of a bicycle is recommended. Meall Mheinnidh is a fine rugged peak sitting snugly between the two Corbetts of Beinn Airigh Charr and Beinn Lair and could be combined with an ascent of one or both Corbetts. The following is a description of the ascent of Meall Mheinnidh only.

Begin at Poolewe to the north-west where a minor tarmac road begins just north of the road bridge over the River Ewe. Cars can be parked a short distance along this road and a bike used from this point. Pleasant cycling following the

*Looking south-east from the summit of Meall Mheinnidh*

*Meall Mheinnidh from Loch an Doire Crionaich*

river leads through natural woodland and out on to open moorland. Pass a recent forestry plantation and a lochan before reaching the farm at Kernsary. About 500m beyond this point, take a minor fork to the right which enters another forestry plantation. The track here is noticeably poorer with many boggy parts. At a large bend in the track, a footpath branches off to the right and bikes should be left at this point. Note that the start of this path can be difficult to locate.

Follow the footpath which descends initially to the Allt na Creige before continuing along the north bank to emerge from the forest at a stile. The path then rises gradually to reveal the enormous craggy profile of Martha's Peak, the imposing rock tower which rises on the south side of Loch an Doire Crionaich and forms the splendid façade of Beinn Airigh Charr. (Martha was a legendary local girl who fell to her death from this tower while tending her sheep.) From this point the well-defined north-west ridge of Meall Mheinnidh is seen to advantage and this provides the best ascent route.

Shortly past a second small lochan, the path begins to turn south into Strathan Buidhe, the glen which separates the two peaks. Cross the stream at the earliest possible convenience and gain the foot of the north-west ridge. The ascent involves nearly 500m of interesting climbing characterised by pleasant grassy terraces with countless crags and outcrops in between. Some scrambling can be found but the whole route can be accomplished with your hands hardly ever leaving your pockets.

The rocky summit contains a small cairn and gives superlative views east into the remote sanctuaries of the Fisherfield and Letterewe Forests which boast some of the remotest Munros in Scotland. The Corbett of Beinn Lair lies 3km to the south-east, its unique bastion of buttresses and gullies only barely glimpsed from this vantage point. The above time is based on a return by the same route, but if time permits it is a good idea to ascend Beinn Airigh Charr by its eastern flank and continue over Spidean nan Clach, which is then descended by its easy west ridge. This option will add about 2 hours to the given time.

**Beinn a' Chaisgein Beag** (Small Quiet Hill); *682m*
*OS Sheet 19; GR 965821*
*35km/700m/6–8hrs (bike)*
*Map 35*

This Graham is the 'little brother' of the higher and remoter Corbett of Beinn a' Chaisgein Mor lying a few kilometres to the south-east. Both hills could conceivably be combined into one expedition via their long rounded connecting ridge and intervening top, but the following is a description of an ascent of the Graham only. By any standards, Beinn a' Chaisgein Beag is a fairly remote and inaccessible hill situated north-west of the main mountain mass of the Fisherfield Forest. The

*View of Meall Mheinnidh from the summit of Beinn a' Chaisgein Beag*

closest approach is from the A832 coastal road to the north where several paths and tracks enter some distance into this wilderness. The Graham's great distance from a road makes an approach by bike a sensible option and the track to Loch na Sealga is suitable for such an option.

Begin immediately west of the bridge over the unnamed river flowing out of Loch na Sealga and follow the track which wends its way delightfully along the south side of the river. This glen gives magnificent views to the rugged peaks of Beinn Dearg Bheag and An Teallach at its head and is consistently interesting with pleasant wooded sections and craggy slopes. The river is popular with fishermen, especially in the summer months. Just over 1km short of Loch na Sealga, the Allt Loch Ghiubhsachain joins up with this river and bikes should be left at this point. Follow the east bank of this second river up into a steep-sided heathery glen for about 1½km to a point opposite a small stream flowing down the opposite hillside. It is possible to follow the west bank of the second river but this involves awkward traversing on steep heather slopes.

Cross the Allt Loch Ghiubhsachain and ascend the stream course to an area of craggy knolls and two small lochans. Just to the south of these lochans, a good stalkers' path winds round the base of some crags. Follow this path in a general south-westerly direction, dropping slightly to cross the Uisge Toll a' Mhadaidh before ascending for 140m to reach the wide bealach south-east of Beinn a' Chaisgein Beag. A short and easy climb of 160m leads to the summit of the mountain. The triangulation pillar lies a short distance from the summit cairn.

Views in all directions are not surprisingly quite superb and suitably varied. Sea views dominate the north-west while to the south-west the intricate jumble of Fisherfield Forest mountains arrest the eye. Sail Mhor, the Corbett outlier of An Teallach, is very prominent to the north-east, and in the opposite direction Beinn Airigh Charr, Meall Mheinnidh and Beinn Lair form a continuous bastion of cliffs across the expanse of Fionn Loch.

The use of a bike obviously necessitates a return to it but this could be suitably varied given time and inclination by completing a high-level circuit of the wild Loch Toll a' Mhadaidh via the unnamed top west of the loch and Creag-mheall Mor to the east. However, this interesting alternative would add at least 2 hours to the above time. For those without access to a bike an approach by the path following the Inverianvie River is recommended as this passes some spectacular waterfalls. This could be combined with the previous route to give a classic round and complete traverse of the mountain.

**Beinn Ghobhlach** (Forked Hill); *635m*
*OS Sheet 19; GR 055943*
*12km/590m/3–5hrs*
*Map 35*

---

Beinn Ghobhlach is a very conspicuous landmark, especially from the A832 road between Aultbea and Dundonnell. Its twin-topped profile belies its modest height, and indeed gives the impression of its being a much higher mountain. It occupies a strategic position on the peninsula between Loch Broom and Little Loch Broom and not surprisingly the views from its airy summit are little short of spectacular.

Take the scenic minor road to Badrallach to the south of the hill, where limited parking is available. From here a recently upgraded footpath follows the coastline for about 8km to the isolated settlement of Scoraig near the tip of the peninsula. Walk along this footpath for about 2km before striking up the steep hillside to reach the twin lochans nestling under the main upthrust of the mountain. The obvious skyline ridge with its band of crags (the west ridge) is the next objective. Reach the foot of this ridge by circling round the south of Loch na h-Uidhe, crossing its outflow at GR 043933. Climb this easy ridge with its optional scrambling opportunities on the many sandstone outcrops. The summit boasts a small cairn together with a larger stone shelter and is a grand viewpoint. Prominent to the south is the Corbett of Sail Mhor and the pinnacled ramparts of An

*Beinn Ghobhlach from across Little Loch Broom*

Teallach, while to the north the scattered sandstone ridges of Coigach beckon.

Leave the summit and follow the horseshoe ridge pleasantly round to the top at the opposite side. The view out to Scoraig and the end of the peninsula, with the sea pressing in on both sides, gives the feeling of almost being on an island. From this second top drop south into the huge west-facing corrie. The west-facing buttress here is quite steep and may offer good scrambling but this is best avoided on the descent. Make a bee-line across rough moorland followed by a steep descent to reach the coastal path which is reached about 1km beyond the point of ascent. Follow the path back to the starting point, which initially goes round a rocky headland where a retaining wall and fence have been constructed.

**Meall a' Chaorainn** (Hill of the Rowan Tree); *705m*
*OS Sheet 19; GR 136604*
*12km/550m/3–4hrs*
*Map 35*

---

This Graham, lying a few kilometres north-west of Achnasheen, is very much the twin of Beinn nan Ramh lying 6km to the north beyond the Munro of Fionn Bheinn. Both have long, whaleback ridges and are roughly the same height. Meall a' Chaorainn could quite easily be combined with an ascent of Fion Bheinn as they are connected by a high bealach at 520m. However, the following is a description of the ascent of the Graham only. It should be noted that the start of this route requires OS Sheet 25. Note also that Fionn Bheinn is on OS Sheet 20!

Begin on the A832 road north of Loch a' Chroisg where a new forestry track begins at a gate at GR 124588. Follow this track for about 1½km before it becomes a grassy track through the trees. A short distance further on, the track emerges from the forest and develops into a reasonable stalkers' path up the steep-sided glen between Meall a' Chaorainn and An Cabar. Pass the odd rowan tree which no doubt gives the hill its name.

At the head of the glen the path climbs north and becomes very indistinct as it traverses round the broad, heathery north-west ridge of the hill. This is the signal to climb to the crest of the ridge and to begin the long haul of 2½km to the summit. Most of this is extremely easy walking on close-cropped heather and moss interspersed with stony patches. Slabs of rock form the cairn at the summit and it is a fine viewpoint for Slioch and the Fisherfield Forest Munros to the north-west.

It is best to return by the route of ascent but this can be shortened by descending early from the ridge and dropping down steep heathery slopes to the path in the glen. Note, however, that there are numerous crags on these slopes and in wet, misty or winter conditions this option may not be practical.

**Beinn nan Ramh** (Hill of the Oar); *711m*
*OS Sheet 19; GR 139662*
*28km/660m/4½–6hrs (bike)*
*Map 35*

Beinn nan Ramh is a fairly remote hill situated at the western end of Loch Fannich and south-west of the main Fannich range of Munros. Its summit is only just on OS sheet 19, and map 20 is the main map used for the ascent from the A832 road east of Achnasheen. As with other hills bearing the name 'Ramh', the mountain is characterised by a long whale-back ridge, with this one running roughly east to west. An approach by bicycle is recommended, using the track which begins at GR 198599 (OS Sheet 25).

The track begins between two forestry plantations and a locked gate at the start requires bikes to be lifted over. Follow the forest edge upwards for about 1½km before crossing a bridge to gain more open moor. Climb steadily for another 1½km before starting the long exhilarating run down to the southern shore of Loch Fannich. Continue along the pleasant lochside with the eastern ridge of the Graham plainly visible ahead. Shortly after a bridge and pipeline, another much more recent track breaks off to the north to contour the eastern flank of Beinn nan Ramh. This is not shown on the current OS map but should be indicated on any subsequent ones. Follow this track until roughly at the foot of the grassy east ridge.

*On the summit ridge of Beinn nan Ramh*

Leave your bikes at this point and begin ascending the ridge for about 250m before levelling off at an area of peat hags and bog. Continue along the crest before reaching a steeper, narrower section with craggy cliffs on the north side. Beyond this the ridge widens and rises almost imperceptibly to the summit cairn in about 1½km. On a clear day (which unfortunately did not accompany the author's ascent) the view must be quite outstanding with the marvellous array of the Fisherfield Forest mountains lying to the north-west. The mountain also gives views of the secluded southern corries of the Fannich range. Return by the same route.

## SECTION 15

# *Loch Broom to Easter Ross*

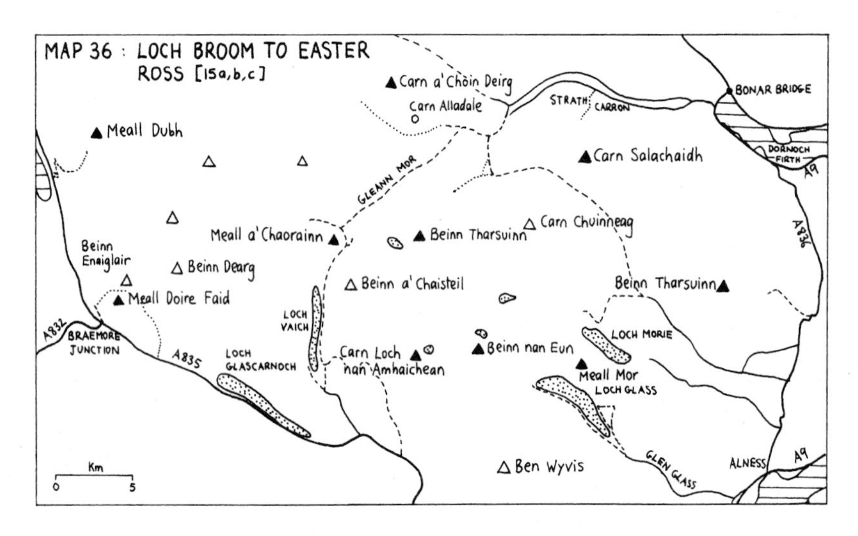


**Meall Dubh** (Black Hill); *667m*
*OS Sheet 20; GR 225886*
*23km/660m/3–5hrs (bike)*
*Map 36*

Meall Dubh is a flat-topped featureless hill lying north-west of the massive collection of the Inverlael Forest Munros and it merits little more than a passing glance on the OS map of the area. In fact, the actual summit is not named at all and the name Meall Dubh applies to a subsidiary top 2km to the north-west. However, despite these negative comments, the hill does possess a fine spacious feel and it commands excellent views of the surrounding higher peaks. It also makes an ideal objective when perhaps the Munros are immersed in cloud.

An approach by bike is highly recommended. Begin at the A835 road at Inverlael and take the forestry track south of the river. Cross the river by a bridge after less than a kilometre and turn left at the junction. Three successive hair-pin junctions lead on to the upper forestry track which should be followed eastwards to near its termination. It should be noted that most of the Inverlael Forest tracks are officially recognised cycling routes. Near the end of the upper forestry track, a track rises steeply upwards to the left, emerging from the forest at a locked gate, and bikes are best left at this point. Beyond the gate, follow the track, which makes a rising traverse round the southern slopes of the unnamed top to the end of the broad tussocky southern flank of the Graham. By this time, fine views would have opened out to the complex topography of the higher mountains to the south and west. From the end of the track take a direct line north of north-east across boggy tussocky terrain which rises gradually to reach the flat summit area containing a small lochan. The summit lies just north-east of this lochan and is a fine perch to admire the arc of higher peaks. To the east lies some of the remotest country in the High-

*On the summit of Meall Dubh*

lands and the Munro of Seanna Bhraigh is one of the remotest in Scotland. Return by the route of ascent, with the cycling section offering a quick, cooling and invigorating end to the expedition – almost all downhill!

**Meall Doire Faid** (Hill of the Lumpy Thicket); *730m*
*OS Sheet 20; GR 221792*
*7km/500m/3–4hrs*
*Map 36*

This little hill is conveniently situated 2km north-east of Braemore junction and is a pleasant short objective perhaps while *en route* to the north-west. It could ideally be combined with its Corbett neighbour of Beinn Enaiglair lying only 1½km to the north. Meall Doire Faid would be a fine mountain to climb in the winter with its grandstand views of the Fannich range to the south.

Begin at the parking area at Braemore Junction where a track leads north-west through a forestry plantation. At the time of writing, hillwalkers are strongly discouraged from using this track as a new lodge has been built at its end, and the owners have rather heavy-handedly erected a clutter of 'Private' and 'Beware of Dogs' signs to ward off unsuspecting walkers. The unsatisfactory alternative is to climb a stile at the edge of the forest and to follow the often boggy forest edge to the path leading up the hill from Home Loch. The author is of the opinion that this is not a viable alternative unless a properly constructed

*Looking down Strathmore to Loch Broom from Meall Doire Faid*

path comes into being.

If you are using the track, turn right at a fork after about 1½km which is just beyond a renovated building on the right. Just beyond is a track which zigzags out of the forest to a gate. Beyond the gate, a good stalkers' path can be followed past Home Loch and this leads after about 2½km to a col north-east of the Graham. From here it is only a short climb of 180m on grass and heather to the cairn at the summit which is a grand viewpoint.

The shortest return route is to descend directly down the south-western flank of the hill to Braemore Junction. However, the ridge heading south-east from the summit makes a pleasant traverse over Meall nan Doireachan which can be descended by its south-eastern ridge to the carpark on the A835 road. A road walk of 2km then leads back to Braemore juntion. This alternative would add about 1½hrs to the above time.

**Meall a' Chaorainn** (Hill of the Rowan Tree); *632m*
**Beinn Tharsuinn** (Transverse Hill) (north-east of Loch Vaich); *710m*
*OS Sheet 20; GR 360827, 412829*
*43km/820m/7–10hrs (bike)*
*Map 36*

These two extremely remote hills lie at the heart of one of the most unfrequented corners of Easter Ross. The Corbett of Beinn a' Chaisteil is reasonably close to each of them and the very fit could tackle all three on a long summer's day. The two Grahams above, however, should provide enough of a challenge for most but the use of a bike is strongly recommended. Various approaches are possible and the one from the south via Loch Vaich is described here.

Begin at the A835 near Black Bridge where a tarred road leads after a few kilometres to the dam at the southern end of Loch Vaich. A parking space is available a short distance along this road just before a gate. Cycle for about 3km before taking a right-hand fork just before a bridge. Climb a gate and follow the now stony track all the way up the east side of Loch Vaich where there are grand views up the loch to Meall a' Chaorainn. Beyond the north end of the loch the track climbs steadily for a few kilometres to contour round the east flank of Meall a' Chaorainn. An ascent can be made from the highest point on the track where a second track branches off. A stiff climb of about 300m on steep heathery slopes leads to a rather flat and uninspiring summit.

Descend to the track junction and cycle for just over 1km to the end of the second track at GR 373832 where there is a small hydro dam and pumping system. Leave the bike and follow the stream eastwards for about 2½km, gaining height gradually until the ground levels off at Crom Loch, a beautifully secluded hill loch which is fished on occasion. Directly beyond the

*Loch Vaich and distant Beinn Tharsuinn*

loch is Beinn Tharsuinn. Walk along the north shore of the loch across difficult peaty terrain and ascend the easy western slopes of the hill. Higher up the going becomes easier on close-cropped heather and moss. The summit area is flat and almost Cairngorm-like in character. The view to the west is dominated by the Beinn Dearg group of Munros. Return by the route of ascent.

Beinn Tharsuinn can also be approached by Glen Calvie to the north-east, which is probably the more natural way to climb the mountain if a bike is not available. A better idea of the topography of the hill can be appreciated from this direction. Both hills could also be climbed using the track along Gleann Mor to the north which is really an extension of the track described initially. Both these options begin at Strathcarron.

**Carn a' Choin Deirg** (Hill of the Red Dog); *701m*
*OS Sheet 20; GR 397923*
*22km/650m/6–8hrs (bike)*
*Map 36*

---

This fine remote hill lies at the heart of some extremely wild country north-east of the Freevater Forest which contains the remote Munro of Seana Bhraigh. Carn a' Choin Deirg is the highest of a series of tops forming a broad curving ridge which begins at the prominent Carn Alladale to the south. The most convenient approach is from Strathcarron to the east, the entrance to which is at Ardgay near Bonar Bridge on the Dornoch Firth. It is regrettable to have to say that Alladale Estates have seen fit to instigate a blanket ban on hill-walking, cycling and camping between 1 July and 15 February, the period they have decided is the hunting season. The author knows of no other estate in Scotland where such a complete unconditional outlaw on recreational activities for almost eight months of the year is in operation. (A conditional ban between mid-August and mid-October for stag shooting is acceptable and is the norm on most estates, with the proviso that intending hill-users contact the estate to check if shooting is taking place. The position taken by Alladale Estates can only serve to cause unwanted friction between them and recreational hill-users. It is left to the reader to decide on the stand he or she wishes to take on this issue. The author has already expressed concern to Alladale Estates!)

The OS map indicates a public road to The Craigs at the head of Strathcarron where a small corrugated iron church and a telephone box are situated. Turn left here and cross the bridge where a tarred road continues for over 2km to just beyond the entrance to Glencalvie Lodge. Cars should be left here. Continue along the track, passing through delightful wooded scenery by the north bank of the cascading River Carron. Pass the entrance to Alladale Lodge, climbing all the while before reaching a locked gate with a sign indicating the estate's instructions to hill-walkers. Beyond this point, the

*Welcome to Alladale Estate!*

track descends steeply to end at the MBA's Alladale bothy. Bikes are best left at this point.

The first objective is Carn Alladale whose summit is easily gained by a gentle climb up the eastern spur on mainly firm close-cropped heather for almost 2km. The small cairn on top gives unusual views out to the peaks of Coigach and Assynt to the far north-west. Suilven is just visible beyond a foreground ridge. The summit of Carn a' Choin Deirg is still 3km distant along a pleasant undulating broad ridge with three intervening tops. Two small lochans are passed *en route*, one just below the actual summit. Beinn Dearg is very prominent to the south-west while the full linear array of the Coigach and Assynt peaks are scattered along the horizon to the north and west from Beinn Ghobhlach to Canisp. The serrated outline of An Teallach is also visible.

To vary the descent, return to the small lochan below the summit and contour round to the spur at GR 393920 before dropping down easy heather slopes to pick up the path which follows the north side of the Allt a' Chlaiginn. This path used to be a well-constructed stalkers' path, but it has now deteriorated somewhat, and another 'track' nearer the river is nothing more than a muddy trail left in the wake of an all-terrain track vehicle, the means to an offensive and lazy solution to stalking. The glen between Carn Alladale and Meall nan Fuaran is a classic example of a U-shaped valley and contains picturesque stands of Scots pine at its junction with the main glen containing the Alladale River. Follow this pleasant path for about 6km back to the bothy from where the track leads back to the start of the route. Note that an alternative approach from Strath Cuileannach to the north-east is not recommended as there is much peat-hag terrain and it is less scenic.

**Carn Loch nan Amhaichean** (Hill of the Neck-shaped Loch); *697m*
**Beinn nan Eun** (Hill of the Bird); *743m*
*OS Sheet 20; GR 411757, 448759*
*34km/900m/5–7hrs (bike)*
*Map 36*

---

These two fairly isolated hills lie north-west of the Ben Wyvis range in the Inchbae forest. A long approach is involved from any direction but that from the south near Inchbae Lodge is the most convenient, especially for Carn Loch nan Amhaichean. Beinn nan Eun, which is the remoter of the two, could be left as a separate excursion from Loch Glass to the east. The route from Inchbae Lodge via Strath Rannoch is described here, and takes into account the use of a bike as far as Strathrannoch.

Begin on the A835 road a short distance past Inchbae Lodge where a track heads north just before a bridge. This track is easily cycled to the farm at Strathrannoch through mainly sitka forest initially and then on open hillside. The view up Strath Rannoch is dominated by Meall a' Ghrianain, the southern outlier of the Corbett of Beinn a' Chaisteil, but Carn Loch nan Amhaichean is not prominent. Just beyond a gate at a sharp bend in the track a faint path initially follows the left bank of the Allt a' Choire-rainich and bikes should be left near the junction of this path.

The path is not at all distinctive at the start but becomes more obvious later on. After about a kilometre it crosses the stream before recrossing it to peter out after about a kilometre north-west of the summit of Carn Loch nan Amhaichean. From here make a gradual ascent through deep heather to reach the small lochan lying at the foot of the north ridge of Carn Loch nan Amhaichean. Drop down about 30m in height to the north shore of Loch nan Amhaichean and follow its outflowing stream east before gradually contouring round to the south. Cross the Abhainn Beinn nan Eun (which may be a problem in spate conditions) and climb the easy western spur of Beinn nan Eun. As height is gained, more boulders dominate the terrain. The cairn at the summit is reached beyond a level shoulder, and the views are extensive, especially east and south to Loch Glass and the Ben Wyvis group.

A return should be made to the small lochan mentioned previously before ascending the steep north ridge of Carn Loch nan Amhaichean. Of the two Grahams this is the shapelier summit and offers fine views to the west. Follow the ridge to the south-west, gradually descending past a huge erratic boulder and continue down the western slopes to reach the edge of a new forestry plantation and Strathrannoch. It is a grand, mainly downhill cycle back through Strath Rannoch to the starting point.

For those without a bike who are wishing to complete a circular route, Carn Loch nan Amhaichean could be ascended first and a return made by the Abhainn Beinn nan Eun path and the Loch Bealach Culaidh path. This latter path ends less than 4km from the A835 road, which can be reached by the wide fire-break east of the starting point.

**Meall Mor** (Big Hill); *738m*
*OS Sheet 20; GR 515745*
*15km/540m/4–6hrs*
*Map 36*

Meall Mor is one of a sprinkling of Grahams forming a wide northern arc round the sprawling mass of Ben Wyvis. In addition to providing fine views of the northern aspect of this complex Munro, it is a worthy objective in its own right, being delightfully positioned between Loch Glass and Loch Morie. Given a few days and a full rucksack, it is an ideal hill to traverse, perhaps along with Ben Wyvis, but the route described here is a 'there and back' from Glen Glass to the south-east.

From Evanton on the Cromarty Firth drive up Glen Glass to the end of the public road at Eileanach Lodge, where there is a small parking area in front of some wrought-iron gates. It is also possible to park about 300m back along the road at a large metal gate which may be used as an alternative starting point. This second starting

*The summit of Carn Loch nan Amhaichean*

point follows the forestry track north of the River Glass, while the Eileanach Lodge start follows the more attractive track south of the river, with the additional advantage of having good views of the intended objective, Meall Mor. Both routes converge at the weir to the south of Loch Glass, which should be crossed if the southerly track has been taken.

A short distance beyond the weir, branch off to the right along a rough forest track which heads north, steadily climbing the forested southern slopes of Meall an Tuirc. After about 2½km this track emerges from the forest and continues almost to the wide bealach between Meall an Tuirc and Meall Mor. This latter continuation is not marked on the OS map. From the bealach follow the ridge north-west on often tussocky boggy ground over a subsidiary top, before following a fence round to the true summit marked by a trig point. A large flattened cairn lies about 50m east of the trig point next to the fence.

Continuing along the ridge a short distance from the trig point offers superb views of the northern end of Loch Glass and its wild hinterland. As well as Ben Wyvis, the Fannichs, the Torridon peaks and An Teallach are all visible on a clear day. Return by the route of ascent.

*Meall Mor from Loch Glass*

**Beinn Tharsuinn** (Transverse Hill) (west of Dornoch Firth); *692m*
*OS Sheet 21; GR 606792*
*13km/520m/3½–5hrs*
*Map 36*

Beinn Tharsuinn is a rather isolated Graham lying between the Cromarty and Dornoch Firths and is in fact the only hill over 2,000ft on OS Sheet 21, apart from its two associated tops to the south of the hill. From most directions it appears as a large, rounded heathery dome and has little to commend it other than its fine summit views.

Begin on the A836 road north of Alness at a large parking area just north of the bridge over the Strathrory River. A well-made track begins here which passes a large gravel pit and can be followed for about 4km to its termination at a gravel quarry on the lower slopes of Torr Leathann, the Graham's south-eastern top. A bike would be useful for this first section. (A large metal barrier excludes motorised vehicles from using this track.)

Climb the eastern slopes of Torr Leathann on initially very boggy and tussocky terrain, and either reach the top or contour round to the col between it and Beinn Tharsuinn. From the col a short but tiring ascent of 100m leads to the spacious summit topped by a triangulation pillar. On a clear day the finest views are south-west to the Ben Wyvis range. Descend by the broad heathery east flank and cross a stream to regain the quarry track used on the ascent.

**Carn Salachaidh** (Dirty Hill); *647m*
*OS Sheet 20; GR 518874*
*13km/650m/3–5hrs*
*Map 36*

This isolated hill standing south of Strathcarron is of little topographical merit, but on a clear day the extensive view north-west to the peaks of Coigach is well worth the effort of ascent. The closest approach is from Strathcarron to the north where a good stalkers' track begins just south of Gruinards Lodge.

The path begins in a wooded area at a metal gate and is to be followed uphill through trees on to open grouse moor. After a gain in height of about 150m, the path levels off significantly, skirting round the east side of Carn Mor, before descending to the Allt a' Ghlinne. The map shows the path to end at this point but it does in fact continue for some distance beyond, gradually petering out on the northern slopes of Carn Salachaidh.

Follow the path's continuation and climb easily to the broad north-west ridge of the hill at a height of around 450m. Follow this ridge over a minor top to the summit of Carn Salachaidh, which is a chaotic jumble of huge granite blocks, the actual summit being such a block with the triangulation pillar nearby. Two other lower tops lie east and west of the main summit.

The Corbett of Carn Chuinneag is the prominent double summit to the south-west, while further west the remote hills of the Freevater and Inverlael Forests jostle for attention.

However, it is to the far north-west that the eye is drawn, with the distinctive painted profiles of Cul Mor, Suilven and Ben More Assynt stealing the scene. Descend by the same route.

Carn Salachaidh can also be approached from Strath Rusdale to the south-east but this involves a long walk along an estate track which continues to the public road in Strathcarron. If a bike is available, then the use of this track is worth considering.

## SECTION 16

# *Coigach to the Pentland Firth*

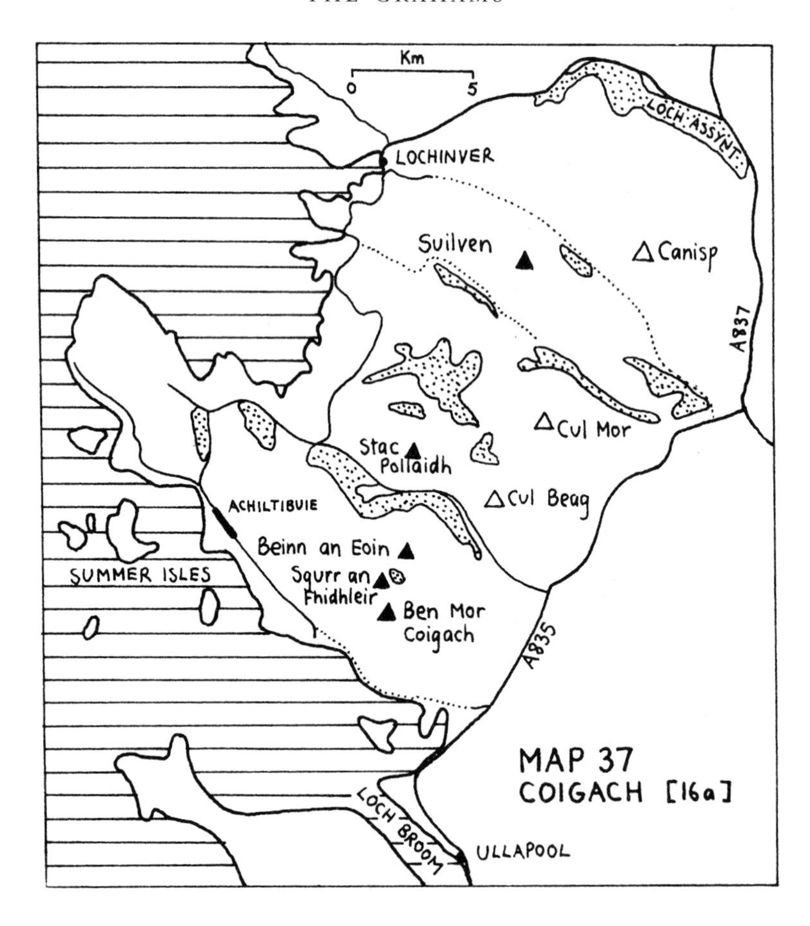


**Ben Mor Coigach** (Big Hill of Coigach); *743m*
**Sgurr an Fhidhleir** (Peak of the Fiddler); *703m*
*OS Sheet 15; GR 094042, 094054*
*11km/770m/4–6hrs*
*Map 37*

---

The extensive sprawling mountain range which includes the above two Grahams is a dominant feature from Ardmair Bay, north of Ullapool, where the long south-western ridge of Ben Mor Coigach totally dominates the scene beyond the bay. What is not evident from this viewpoint is the complex topography of the range with its steep sandstone cliffs, narrow ridges, shapely summits and grand corries. These assets, combined with the close proximity of the sea and numerous islands, make the traverse of the above two peaks one of the finest hillwalking jaunts in the north-western Highlands.

The most convenient starting point is Culnacraig at the end of the Achiltibuie road to the south-west of the range. From here, a good coastal path may be followed for a short distance before breaking off to the left to climb the steep heathery slopes of Garbh Choireachan. Higher up it is possible to enjoy some worthwhile scrambling on the many sandstone outcrops, but these can be avoided if so wished.

After a relentless ascent of over 600m, you will finally reach the summit ridge of Ben Mor Coigach. This is a good point to stop for a breather and to enjoy the glorious views out to the scattered jewels of the Summer Isles. From there the summit of Ben Mor Coigach lies just over 1km away along a delightfully narrow crest containing several easy sandstone towers, all avoidable but adding more to the fun if taken directly. The actual summit contains a large shelter cairn situated on a small plateau standing out north of the main ridge line. Not surprisingly, the summit views are outstanding. To the north is the prow of Sgurr an Fhidhleir looking very prominent with Beinn an Eoin visible just beyond.

To continue to Sgurr an Fhidhleir, simply adhere to the ridge which makes a sharp turn to the north less than 1km further on, before dropping fairly steeply to the wide col between the peaks. From this col, at a height of about 550m, it is an easy ascent of 150m to the airy summit perch of Sgurr an Fhidhleir. The small cairn teeters on the brink of an almost sheer precipice dropping 550m to the waters of Lochan Tuath. The direct ascent of this prow was only made as recently as 1962. To the north, grand views of Coigach's

*The peaks of Coigach*

other dramatic peaks can be enjoyed with Stac Pollaidh being particularly prominent.

Descend by the long grassy south-west ridge which leads in just over 3km to the road's end at Culnacraig.

These two peaks can also be climbed from the bridge at Drumrunie just off the A835 road but the going is initially wet and boggy and involves a much longer day. If an obliging driver is available, a complete traverse of the range from Culnacraig to Drumrunie via Beinn Tarsuinn would make an interesting outing.

**Beinn an Eoin** (Hill of the Bird);
*619m*
*OS Sheet 15; GR 105064*
*10km/680m/4–5hrs*
*Map 37*

---

Beinn an Eoin is a beautifully wild, little-frequented hill lying between Ben Mor Coigach and Stac Pollaidh. It consists of two separate tops, the southern one of which is the highest point and therefore the actual Graham. The route described below traverses both tops and is in effect a clockwise round of the large eastern corrie facing Loch Lurgainn.

Begin at the southern end of Loch Lurgainn, where there may be some difficulty in parking a car. A rather boggy footpath starts just east of the bridge, which is to be followed until it reaches the south bank of the Allt Claonaidh. Cross this and make an ascent on steep heather and slabs of the prominent Cioch Beinn an Eoin, the rocky bluff which marks the start of the ridge. Already there will be glorious views of the surrounding Coigach peaks, particularly Stac Pollaidh and Cul Beag. From here it is a pleasant ridge walk on mainly rough sandstone slabs before the final steep rise onto the summit of Sgorr Deas, literally meaning 'South Peak'. The view south over secluded Lochan Tuath to the dramatic prow of Sgurr an Fhidhleir is particularly fine, while to the north the isolated sandstone sentinels of the Inverpolly Forest form a stark but striking skyline.

Follow the ridge north-west for about 500m before descending to the right to reach the lochan nestling in a hanging corrie between the south and north peaks. It is essential not to leave this descent to the right too late, as the ridge beyond ends sharply in a series of steep crags. The lochan is a delightfully wild and remote spot to spend some time before the final climb up to Sgorr Tuath (North Peak). Some intermittent scrambling on the sandstone outcrops may be enjoyed on the ascent.

The summit area of Sgorr Tuath is split by a deep fissure, and beyond the summit some Stac Pollaidh-like sandstone pinnacles provide a good foreground for the view north. From the summit take a line south-east down easy heathery slopes and skirt round the northern slopes of Cioch Beinn an Eoin to reach the route followed during the walk in.

**Stac Pollaidh** (Peak of the Peat Moss); *612m*
*OS Sheet 15; GR 107106*
*3km/550m/2–4hrs*
*Map 37*

---

The above translation and others such as 'Lumpy Peak' and 'Muddy Stack' do little justice to what is arguably the finest small mountain in Scotland. If anyone has climbed only one Graham, then this is probably it. Stac Pollaidh, with its distinctive skyline of weathered sandstone pinnacles, probably attracts more walkers than any other mountain in the north of Scotland. It is well seen on the drive north from Ullapool and is situated north of Loch Lurgainn and the minor road to Achiltibuie. The mountain's growing popularity has resulted in a large purpose-built carpark being constructed on this road south of the hill and this is the start of the route.

From the carpark a path can be followed directly up the hillside which forks about halfway up. The left fork ascends directly to the main saddle on the ridge via a highly eroded 'path' which is steep and unpleasant. The right fork, however, is recommended and leads round to the east side of the mountain where it is possible to begin a complete traverse of the summit ridge. Leave the path before it begins to traverse round the north side of the peak and ascend the easy heathery slopes to the main ridge. The actual summit of Stac Pollaidh lies at the western end of the ridge and the next part of the route is one of the most delightful scrambles in Scotland. Having said this, it is possible to avoid almost all of the crags and towers by easier low-level paths but this would be missing out on the fun.

The crux of the entire route is a small rock tower which blocks the passage to the true summit and cannot be avoided. The easiest line involves dropping down the gully to the left for a few metres and then scrambling up a steep slab with scant holds. Remember also that this will have to be reversed as there is no easy descent route on the west side. It is also possible to climb the tower direct, which may be preferred by some; but the preceding alternative is recommended on the return.

The finest features of the mountain are the weirdly sculpted sandstone pinnacles, many resembling grotesque human-like forms, with names such as 'The Sphinx', 'Tam o' Shanter', 'Lobster Claw' and 'Andy Capp'. Even if the main summit is not reached, these unusual pinnacles form the highlight of the climb, and the views, not surprisingly, are magnificent. Descend from the main saddle on the steep eroded path leading to the carpark.

**Suilven** (The Pillar); *731m*
*OS Sheet 15; GR 153183*
*21km/700m/6–9hrs*
*Map 37*

---

The bold and prominent profile of Suilven rises up in isolated grandeur from the surrounding lochan-strewn moorland. Though actually slightly

*Pinnacles on Stac Pollaidh*

north of the district known as Coigach, Suilven's distinctive character has more in common with the Coigach peaks than that of Assynt. This distinction has made it one of the most well-known and most photographed peaks in the British Isles. In essence, Suilven is a triple-topped ridge running from south-east to north-west with the highest top, Caisteal Liath (Grey Castle), lying to the extreme north-west. Whether from the north or south, Suilven's summit ridge is well seen, while from the east and west the mountain appears to rise up as a single unassailable 'Pillar', the name given to it by Viking invaders from the sea.

From any direction Suilven involves a long approach and unlike Stac Pollaidh it involves much more commitment than a short climb from the road. The most convenient starting point is near Lochinver to the north-west, where a single-track road leads east to Glencanisp Lodge. About 1km short of the lodge gate there is a parking area and this marks the start of the route.

Follow the track through the lodge grounds and branch off after the eastern end of Loch Druim Suardalain along a well-made stalkers' path, taking the right-hand path at a cairned fork some 3½km further on. Suileag Bothy is situated a short distance north of this point along the left fork. Continue for 2km along the north bank of the river, crossing it by a footbridge, before following the path along the south side to the footbridge at the north-west end of Loch na Gainimh. A rough path heads south-west from here, leading up to an area of idyllic little lochans which in turn leads to the foot of the steep scree gully below the Bealach Mor, the lowest point on Suilven's ridge. Reach this point and climb up the gully to the bealach. Turn right here and go through a gap in a drystane dyke which had oddly been constructed across the ridge. A well-used path follows the line of the ridge to the spacious summit of Caisteal Liath, the highest point of Suilven. Not surprisingly, the views from this magnificent perch are quite stunning, particularly to the west.

The return journey follows the route of ascent but if time and inclination permit it is well worth continuing south-east along the ridge from Bealach Mor where some mild scrambling leads to the central peak of Meall Mheadhonach, whose top is unusually flat and grassy. From here the ridge descends steeply to a col where a fairly exposed scramble on the left leads to the top of Meall Bheag. It is possible to continue along the ridge from this top by passing an obvious gap and descending the south-eastern spur of Suilven. The path along the north side of Loch na Gainimh can then be reached, which leads north-west to the footbridge mentioned previously. Note that this extension will add about another 2 hours to the time given above. A grand way to tackle Suilven is to begin at Glencanisp Lodge and to complete the above route using the path via Lochan Fada and Cam Loch to the A835. This would require two cars or an obliging driver.

*Suilven from Cul Mor*

**Meall an Fheur Loch** (Grassy Hill of the Loch); *613m*
**Meallan a' Chuail** (Hill of the Cudgel); *750m*
*OS Sheets 15, 16; GR 361310, 344292*
*12km/760m/4–6hrs*
*Map 38*

---

These two hills lie to the west of Loch Merkland and east of the Corbett of Beinn Leoid. All three summits are easily attainable in a day's walk from the A838 road between Loch Merkland and Loch More; although the following route description does not include an ascent of Beinn Leoid. The finest of the three is undoubtedly Meallan a' Chuail, whose elegantly curving summit ridge drops sharply to the east to a pair of lochans.

Halfway between Loch Merkland and Loch More a well-constructed stalkers' path zigzags upwards between two forestry plantations and this can be gained via a small wooden footbridge over the Allt Ceann Loch. Ascend the path easily for about 1½km until it begins to level out at an area of knolls and lochans. At this point, leave the path and head roughly south-east, climbing steadily for 150m to reach the extensive flat summit area of Meall an Fheur Loch. The cairn at the actual summit lies just off OS map 15 and is not particularly easy to find in misty conditions (from experience!).

To reach Meallan a' Chuail, head south for a few hundred metres before gradually curving to the west to arrive at the northern end of Loch Lol-ghaoith.

A further descent of about 70m, followed by an ascent of 100m, leads to the broad shoulder at the foot of the north ridge of the hill. The last 180m of ascent follow the well-defined crest of the north ridge with a final steep incline before the cairn at the summit. The views from this airy perch must be quite grand but, unfortunately, the author was accompanied by low cloud and drizzle!

To return, retrace steps down the north ridge and continue north from the shoulder for 1½km to reach the end of the path used on the ascent. A large cairn marks the end of this path. Follow the path easily back to the starting point.

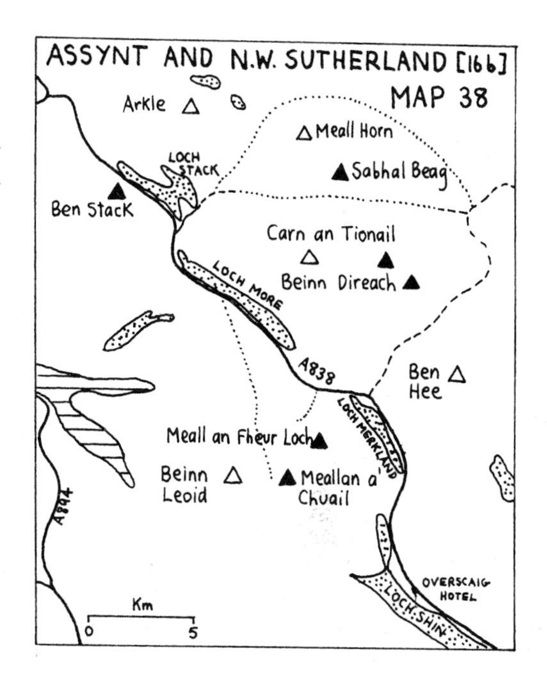


**Carn an Tionail** (Hill of the Gathering); *759m*
**Beinn Direach** (Straight Hill); *688m*
*OS Sheet 16; GR 392390, 406380*
*18km/790m/5–7hrs*
*Map 38*

---

Between the Corbetts of Ben Hee and Meallan Liath Coire Mhic Dhugaill these two hills occupy a fine position north of Loch Merkland and make a delightful horseshoe route from West Merkland, the usual starting point for the ascent of Ben Hee. Carn an Tionail in particular is an elegant and striking mountain with a long southern ridge and is in many respects a more interesting climb than Ben Hee.

A good Land Rover track begins at West Merkland near the bridge and there is a locked gate at the entrance. The track passes through Bealach nam Meirleach (Robber's Pass) and was originally an old drove road. Walk up the track for about 2½km before crossing the Allt na Glaise on a footbridge. This provides access to the grassy slopes leading up onto the south ridge of Carn an Tionail. Once established on the ridge it is a pleasant airy walk to the flat and stony south top of the hill. Continue north to the col below the actual summit where there is a tiny well-constructed stone shelter. This hill is very popular with deer and many gather here and around the summit to graze – hence the name of the mountain.

The stony summit contains a fair-sized cairn and is a grand panoramic viewpoint for the surrounding peaks. The most prominent mountain is Ben Hope whose craggy western profile is unmistakable to the north-east. To the east is Ben Loyal and the twin cones of Ben Griam Mor and Ben Griam Beg, while Morven and Maiden Pap are just visible on the horizon.

Continue beyond the summit in a north-easterly direction and gradually curve back, descending all the time to reach the rough bealach below Beinn Direach. This bealach is a mass of huge boiler-plate slabs and is a wild and lonely spot. A short ascent of only 150m leads to the spacious rock-slabbed summit which is topped with a recently built cairn. Beinn Direach just scrapes in as a Graham with exactly 150m of relative height. Descend the grassy southern slopes and either climb to the top of Meall a' Chleirich or drop south-west then south to reach the track which is followed back to the A838 at West Merkland.

**Sabhal Beag** (Little Barn); *732m*
*OS Sheet 9; GR 373429*
*23km/730m/5–8hrs*
*Map 38*

---

Sabhal Beag is a relatively insignificant little peak tucked away in the south-eastern corner of the massive mountain complex dominated by the sprawling ridges of Arkle, Foinaven and Meall Horn, all of which are Corbetts. Given plenty of time and good conditions this Graham can ideally be combined with Meall Horn via the subsidiary top of Sabhal Mor (Big Barn), which is actually smaller than Sabhal Beag by 2½km. The shortest and most interesting approach is from the west at Loch Stack and the following is a description of the ascent of Sabhal Beag only. Bike owners should note that most of the following route can be cycled and this option would considerably shorten the time given above.

At the southern end of Loch Stack, a track (which is partly tarmacked) begins from the A838 and leads to Lone after 2½km. Cars are discouraged on this section and should be parked just before the bridge. Follow the pleasant track to Lone with Arkle's south-western defences dominating the view to the north. At Lone, the track deteriorates somewhat but is still cyclable. Follow it east over initially level ground before climbing steeply through a gap into Strath Luib na Seilich. The track now meanders pleasantly along the river for 3km before climbing steeply to the Bealach na Feithe at 450m. The summit of Sabhal Beag lies exactly 1km north of this point with a height gain of almost 300m. Climb initially steep boulder-strewn slopes before levelling off at the summit plateau and the low slabby cairn. Return by the same route.

If you are continuing on to Meall Horn, it should be noted that another track following the Allt Horn can be used on the descent. An approach from the east in Strath More is also possible, but it is longer and less interesting.

**Ben Stack** (Steep Hill); *721m*
*OS Sheet 9; GR 269423*
*7km/670m/3–5hrs*
*Map 38*

Ben Stack's rocky conical profile is unmistakable during the drive north along the west shore of Loch More. It rises steeply in tiers of rock from the southern shore of Loch Stack but its north-west to south-east alignment makes approaches from either of these directions the likeliest options. Ben Stack is the most northerly Graham and not surprisingly has marvellous views from the summit.

The easiest approach is from the south-east on the A838 road anywhere near the turn-off to Lone just south of Loch Stack. Head north-west across initially boggy ground, which soon gives way to tussocky heather and rocky outcrops as height is gained. After about an hour, you will reach a small false summit at a height of 540m. A fine view of the final grassy summit pyramid can be gained from this point.

This last section is the easiest part of the climb, which is on close-cropped grass almost all the way to the top. The summit area is split by a fissure with a trig point at 718m on the southern side while the cairn at the actual summit lies on the northern rib just beyond a small transmitter aerial powered by solar panels. To the north-east the quartzite screes and crags of Arkle and Foinaven totally dominate the view, while directly north the bare lochan-studded gneiss table land appears to stretch indefinitely

*Ben Stack from Loch More*

to the blue haze of the sea. On a calm sunny day it is quite an effort to have to descend from this grand viewpoint. Return by the route of ascent.

Ben Stack can also be ascended from the north-west by a ruined roadside cottage where a stalkers' path climbs up to the east of Loch na Seilge. The route then climbs steeply up the north-west spur of the mountain. The ideal way to tackle the hill is to combine both these routes in a traverse but this would involve some walking along the road or a second car.

**Beinn Dhorain** (Hill of Torment or Hill of the Otter); *628m*
*OS Sheet 17; GR 925156*
*3km/360m/1–2hrs*
*Map 39*

This hill of old red sandstone presents a steep and quite craggy east face to Glen Loth which connects the A9 coast road to the Strath of Kildonan. The track through Glen Loth has only recently been upgraded to a tarmacked road and it is now possible to drive to within 1km of the summit. Cars can be parked at a point on the road almost exactly due east of the hill.

Climb a metal gate in the deer fence and zigzag up the steep grassy and heathery slopes, keeping to the right to avoid a girdle of crags. Reach a large cairn which is not at the actual summit though it is a better viewpoint than the true summit which lies some 300m to the north-west and is crowned by a smaller cairn. The view to the north-east is dominated by the conical scree of Morven, which looks much higher than its 706m would suggest. Just visible to the south on a clear day is the subject of much ill-feeling, the Duke of Sutherland's statue standing high on Beinn a' Bhragaidh above the coastal town of Golspie. The Duke was responsible for the eviction of thousands of crofters during the grim period of the Clearances, and Ben Loth's desolation is a sad reflection of these mass evictions.

The best descent route is to head north to the col between Beinn Dhorain and Ben Uarie which may also be ascended with an extra height gain of only 40m. Drop down the corrie between the two summits to reach the road and the starting point. This corrie could also be used as an ascent route.

**Creag Mhor** (Big Rock); *713m*
**Ben Armine** (Hill of the Warrior); *705m*
*OS Sheet 16; GR 698240, 695273*
*46km/850m/7–10hrs (bike)*
*Map 39*

These hills are two of the remotest Grahams in the whole of Scotland and their ascent is a major challenge for the fit walker, who preferably also has access to a bike. Both hills are part of a long, undulating poorly drained ridge running from the north-eastern end of Loch Choire at Loch Choire Lodge to Ben Armine Lodge, two of only three habitations in an area covering nearly

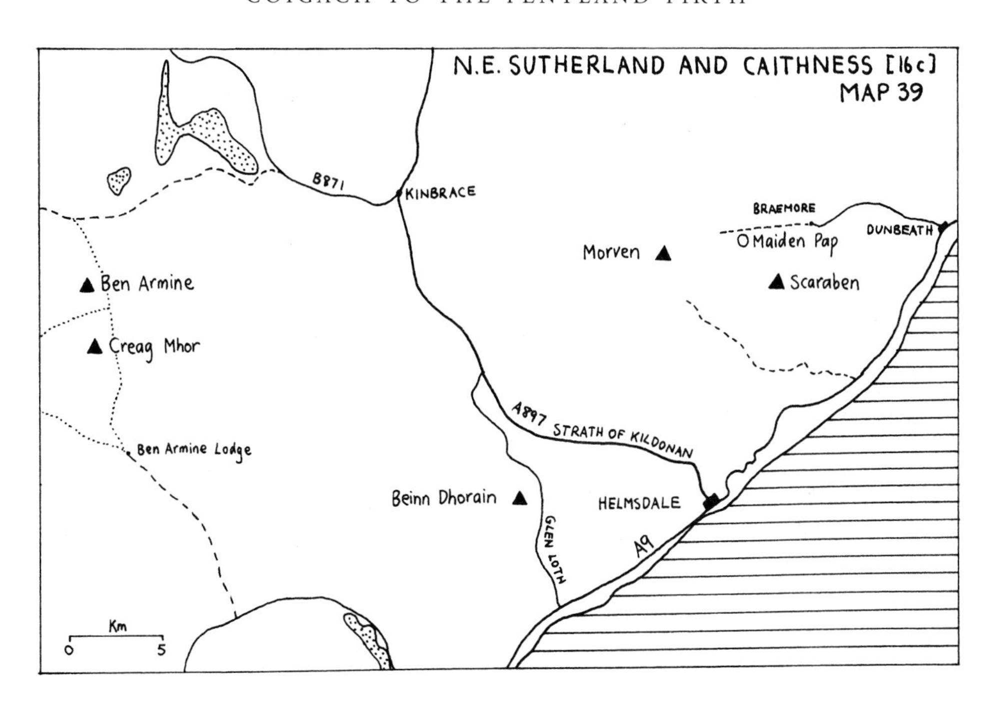

*Beinn Dhurain from Glen Loth*

400sqkm. The Ben Armine Forest is deer country and an excellent system of tracks criss-crosses the area, many of which are ideal for the use of a mountain bike.

The most convenient approach begins on the B871 Kinbrace to Bettyhill road where an excellent gravel and sand track begins near Badanoch Lodge (OS Sheet 17). This track is well maintained by Loch Choire Estate and, although there are no locked gates, unauthorised vehicles are prohibited beyond the second bridge south of Loch Badanoch. However, the track is ideal for cycling and the 14km run is an interesting prelude to the walk ahead.

Go to the area marked as GR 687310 where a well-constructed stalkers' path gradually ascends the hillside to the south and passes along the steep eastern face of Ben Armine and Creag Mhor. This track can be cycled, but as the route described below involves minimal backtracking it is best to leave your bikes near the track junction.

Follow the track southwards under the imposing craggy east face of Ben Armine with Gorm-loch Beag appearing on the left. Shortly beyond this point, another track heads west, gradually ascending easy slopes to the wide bealach between Ben Armine and Creag Mhor. Descend south for about half a kilometre before tackling the relentless grassy northern slopes of Creag Mhor. You will finally reach the triangulation pillar which is a grand viewpoint. The two obvious landmarks to the east are Morven and Ben Griam Mor. The latter peak fails to reach Graham status by a mere 20m. The sense of absolute remoteness on this isolated outpost is quite profound.

Retrace your steps to the bealach and ascend 200m on heather and moss to the flat summit of Ben Armine, known as Creag a' Choire Ghlais. There is no cairn at the highest point. From the summit head north-west to the boggy col below Meall nan Aighean before making a rising traverse north-east to reach the grassy eastern slopes of this top. Descend directly to the stalkers' track and follow it back to the main track. If the cycle in was quite a burden, the cycle out will most definitely be the opposite. Much of the route goes gradually downhill and the easy run past the numerous large fishing lochs is a delightful and relaxing ending to a tiring but satisfying day.

The two hills could also be approached from the south at Sciberscross, north of the River Brora, where a track leads in to Ben Armine Lodge. However, this track is more undulating and is not easily cycled.

**Morven** (Big Hill); *706m*
**Scaraben** (Divided Hill); *626m*
*OS Sheet 17; GR 004285, 066268*
*24km/1,050m/8–10hrs*
*Map 39*

---

These two hills together with the 'miniature Morven' of Maiden Pap form a distinctive trio in the south-east corner of Caithness. Morven is a prominent cone of old red sandstone and is the most recognisable of the three, as well as being the highest point in Caithness. In complete contrast, Scaraben is a long undulating ridge of three distinctive rounded tops of white quartzite, the central one being the true summit. Between Morven and Scaraben is another hill known as Smean, which possesses an unusual sandstone outcrop and it is included in the round about to be described.

The most convenient starting point is Braemore to the north-east, which can be reached by a single-track road from Dunbeath on the coast. Cars should be parked just before the bridge near the telephone box. Follow the track over the bridge through a pleasant wooded section with Maiden Pap and Morven rising tantalisingly ahead. At the keeper's cottage at Braeval, keep to the right and walk up the track which passes through a small plantation of sitka spruce. The track stays to the north of Maiden Pap which by this time will look like a prominent little rocky cone and it is well worth climbing if there is time. At the bothy known as Corrichoich, the track ends but a faint path follows the south bank of the Berriedale Water to a small grassy knoll with an assortment of small standing stones. This is the remains of a prehistoric circular con-

*Morven from near Braemore*

struction known as a wheelhouse, and is a suitable foreground to the mighty Morven, which now totally dominates the landscape.

From the wheelhouse head south-west across tussocky heather and bog to reach the wide col between Morven and Smean. From this col it is a straight-forward but fairly steep ascent on heather and rock for 400m to the summit. An obvious rocky crag of sandstone conglomerate bars the way to the short summit ridge but it can be bypassed on either side. However, a direct ascent gives an interesting scramble of 15m with plenty of rough holds. The actual summit lies a few hundred metres beyond on a rocky plinth with a small cairn. On a clear day the views are tremendous with Hoy and Orkney Mainland visible to the north. This airy perch also gives a good idea of the work still to be done to reach Scaraben and some may elect to leave this for another day!

To continue to Scaraben retrace your steps to the col and ascend the easy western slopes of Carn Mor, the small top north-west of Smean. Continue south-east to the obvious sandstone tor which can be climbed by a pleasant short scramble. From Smean drop roughly south-east for 200m to reach the wide saddle below Sron Gharbh, the westernmost of Scaraben's three tops. Ascend this top as far as the broad shoulder which projects from its northern slopes at about 450m. From here either make a direct ascent of the western top, or make a rising traverse on quartzite scree to reach the col west of the main summit. From the col it is an easy 100m ascent on quartzite boulders and heather to the spacious summit crowned by a triangulation pillar.

The best route of return is to continue east to the col between Scaraben and East Scaraben and descend directly north over rough moorland to Braemore and the start point. Alternatively, continue over East Scaraben and descend by the east ridge which leads to a path following the south bank of the Berriedale Water back to Braemore. This is a longer option, however.

Both Morven and Scaraben could be tackled from the south-east at Berriedale on the A9, but this involves a much longer approach by the track up the Langwell Water.

If climbing Scaraben as a separate excursion, it is best to begin at GR 084300 where a track descends through a farmyard to the Berriedale Water and crosses it by a small suspension bridge to reach the path on the south bank.

## SECTION 17

# *The Islands*

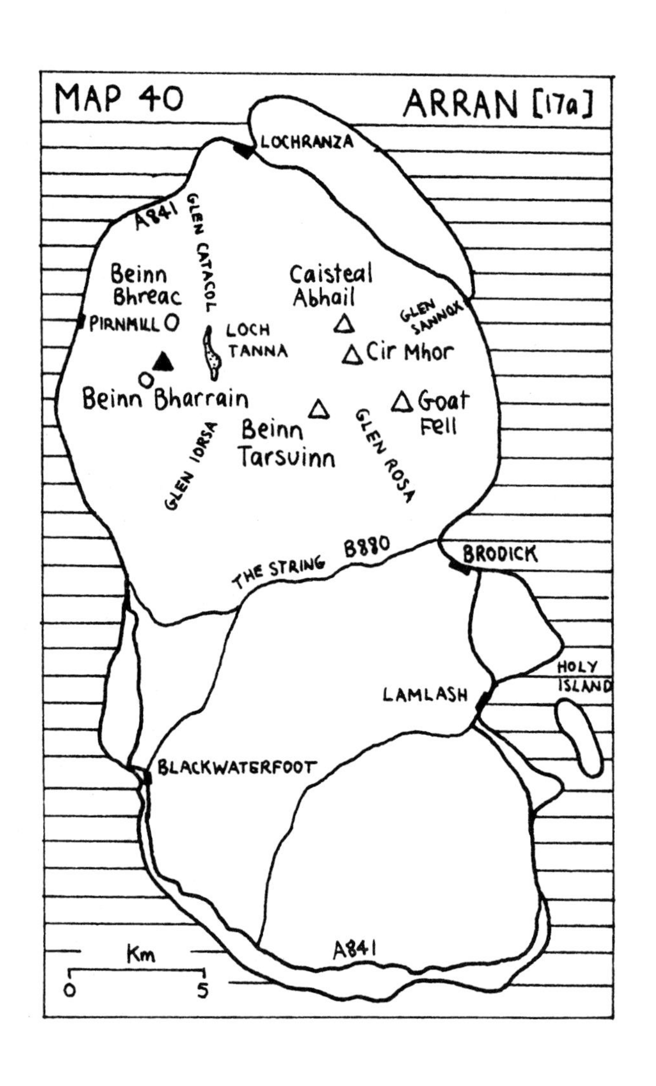
MAP 40
ARRAN [17a]
LOCHRANZA
A841
GLEN CATACOL
Beinn Bhreac
Caisteal Abhail
GLEN SANNOX
PIRNMILL
LOCH TANNA
Cir Mhor
Beinn Bharrain
Goat Fell
Beinn Tarsuinn
GLEN IORSA
GLEN ROSA
THE STRING
B880
BRODICK
HOLY ISLAND
LAMLASH
BLACKWATERFOOT
A841
Km
0
5

**Beinn Bharrain** (Barren Hill); *721m*
*OS Sheet 69; GR 901427*
*14km/850m/3½–5hrs*
*Map 40*

The western hills of Arran are unfairly neglected in favour of the castellated ridges and pointed summits of the highly popular Goat Fell range across Glen Iorsa to the east. It is true that the Beinn Bharrain range does not possess the same grandeur as its eastern counterparts but it does contain a miniature A' Chir-type ridge which gives some enjoyable scrambling. The traverse of all the main tops of Beinn Bharrain is a delightful outing far from the madding crowds to the east. The route described below begins at Pirnmill and is a pleasant horseshoe taking in Beinn Bharrain and the north-easterly top of Beinn Bhreac.

At Pirnmill a farm track leads up the hill just north of the bridge. Follow this round a left then a right bend until it again bends to the left to a farm. At this point leave the track and cross a stile to a muddy path going through an area of small birch trees and hazel coppices. The path crosses several more stiles, becoming established on the north side of the Allt Gobhlach (Forked Stream) where a fine waterfall and a deep gorge maintain interest until the prominent north-western ridges of Beinn Bharrain make their appearance. Cross the burn higher up and head for the entrance to Coire Roinn which is enclosed by two obvious ridges.

The miniature A' Chir-type ridge mentioned previously is to the left and it forms the north-east wall of the corrie and provides the most sporting ascent to the summit. The right-hand ridge forms the south-western boundary of Coire Roinn and gives an easy walking ascent to Beinn Bharrain's south-west top. The recommended route is by the left-hand ridge whose approach is made easy on huge granite slabs. Thereafter the angle steepens on good granite blocks and heather with scrambling beginning at an obvious outcrop marking the beginning of a narrow, more level, section. Most difficulties can be avoided by traverses on the right, but keeping to the crest of the ridge gives the finest situations with small pockets of entertaining scrambling.

The final step to the easy summit slopes is not easy to avoid and is best tackled directly. The cairn at the summit and the triangulation pillar are only a short stroll of a few hundred metres beyond the top of the ridge. If a visit to all of Beinn Bharrain's tops is to be made, then a detour south-west will be necessary to climb the south-west top which is guarded by some fine granite slabs and tors. The only advantage of ascending the non-scrambling ridge mentioned earlier (on the south-west side of Coire Roinn) is that a traverse of all three tops can be made without any backtracking.

From the highest point, descend north-eastwards to Bealach an Fharaidh, whilst enjoying grand views of Loch Tanna and the main Arran ridges to the east. Follow the broad ridge round and up on to the summit of Beinn Bhreac, which is topped by a huge cairn. Continue northwards along the ridge to a minor top of 653m. Finally, descend the broad heathery west ridge of this top to the Allt Ghobhlach and the path of ascent.

An interesting 'added extra' to this trip is to make a visit to Arran's finest high-level lochan which is beautifully situated below steep granite cliffs and scree to the north of the minor top mentioned previously. Fhionn Lochan, as it is called, can be reached by either descending north or west from the minor top, but gradually turning north if the latter option is chosen. Both these routes of descent essentially follow the lip of the corrie which encloses the lochan. The crystal clear waters of Fhionn Lochan are the home to red-throated divers which nest beside the loch. Eagles have also been spotted in this idyllic spot. From the lochan a good path descends to Mid Thundergay, which lies nearly 3km north of Pirnmill.

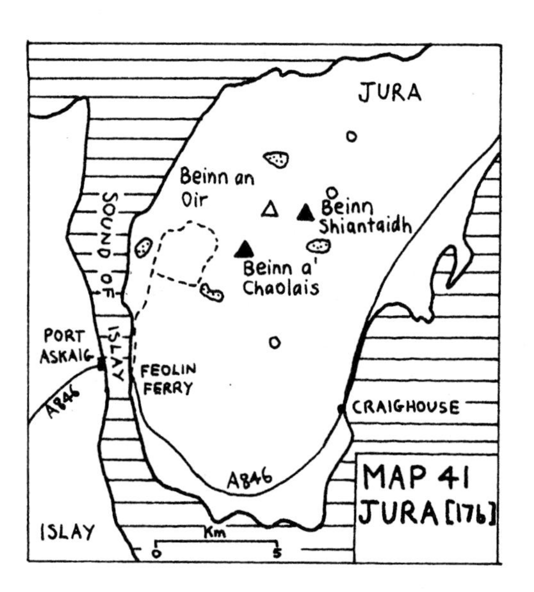


**Beinn Shiantaidh** (Holy Hill); *757m*
**Beinn a' Chaolais** (Hill of the Narrows); *733m*
*OS Sheet 61; GR 513747, 488734*
*19km/1,320m/7½–10hrs*
*Map 41*

---

The distinctive trio of scree-covered domes known as the Paps of Jura are a prominent landmark from both the mainland and its neighbouring islands. They comprise one Corbett (Beinn an Oir) and two Grahams (above), and since the Corbett lies between the other two an ascent of all three is described below. This is by no means an easy outing as there is much ascent and descent involved, but it is possible to climb each separately.

Begin on the A846 road at the start of the Glen Batrick path which can be followed for about 2km before making a rising traverse west to reach the lochan-studded col between Corra Bheinn (sometimes known as 'The Fourth Pap') and Beinn Shiantaidh. The south-east shoulder of Beinn Shiantaidh offers the best line of ascent, although some scree climbing is unavoidable at the start. Towards the top the shoulder develops into a pleasant ridge and leads directly to the cairn at the summit, where there are grand sea views in all directions.

Descend the west ridge of the hill which comprises large angular blocks

*The Paps of Jura from Islay*

with some crags lower down, and you will reach the wide grassy bealach below Beinn an Oir. This can be climbed more or less directly by a series of large slabs initially, which offer some reasonable scrambling. Alternatively, climb a grassy ramp which runs upwards from left to right. Reach the main north-east ridge where there is an interesting rib of reddish-coloured rock higher up. The final section to the summit follows a stony path leading past two drystane shelters to the triangulation point.

Descend Beinn an Oir by its south ridge, which is quite rocky and complex, particularly in a mist. A short distance down, a minor spur to the south-east branches off from the south ridge and care should be taken not to confuse this with the south ridge. Now walk to the more southerly of two lochans which nestle in the bealach below the final hill of Beinn a' Chaolais. This can be ascended by its north-east shoulder which contains the usual unavoidable angular quartzite scree, though the final upper section is on more amenable mossy terrain. The summit is a grand place to contemplate the wild rocky uninhabited north-western coastline of Jura and the hills already climbed.

The quickest descent route will involve retracing your steps on Beinn a' Chaolais before descending to Loch an t-Siob and following the Corran River until it turns south. At this point, head east across open moor for 1km to reach the start of the Glen Batrick path.

Beinn a' Chaolais can also be ascended from the west, where a rough track traverses the lower slopes of the hill and descends to Cnocbreac and Inver Cottage north of the Islay Ferry at Feolin.

**Ben Buie** (Yellow Hill); *717m*
**Creach Beinn** (Hill of Spoil); *698m*
*OS Sheet 49; GR 604270, 642276*
*10km/1,270m/6–8hrs*
*Map 42*

---

These two splendid rugged peaks lie south of Glen More and are the most southerly of the Mull Grahams. In particular Ben Buie presents an awe-inspiring rocky profile on the final approach to the little village of Lochbuie, and the mountain contains much gabbro and rhyolite, which give some excellent scrambling in the upper reaches. Across the deep gash of Gleann a' Chaiginn Mhoir to the east lies Creach Beinn, another craggy mountain, whose complex south-east face is seen to advantage during the drive along the north shore of Loch Spelve *en route* to Lochbuie. This secluded village is the ideal starting point for the traverse of both peaks, despite the almost sea-level start.

Leave the Lochbuie road near the telephone box below the steep slopes of Ben Buie and generally head in a northerly direction by aiming for the level shoulder east of the main summit. The line direct from this shoulder to the summit contains the best scrambling, with numerous outcrops of beautifully rough gabbro and rhyolite, which is almost Cuillin-like in character. A non-scrambling route to the summit can be effected if so wished by following the left side of the burn (from the telephone box) which follows the vague curving south ridge of the mountain. This route, however, contains much loose scree in the upper reaches; the final girdle of crags can be avoided by a shallow rake running from left to right. The main summit of Ben Buie is crowned by a large cairn and is not surprisingly an excellent viewpoint on a clear day. About 500m to the north is a second summit 3m lower, which will have to be reached before the descent into Gleann a' Chaiginn Mhoir. It should be noted that there is local magnetic variation on the summit area of Ben Buie and the compass cannot be relied upon.

From the lower north summit, head north for about 150m before turning east to descend the obvious east spur of the mountain which was visible on the ascent. This spur is composed of large apron-like slabs at an easy enough angle to make the descent a delight. During the descent, there is a marvellous vista of the string of lochs at the floor of the glen and the shapely cone of Beinn Talaidh rising beyond comes into view. After what seems an age, you will finally reach the southern end of Loch Airdeglais and the path which runs through the glen.

An initially steep ascent of 300m, with possible pockets of scrambling, is the first stage in reaching the next summit of Creach Beinn. Once this is

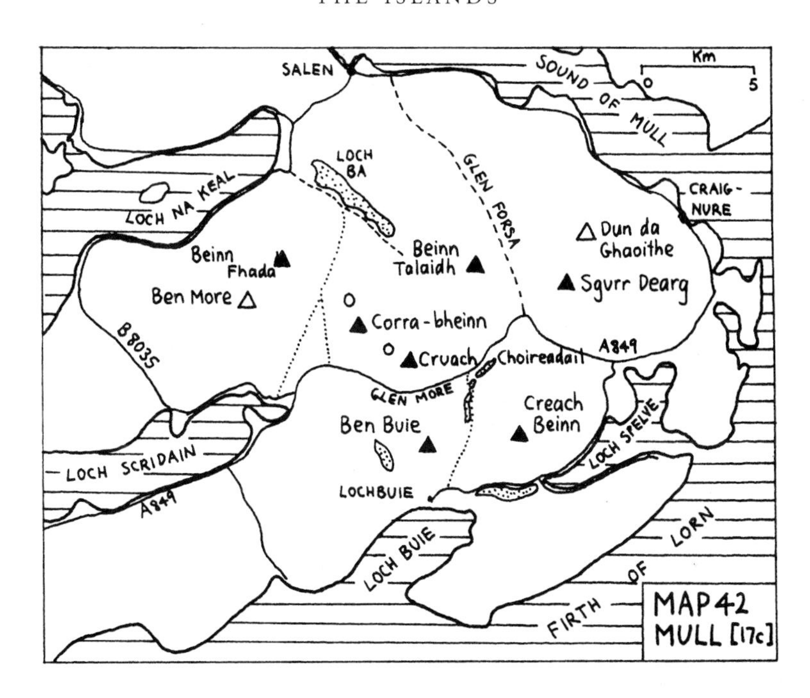

*Ben Buie from Loch Uisge (Mull)*

accomplished, you will reach a wide flattish area containing much rock and a small lochan. Climb gradually west through this area to reach the rocky north ridge which leads directly to the cairn at the summit and trig point. The view south-east across Loch Spelve and the Firth of Lorn to the mainland peaks is particularly fine.

The most natural descent route is to follow the long twisting south-west ridge which ends at Lochbuie, but care should be taken here in mist as the route has many false tops and twists and turns. The tiny lochan at GR 624263 is a good point to aim for before the final descent south-west to the beginning of the path through the glen.

It is, of course, quite possible and perhaps preferable to climb each of these Grahams on separate excursions. If this option is taken, then the south-west ridge of Creach Beinn would provide a good ascent route. Its continuation over Meall nan Capull and Glas Bheinn, followed by a south-easterly descent to the road, would make an interesting addition. The classic way to tackle Ben Buie would be a south to north traverse, descending by its long north ridge to the road in Glen More. This option would, of course, require a kind driver. The north ridge would also provide an easy ascent route but it does not show the best side of the mountain.

**Beinn Talaidh** (Hill of the Cattle); *761m*
**Sgurr Dearg** (Red Peak); *741m*
*OS Sheet 49; GR 625347, 665339*
*11km/1,300m/5–7hrs*
*Map 42*

---

The prominent cone of Beinn Talaidh is second to Ben More as Mull's most distinctive peak and in fact has been mistaken for Ben More on more than one occasion. Until a few years ago its highest point was thought to be 763m (over 2,500ft), thereby giving it the status of a Corbett. However, it is now known to be 761m – and collects the honour of the highest Graham, even though two other Grahams are also credited with 761m of height. Beinn Talaidh's distinctive profile dominates Glen Forsa which lies to the east, whilst Sgurr Dearg rises in less spectacular form to the west of the glen. The traverse of both summits in a day is not a long expedition but it involves considerable descent and re-ascent.

Begin at the large bend on the A849 road through Glen More where a new forestry track can be followed for a short distance before climbing the boundary fence to reach the open hillside. It should be noted that the bulk of Glen Forsa has now been planted out with sitka spruce forest which is not shown on the current (1992) OS Landranger map. Steep grassy slopes lead after 350m of ascent to the shoulder of Maol nam Fiadh, from where an obvious curving ridge continues easily to the summit of Beinn Talaidh. The large cairn lies a short distance south-west of the trig point and provides fine views in all directions.

From the summit, descend north-eastwards on the steep scree slopes to reach the col between Beinn Talaidh and its minor companion, Beinn Bheag. Make a contour round the col to reach the grassy south ridge of Beinn Bheag and descend this to Glen Forsa. Cross the glen by one of the many fire-breaks through the trees to reach the formidable western slopes of Sgurr Dearg.

Almost any line can be taken up these slopes which basically means a relentless slog of nearly 500m to reach the rocky north-west ridge named Beinn Bhearnach on the map. Follow this ridge directly to the summit; there are ever-present views to the left into lonely Coire nan Clach, which is well named as 'Corrie of the Stones'. Across this corrie lies Mull's only Corbett of Dun da Ghaoithe. The cairn at the summit of Sgurr Dearg offers fine views of this peak as well as of Beinn Talaidh across the glen. The most natural descent route goes south to the col below another Beinn Bhearnach, following an old drystane dyke into Coire nan Each where deer can often be seen. Easy slopes lead directly down to the road at the ruin of Torness, from where it is a short walk to the starting point.

Both of the above Grahams can easily be climbed as separate expeditions, with perhaps the well-defined north ridge of Beinn Talaidh being used as a route of descent followed by a walk back along Glen Forsa. Beinn Talaidh is often climbed by way of this ridge by following an approach from the north, and the MBA bothy at Tomsleibhe can also be used for an overnight stop. Sgurr Dearg can be climbed in conjunction with Dun da Ghaoithe but it should be noted that the north-east ridge of Sgurr Dearg contains a rock step of 6m about 50m below the summit, which is easier to negotiate in the ascent than descent.

**Corra-bheinn** (Hill of the Hollows); *704m*
**Cruach Choireadail** (Rocky Stacked Hollows); *618m*
*OS Sheet 48; GR 573321, 594304*
*12km/1,150m/6–8hrs*
*Map 42*

---

To the east of Ben More a long undulating ridge of four distinct summits can be seen to advantage from the head of Loch Scridain. From left to right, the second and fourth of these tops have been granted Graham status, and the traverse of the whole ridge makes a grand expedition despite the significant drop between the summits.

The best starting point is at the old bridge at GR 564306 in Glen More where a path wends its way up Sleibhte Coire for 3km to the col west of Cruachan Dearg at a height of 332m. This path can be followed right to the cairn at the col although it might be tempting to cut off to the right before the col to gain quicker access to the west ridge of Cruachan Dearg. A stiff climb

*Ben More from Cruachan Dearg (Mull)*

on grass and rough crags will lead eventually to the marvellous viewpoint of Cruachan Dearg, from whence Ben More and its satellites, A'Chioch and Beinn Fhada, can be well seen on a clear day. Descend the south-eastern slopes on mainly scree to the col below the first Graham of Corra-bheinn, and then ascend it easily to the trig point at the summit. Corra-bheinn contains many rocky crags and outcrops and in its upper reaches these are composed of gabbro, which, as Cuillin lovers know, is a delight to climb on.

The drop from Corra-bheinn to the col below the third top of Beinn a' Mheadhoin is the greatest descent on the ridge (over 300m) and this is best achieved by continuing along the summit ridge of Corra-bheinn for about 300m before descending on grass and scree to the south-east. Follow the pleasant north-west ridge of Beinn a' Mheadhoin to its summit, which is probably the least interesting top on the ridge. Head east from the summit before dropping down easily to Mam Choireadail, the col below the second Graham and the last top of the ridge. Cruach Choireadail has two tops, with the southerly one being the higher, and from the col a rising traverse can be made to the dip between the two. Ascend on rock and scree to the spacious summit and cairn; across Glen More, Ben Buie and Creach Beinn are both prominent on a clear day.

Descend from the summit in a general south-westerly direction, keeping west initially to avoid a girdle of

*On Beinn Fhada (Mull)*

crags which surround the south of the hill. Care should also be taken lower down the hill where numerous rocky outcrops have either to be negotiated or avoided. On reaching the road, it should be no more than a walk of 2km back to the starting point.

**Beinn Fhada** (The Long Hill);
*702m*
*OS Sheet 48; GR 540349*
*10km/700m/3–4hrs*
*Map 42*

---

This hill is to a large extent overshadowed by Ben More and A'Chioch to its south-west, but, despite this, it is a fine objective in its own right. The ascent of Beinn Fhada makes an ideal prelude to the traverse of Ben More and A'Chioch and the ascent of all three peaks can be made in a natural horseshoe route around Gleann na Beinne Fada. The ascent of Ben More has already been well documented in other sources.

The following route description assumes only the ascent of Beinn Fhada, although this can easily be extended to include the other two peaks. The ideal approach is from the bridge at the mouth of the Scarisdale River on the shores of Loch na Keal. If the complete round of Gleann na Beinne Fada is the objective, then the bridge over the Abhainn na h-Uamha to the south-west will be more advantageous.

Follow the south bank of the Scarisdale River to a fine gorge before turning south up the grassy ridge to the small cairn on the north-west top (563m). The long ridge of Beinn Fhada, which gives the hill its name, is now to be followed for about 1½km over several minor bumps to the final steepness below the main summit. Climb up to the top on grass and shattered rock where there are two cairns only a short distance apart. The view to A'Chioch and Ben More is immediately arresting. Descend to the col below A'Chioch on slopes mainly of grass and scree before dropping west into Gleann na Beinne Fada, where a faint path follows the south bank of the Abhainn na h-Uamha to the bridge at its mouth.

A second fine horseshoe route involving Beinn Fhada can be made by ascending the prominent little peak of Beinn Ghraig (591m) from the west and continuing round to Beinn nan Gabhar and finally up Beinn Fhada by its east ridge. The ascent route of Beinn Fhada which has been described above must then be followed in the reverse. On a day when low cloud is plaguing Ben More, this option will have much to commend it.

**Trallval**; *702m*
*OS Sheet 39; GR 377952*
*22km/2,000m/9–12hrs*
*Map 43*

---

Trallval is the only Graham on the Isle of Rum, and is one of the five main peaks which, together with their intervening ridges, forms the Rum

Cuillin. For many people a visit to this magical island is a once-in-a-lifetime experience and, weather permitting, a complete traverse of the ridge is a must for the fit and competent hillwalker. As Trallval is the central peak of the five, it is doubtful if it would ever be ascended singly for its own sake, though this would certainly be possible by a rather circuitous route. For this reason, the above statistics refer to a complete traverse of all five peaks which also, incidentally, includes two Corbetts, Askival and Ainshval.

The island of Rum is a National Nature Reserve under the control of Scottish Natural Heritage, and permission to go there must be obtained from the chief warden, who can also advise as to accommodation and camping. Full details are available by directly contacting the warden (White House, Isle of Rum, Inverness-shire, PH43 4RR, tel. 01687 462026). Access to Rum is by Caledonian MacBrayne ferry from Mallaig or Bruce Watt Cruises, also in Mallaig. No cars are allowed on the island.

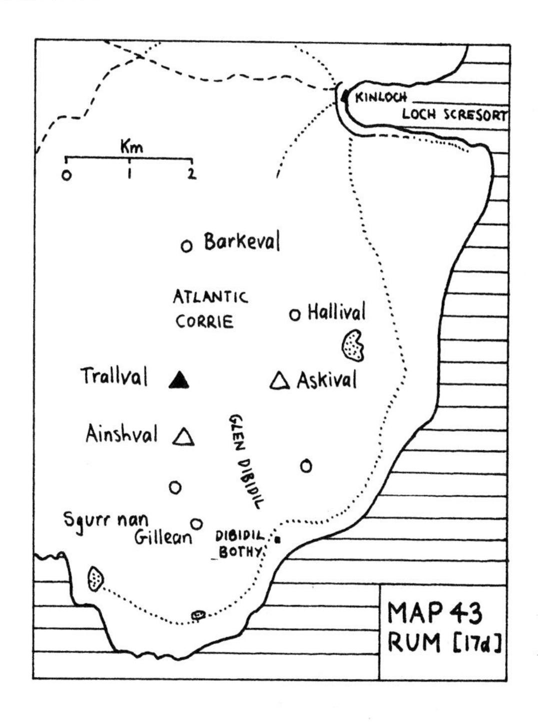

*Trallval from Askival (Rum)*

The usual starting point for the Cuillin traverse is Kinloch, the only settlement on the island. Just south of Kinloch Castle take the Coire Dubh path, which is signposted, and follow it up to Bealach Bairc-mheall. A well-defined ridge then leads south-east to the first summit of Hallival with a steep rocky section just below the top. The numerous holes around the summit are entrances to mountain-top burrows used by Manx Shearwaters.

Descend the south ridge of Hallival which is quite steep initially with its numerous rocky steps, before tackling the north ridge of Askival. This contains the Askival Pinnacle, a massive slabby step in the ridge, which can be avoided by a path on the left or tackled directly by a Moderate rock climb. Easy scrambling leads to the summit of Askival, the highest point on Rum and a marvellous viewpoint on a clear day.

Askival's west ridge leads easily down to Bealach an Oir (Pass of Gold), from where Trallval can be climbed by its east ridge. This provides some easy scrambling to reach the slightly lower eastern summit, from where you can traverse the exposed, airy ridge which connects it with the true summit, another magnificent vantage point for the other peaks in the range. The descent from the summit of Trallval south to Bealach an Fhuarain is quite steep and rocky and will require care and the location of a good route.

The Bealach an Fhuarain is a good point from where to make a descent into Glen Dibidil if enough ascent has been done for one day. Otherwise, another two peaks, Ainshval and Sgurr nan Gillean, still await the fit hillwalker. The lower rocky buttress of Ainshval's north ridge can be climbed directly by a good scramble or avoided by going to the right. Higher up, the ridge narrows with some fine easy scrambling near the top. The ridge from Ainshval to Sgurr nan Gillean is mainly grassy and crosses a subsidiary top. Enjoy memorable views to Eigg and Skye from this far-flung point before descending by the south ridge to the coastal path. From here, it is still a long but scenic walk back to Kinloch.

**Ben Aslak** (Breast Mountain);
*610m*
*OS Sheet 33; GR 750191*
*4km/330m/1½–2½hrs*
*Map 44*

---

Before the promotion of Ladylea Hill in Strathdon to Graham status, Ben Aslak had the dubious honour of being the smallest Graham. The name 'Aslak' is most likely derived from the Gaelic *aslaich*, meaning 'breast' in reference to the mountain's twin summits. 'Breast Mountain' is not a literal translation as the word 'Aslak' is an anglicised corruption of the true name. Ben Aslak is well seen from the Glenelg area, rising as it does to the south of Kylerhea Glen, and it is an ideal objective for a short outing when travelling to or from the Kylerhea Ferry.

The shortest route begins at the Bealach Udal on the Kylerhea Road

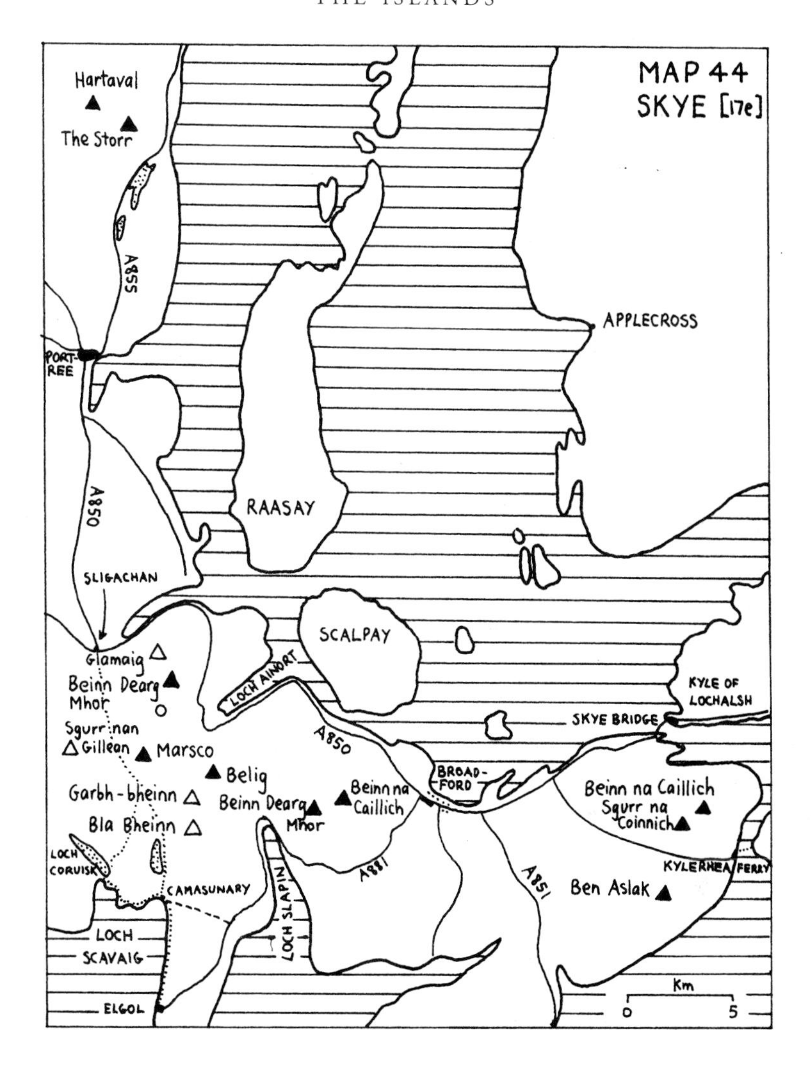


which is already at a height of nearly 280m. Ascend the heathery north-eastern flank of Beinn Bheag, a small top north-west of Ben Aslak, before making a contour to reach the wide bealach between the two. From here, make a direct ascent of the north-western spur, passing an idyllic little lochan *en route.* On a clear day, this point gives marvellous views of the Cuillin Ridge and is a spot at which to linger. The final 150m or so can be livened up with some optional scrambling on the upper crags but an obvious grassy tongue provides an alternative route. The highest point is the western top (to the right) where there is a small cairn. The eastern top, which is only marginally lower, lies about 500m away, and another lochan lies halfway between the two tops. Descend by the same route.

*The summit of Ben Aslak (Skye)*

*Sgurr na Coinnich and Beinn na Caillich from near Glenelg (Skye)*

An alternative route of ascent (or possibly descent) is the long east ridge which leads to Kylerhea at its foot by a path. But this option loses out on the height advantage of the Bealach Udal.

**Sgurr na Coinnich** (Peak of Moss); *739m*
**Beinn na Caillich** (Mountain of the Old Woman) (Kylerhea); *732m*
*OS Sheet 33; GR 762222, 770229*
*6km/710m/4–5hrs*
*Map 44*

---

These two hills together with Ben Aslak to the south form a distinct mountainous upthrust in south-east Skye. They are well seen from the Skye Bridge and also from Glenelg on the mainland to the south-east, and provide wonderful viewpoints. The best starting point is the Bealach Udal on the scenic minor road to the summer ferry crossing point at Kylerhea, which has the advantage of a high start (279m).

From the bealach, climb the heathery southern slopes of Sgurr na Coinnich, with their grand views of Blaven and the main Cuillin Ridge opening up as height is gained. A small lochan lies less than 500m south-west of the summit triangulation pillar. Views from the summit are extensive and the mainland peaks of Beinn Sgritheall and Ladhar Bheinn are particularly prominent.

Descend (without difficulty) to the Bealach nam Mulachag and make a direct ascent of the relatively rocky south ridge of Beinn na Caillich to the cairn at the summit. Again the views are extensive, with the Skye Bridge looking well. A return to the Bealach Udal can be made by following the route of ascent but rather than reclimb Sgurr na Coinnich it is possible to contour round its eastern flank once some height has been gained from the Bealach nam Mulachag.

**Beinn na Caillich** (Hill of the Old Woman) (Broadford); *732m*
**Beinn Dearg Mhor** (Big Red Hill) (Broadford); *709m*
*OS Sheet 32; GR 601233, 587228*
*10km/970m/5–7hrs*
*Map 44*

---

The above two hills, together with the minor top of Beinn Dearg Bheag, are known collectively as the Eastern Red Hills of Skye and they form an undulating horseshoe ridge above Broadford to their east. Beinn na Caillich is the highest of the trio and it totally dominates Broadford, rising in a massive rock and scree cone from the surrounding moorland. The first recorded ascent of any Skye peak was that of Beinn na Caillich in 1772 by Thomas Pennant from the former MacKinnon household at Coire-chat-achan which is the usual starting point.

Coire-chat-achan can be reached by a fairly indistinct path which starts just south of a neolithic chambered cairn north of the A881 Broadford to Elgol road. Alternatively, follow a track for 2km which starts on the main A850 road 1½km beyond Broadford. The decision to do a clockwise or anti-clockwise circuit of the horseshoe round Coire Gorm really depends on the individual. For those who prefer to get long steep ascents out of the way at the beginning of the day, then the anti-clockwise option is preferable, thus climbing Beinn na Caillich first. On the other hand, for those who prefer a more gentle ascent, the clockwise circuit is the best option and the easy-angled east-north-east Ridge of Beinn Dearg Bheag should be aimed for. Note that this second option will entail a steep descent at the end of the day. Taking all things into account, the first option is probably preferable and is described here.

Basically, a fairly direct line from Coire-chat-achan leads across grass and heather to the ever increasing steepness of the eastern slopes of Beinn na Caillich. As height is gained, the heather gives way to large boulders, which make for a quick ascent. Soon, the angle eases off to reveal the huge cairn at the summit. Legend has it that a Norse princess is buried under the cairn. The view from the top is quite magnificent on a clear day and the white houses of Broadford appear as scattered sugar grains far below. Follow the ridge west to the col below Beinn Dearg Mhor and climb easily to its large cairn of pink stones, which is a phenomenal viewpoint for the massive

*On the ridge between Beinn Dearg Mhor and Beinn na Caillich (Skye)*

eastern ramparts of Bla Bheinn and Clach Glas.

The descent to Bealach Coire Sgreamhach is fairly steep on grass and scree, and leads out easily to the final top of Beinn Dearg Bheag, whose cairn is also a fine viewpoint for Bla Bheinn, Loch Slapin and the Sleat peninsula. Finally, descend the easy-angled east-north-east ridge and follow the Allt Beinn Deirg back to Coire-chat-achan.

An alternative, and less-frequented, circuit of the two Grahams begins near Strollamus to the north, where a path can be followed up to An Slugan before ascending the north ridge of Beinn Dearg Mhor. Beinn na Caillich can then be descended by its north-west ridge east of Coire Reidh. This route is slightly shorter and has much to commend it.

**Belig** (Norse origin); *702m*
*OS Sheet 32; GR 544240*
*6km/690m/3–4hrs*
*Map 44*

Belig may be considered to be the true rocky termination of a long south to north ridge made up of the Munro of Bla Bheinn, the Corbett of Garbh-bheinn and, of course, the Graham of Belig. The complete traverse of these 'Cuillin outliers' is a superb expedition and it includes some classic scrambling. It is one

*Looking south-west from the summit of Belig (Skye)*

of the few instances when a Munro, Corbett, and Graham can be naturally combined into one route. However, the route described below is a little less ambitious and is a 'Belig only' option.

Begin on the A850 road at the head of Loch Ainort and cross fairly boggy terrain heading directly for the prominent north ridge. About halfway up the ridge, an obvious crag provides a good steep scramble following a crack fault line up the centre; this can be avoided on either side. Shortly above this crag, the ridge begins to level off along a narrow grassy crest and the airy summit, which is topped by a small cairn, is soon reached. On a warm day Belig is one of the summits where it is possible to linger for hours as the views in all directions are stunningly riveting. The main Cuillin ridge, Bla Bheinn, then Red Cuillin, Trotternish, Raasay, Scalpay, the mainland, Sleat – all are visible on a clear day. Descend the steep south-west ridge by following the line of an old drystane dyke to Bealach na Beiste from whence a further descent has to be made to the Abhainn Ceann Loch Ainort and the starting point.

Note that a natural horseshoe route can be accomplished by continuing from the Bealach na Beiste over the Corbett of Garbh-bheinn and then down the long north ridge which ends at the head of Loch Ainort. It is also possible to ascend Belig from the south at the head of Loch Slapin by its steep south ridge, and this is the best starting point if the objective is to include Garbh-bheinn and Bla Bheinn.

**Marsco** (Seagull Rock); *736m*
*OS Sheet 32; GR 507252*
*10km/720m/2½–4hrs*
*Map 44*

Marsco is a mountain of much individual character and is one of the Western Red Hills lying east of Glen Sligachan. It has a very distinctive profile when viewed from the vicinity of the Sligachan Hotel to the north, and it even vies with Sgurr nan Gillean in its ability to command attention. An approach along Glen Sligachan has much to commend it, but a shorter and easier route begins on the A850 road at the head of Loch Ainort. Cars can be parked at the big bend in the road and an easy route can be followed south-west up the delightfully named Coire nam Bruardaran or Corrie of Dreams. This corrie is wide and grassy initially and offers fine views of the craggy eastern flank of Marsco, though this is certainly not Marsco's best side.

Follow the burn almost right up to the bealach at about 320m where superb views of Garbh-bheinn and Bla Bheinn present themselves. The little craggy peak across Am Fraoch-choire (The Heather Corrie) is the rarely climbed Ruadh Stac (Red Stack at 493m). From the bealach, climb the easy-angled south-east ridge which is initially composed of scree and heather, developing into a fairly narrow rocky crest higher up. After a false summit, the ridge bends slightly west and continues delightfully to the small cairn at the summit which is an unrivalled viewpoint for both the

*On the summit ridge of Marsco looking to Blaven (Skye)*

main Cuillin ridge and the outlier of Bla Bheinn. It would not be overstating things to say that the summit of Marsco is one of the finest viewpoints in the whole of Skye. The north and west aspects of this mountain are fairly steep and craggy and do not offer many easy descent routes, therefore it is best to descend by the route of ascent.

The alternative route from Glen Sligachan is longer but offers the possibility of some scrambling on the fairly well-defined north-western spur which is an obvious feature from the glen. The steep west face of the mountain contains the Fiaclan Dearg or Red Tooth, where two buttresses offer the only significant rock-climbing in the Red Cuillin.

**Beinn Dearg Mhor** (Big Red Mountain) (Glamaig); *731m*
*OS Sheet 32; GR 520285*
*12km/850m/4–6hrs*
*Map 44*

---

Beinn Dearg Mhor and its southerly neighbour, Beinn Dearg Mheadhonach (Middle Red Mountain), form part of the Western Red Hills of Skye – or, simply, Red Cuillin. Both hills are composed of granophyre which wears to a pinkish red colour, and which is especially noticeable in the late evenings of summer when the slanting rays of sunlight accentuate the ridges and corries. The two hills lie south of the massive scree cone of Glamaig (a Corbett) and all three could be climbed together via their connecting ridges. The

*Beinn Dearg Mhor and Glamaig from Beinn Dearg Mheadhonach (Skye)*

route described below, however, does not include Glamaig.

Begin at Sligachan to the north-west, where a long sweeping shoulder known as Druim na Ruaige is well seen and offers a pleasant means of ascent to the summit of Beinn Dearg Mheadhonach. Follow the Glen Sligachan path for about 1km before striking off to the left to gain the foot of the ridge. Once established on the broad crest, an easy walk leads naturally to the top with its twin summits. The summit offers grandstand views of the main (Black) Cuillin Ridge, and Sgurr nan Gillean can be seen to perfection. From the north top, descend easily to Bealach Mosgaraidh before making a relatively steep climb on boulders and small outcrops to the cairn at the summit of Beinn Dearg Mhor, which is perched right on the eastern edge of the hill overlooking the A850 road and Loch Ainort far below.

Descend by the north ridge, which leads out to a small subsidiary top before dropping steeply on scree and boulders to Bealach na Sgairde, which is below the enormous bulk of Glamaig. From here, Glamaig can be ascended by a relentless slog up 350m of scree, but the route described here drops down initially steep scree slopes to Coire na Sgairde to pick up the line of the Allt Darnich, which cascades delightfully through a lower gorge in a series of idyllic little falls and pools. This leads naturally back to Sligachan, where refreshment can be found waiting in the local hostelry.

A quicker route to Beinn Dearg

*The Storr from Loch Fada (Skye)*

Mhor is to go by way of the rocky north-east spur which forms the southern boundary of Coire nan Laogh. This can be reached from the A850 road at its highest point south-west of Druim nan Cleochd.

**The Storr** (The Peak or Pillar); *719m*
**Hartaval** (Rocky Hill); *669m*
*OS Sheet 23; GR 495540, 480551*
*9km/730m/5–6hrs*
*Map 44*

---

The northern Trotternish peninsula of Skye contains for almost its entire length a twisting serpentine ridge which, were it not for its classier Cuillin contender in the south, would be the finest range of hills on Skye. Indeed, the complete traverse of 30km over this undulating escarpment ranks alongside the Black Cuillin traverse as the finest hill-walking day in Skye. In addition, its relative lack of popularity, sunnier climate and remarkable rock architecture give it a magnetism that is hard to resist.

The Trotternish Ridge, as it is known, contains two Grahams, both of which are in the vicinity of the Old Man of Storr, the much-photographed rock pinnacle which is seen to advantage from the Staffin road north of Portree. The Storr is the highest summit on the ridge and rises directly behind the Old Man in a series of fantastic cliffs and buttresses. The remoter Hartaval lies to the north-west of The Storr and remains hidden from most viewpoints. The route described below explores the area known as the Sanctuary, which contains the Old Man and then ascends The Storr and Hartaval in that order. However, this can be varied so that only The Storr is climbed and Hartaval can be left for another day.

Cars can be parked on the A855 road just before a forestry plantation at GR 504525. From here a path follows the edge of the forest for about a kilometre before turning north into the bowl of Coire Faoin and the Sanctuary. Another path goes through the forest but it is often closed due to erosion and lack of drainage, and is not recommended. The collection of bizarre and ghostly pinnacles which surround the equally imposing obelisk of the Old Man of Storr (50m) are an unexpected delight and it is easy to sympathise with W.A. Poucher in his classic, *The Magic of Skye,* when he writes: 'I was so amazed at the weirdness of this display that I stood there in the brooding silence and imagined myself transported back through the ages to the Celtic era, with the fabulous creatures of their mythology lurking at every corner and their priests waiting to initiate some ghastly human sacrifice.'

It is worth taking the time to explore the Sanctuary by using the profusion of paths and sheep tracks, though it should be noted that scrambling is not advisable as the rock is friable and unreliable. Having said that, the Old Man was first climbed in 1955 by Don Whillans and his party, but it is a 'Very Severe Route', both strenuous and very loose. From the north side of the Old Man, a steep descent on loose scree and mud leads to a good path which traverses the northern part of the Sanctuary. It eventually crosses a fence to reach the north-east ridge of The Storr. At this point turn to follow a vague path which lines the tops of the cliffs and buttresses in a south-westerly direction, gradually ascending to the summit of The Storr. The view looking down to the Old Man and the Sanctuary, and outwards to the Isle of Raasay and the mainland peaks beyond, is quite breathtaking.

From the summit trig point, Hartaval lies in a north-westerly direction and is easily gained by descending the grassy slopes to Bealach a' Chuirn for 200m, then hugging the ridge line to the small cairn at the summit. Those opting to omit Hartaval should continue round the top of the Storr cliffs and descend the obvious south-east ridge which commands marvellous views across the Sanctuary. The common meeting point for both of those options is Bealach Beag which can be easily reached from Hartaval by a return to Bealach a' Chuirn followed by a traverse round the grassy east side of The Storr. From Bealach Beag a somewhat loose-stoned path descends the north side of a stream, and provides a suitable chink in the armour of the east-facing cliffs. This then leads easily back to the A855 and the starting point.

**Uisgnaval Mor** (Big Outer Hill);
*729m*
*OS Sheets 13, 14; GR 120085*
*12km/880m/4–6hrs*
*Map 45*

---

Uisgnaval Mor is the highest of the central group of North Harris hills and is usually climbed along with its satellite summit of Teilesval (697m) to the north-east which is connected by a high col at 560m. It is an excellent hill to gain an appreciation of the complex topography of the other North Harris hills and ridges to the east and west.

The ideal route to the summit follows the long curving spine of the mountain's south-west ridge which can conveniently be gained from the head of Loch Meavaig at the beginning of the track which runs north through Glen Meavaig. (This track also provides the return route.) Reach the crest of the ridge near the small lochan at GR 110063 and ascend the remainder of the ridge which is covered by grass and occasional rocky outcrops to the wonderfully airy summit where the cairn is perched right on the edge of a steep crag. From this superb vantage point, you can enjoy fine views of Clisham and its associated tops, and also of Oreval and Ullaval to the west.

Teilesval is easily reached by a short descent of about 170m on steep slopes of grass and rock to the col north-east of the summit, followed by a short climb of 140m with some scrambling opportunities on a small crag some two-thirds of the way up. Descend Teilesval by its north-west ridge above Glen Uisletter and gradually drop down to the mouth of this glen at the 'bridge' over the Uisletter, which is nothing more than a few pipes set in concrete. Grand views can be had from here of the steep rocky

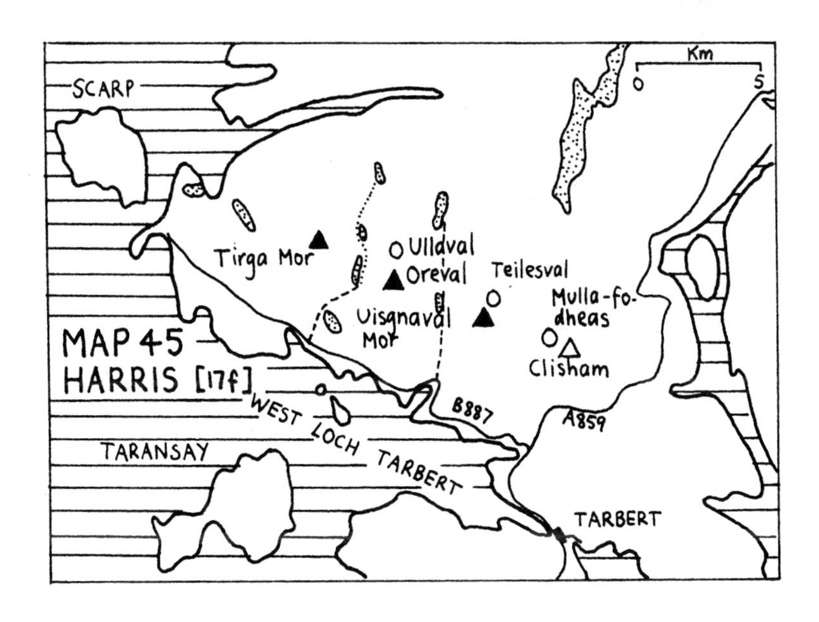

nose of Sron Scourst, which is comparable with the more famous Sron Ulladale to the north-west but which has much less climbing potential. A walk of 4½km along the Glen Meavaig track, which passes the popular fishing spot of Loch Scourst, leads back to the starting point.

It is possible to extend the above outing if you so wish by continuing along the ridge north of Teilesval to Stulaval and descending its north-west ridge to the termination of the Glen Meavaig track. This would add on a good two to three hours to the above itinerary.

**Tirga Mor** (origin unknown); *679m*
**Oreval** (Moorfowl Hill); *662m*
*OS Sheets 13, 14; GR 055115, 083099*
*17km/1,320m/7–9hrs*
*Map 45*

---

These two hills are the highest points of the western group of hills in North Harris which collectively contains Loch Chliostair as its central hub. Oreval is the highest summit of a long south to north ridge lying east of Loch Chliostair, whose northerly termination is the celebrated overhanging crag of Sron Ulladale, which has been described as the most awe-inspiring crag in the British Isles. Tirga Mor is higher and more rugged than Oreval and lies on the west side of Loch Chliostair. If both are

*On the summit of Uisgnaval Mor looking to Teilesval (Harris)*

climbed together in a circuit of the loch, with a possible extension to view Sron Ulladale, this would rank as a classic – if not the classic hillwalking day on the Outer Isles.

Begin on the B887 road at the end of the track which leads to the dam at the southern end of Loch Chliostair. Follow the track to the dam and cross the dam to gain the foot of the south-east ridge of Tirga Mor. Initially the ridge is quite grassy and full of boulders; but higher up, it becomes steeper with more rocky slabs and provides some reasonable scrambling in places. The last part of the ridge is broad and grassy and leads directly to the mossy triangulation pillar and surrounding cairn. As expected, the views from the summit are quite exceptional.

Descend by the broad north-east ridge over a minor flat top and drop easily down grassy slopes to the north end of Loch Ashavat, the small loch which lies above and north of Loch Chliostair. Note that the small fishing hut marked on the map at this point is no longer there. At this point, if time and inclination permit, it is worth heading north along the path for about 1½km to view the huge overhanging cliff of Sron Ulladale – although for some the thought of the descent and re-ascent involved may be too much – unless, of course, you have decided to leave Oreval for another day. From the north end of Loch Ashavat, the best way to tackle Oreval is to climb east up the easy slopes for only 170m in order to reach the wide grassy col between Ullaval and Muladal. From here, follow the ridge south over Ullaval and onto Oreval, which has two cairns at its summit and some marvellous views.

From Oreval, continue south along the delightful grassy ridge to the minor top of Bidigi, before finally arriving at the last top of Cleiseval, which is crowned with a triangulation pillar and which has magnificent views south to various scattered islands and distant white beaches. At the end of a long summer's day on the Harris hills, it is difficult to leave this unparalleled vantage point. From the summit of Cleiseval, drop south-west down the easy grassy slopes to the road, from where it is only a walk of 2km back to the starting point.

Both the Grahams described above could easily be climbed on separate excursions using the excellent stalkers' path which runs along the east side of Loch Chliostair and the west side of Loch Ashavat. This would certainly give more time for viewing Sron Ulladale and for generally taking in the atmosphere of this wild and beautiful part of Harris.

**Beinn Mhor** (Big Hill); *620m*
*OS Sheet 22; GR 808310*
*12km/650m/4–6hrs*
*Map 46*

The major hills of South Uist form a twisting spine on the eastern side of the island between the large sea lochs of Eynort and Skipport. From the vast

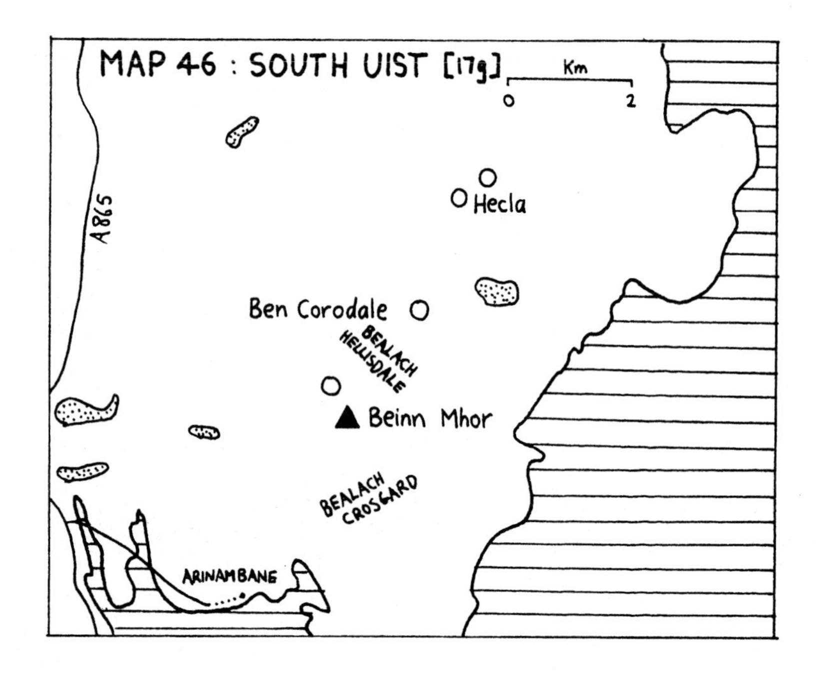


sandy beaches and *machair* of the west to the mountains of the east lies an area of peaty bogland peppered with countless lochs and lochans – a fisherman's paradise. South Uist's lifeline, the A865 road, runs the entire length of this area, with many minor roads branching off to the isolated communities in the west. Precious few roads, however, penetrate east towards the mountains and the two that do reach the two sea lochs mentioned above.

Beinn Mhor is the highest and most southerly of the three distinct summits and it is more easily reached from the Loch Eynort road to the south. If suitable transport arrangements can be made, and if the time is available, then the ideal way to tackle the group would be to make a complete traverse of Beinn Mhor, Ben Corodale and Hecla, by beginning or ending at either Loch Eynort or Loch Skipport. This is a long day, however, and involves 1,200m of ascent, with tricky terrain to negotiate near the summit of Ben Corodale and south-west of Bealach Hellisdale.

For those with more modest intentions, an ascent of Beinn Mhor only is an interesting excursion and gives a fine appreciation of the surrounding country. The ideal outing is a complete traverse of the summit ridge which connects Bealach Crosgard in the south with Bealach Carra Dhomhnuill Ghuirm in the north but again this may create transport problems. Loch Dobhrain on the A865 road is a good starting or finishing point if this option is taken, and it is also a suitable starting point for the traverse of all three summits if the finishing point must be

*Beinn Mhor from Arinambane (South Uist)*

at the same place. The following describes the ascent of Beinn Mhor only and assumes a return to the starting point.

Begin at the end of the public road north of Loch Eynort where cars can be parked opposite a house. A good path goes through a gate and a small wooded area to eventually reach the ruin and small wooden bothy of Arinambane. The path continues beyond this point although this is not indicated on the map. Follow the path round the coast, and cross a small stream by a wooden bridge and stile, where the going gradually becomes boggier and the path less distinct. You will then reach a beautifully positioned ruined shieling which is perched on a small headland. (The shieling is a poignant reminder of the forced eviction of thousands of crofters from South Uist on the insensitive whim of Colonel Gordon of Cluny, who bought the island together with Benbecula and Eriskay in 1838.) From here you may enjoy grand views of Beinn Mhor with its long south ridge sweeping down to Bealach Crosgard and the route of ascent.

Continue on the path which hugs the western shore of a small inlet and cross the stream at its head. From here the path ceases to exist and over a kilometre of poorly drained boggy ground must be traversed before reaching the steep heathery slopes leading to Bealach Crosgard. In wet conditions, these slopes can be extremely slippery and care should be taken. Towards the top, a jumble of large boulders liven up the ascent. In terms of height, this bealach is only halfway up at a little over 300m above sea-level, but the easy grassy ridge between this point and the summit can be ascended in less than an hour. During the ascent there is one short, level section which precedes the final steep grassy ridge leading to a large cairn.

The actual summit lies almost 500m beyond this and boasts a trig point surrounded by a drystane dyke. Here you may enjoy the dramatic views of the wild and fairly inaccessible Glen Hellisdale to the east with its precipitous array of buttresses forming a continuous wall on the south side of the glen. This glen is a true wilderness camper's delight and is an ideal base for exploring the remote eastern corries and ridges of these hills which all face out to the open sea.

The quickest means of descent is to return by the same route but this would omit the finest part of the ridge, which narrows significantly beyond the summit with steep drops on either side. If you traverse this section of the ridge after a short descent from the summit, you will encounter several boulder outcrops *en route*. You will then reach a subsidiary summit (608m) after two-thirds of a kilometre. The ridge continues beyond this point and should only be taken by those ending the walk at Loch Dobhrain or continuing on to the other two hills.

Leave the ridge and descend west down heathery slopes for 250m to the little lochan below Spin, which is a subsidiary summit (356m) lying west of Beinn Mhor. The broad southern shoulder of Spin can then be descended on pockets of rough ice-scoured gneiss leading down to Loch nam Faoileann and the coastal path used on the walk in. Note that it may be preferable to execute the above route in reverse, but each has its advantages and disadvantages.

# INDEX OF GRAHAMS